In Memoria

There are only a few organizational men in each generation who make the kind of impact that changes the way the rest of us respond to that organization's purpose and direction. Dr. Jim Tresner was one such man. His simple and profound love for Freemasonry inspired almost every man who knew him to make a study of Freemasonry a lifelong experience.

He understood Freemasonry as a way of life. And his greatest hope in men was that they would feel the same. He was internationally known as a Masonic author, writer, speaker and scholar. But every brother who was personally acquainted with Jim was simply proud to call him "My Brother." We can only wish that more of us could approach the understanding of servant leadership that seemed just to come naturally for Jim every day of his life. We can be assured our fraternity has been made better because of him.

This book is dedicated to the memory of
Dr. James Tracy Tresner, II, 33°, G∴C∴
1941-2018

The Journey of the Elu to Enlightenment

A Contemporary Interpretation of the Teachings of the Scottish Rite

Full Color Edition

Robert G. Davis, 33°, G∴C∴

Building Stone Publishing
Guthrie, Oklahoma

Copyright© 2019 Robert G. Davis

All right reserved. No part of this publication may be reproduced or transmited in any form or by any means, electronic or mechanical, including photocopying, recording or any information storage or retrieval system, without prior permission from the publisher.

ISBN: 978-1-7990665-5-2

Full Color Edition

Published by:

Building Stone Publishing
Guthrie, OK 73044

Table of Contents

	A Matter of Character	7
	Foreword	9
	Preface	12
I	Introduction	21
II	The Scottish Rite as a Vehicle for the Transformative Art	27
III	What Is Enlightenment?	35
IV	What Is Freedom?	49
V	What Is Toleration?	61
VI	Six Major Themes of the Scottish Rite	71
VII	The Quests, or Thematic Journeys of the Scottish Rite	101
VIII	Historical Timeline of High Degrees	111
IX	Lodge of Perfection	119
X	Chapter of Rose Croix	211
XI	Council of Kadosh	247
XII	Consistory	345
XIII	Whither Are We Traveling?	365
	References Cited	370

Illustrations

The Illustrations on the opening pages of each Chapter or Degree Explanation were taken from the Liturgy of the Ancient & Accepted Scottish Rite of Freemasonry, for the Southern Jurisdiction of the United States, Parts II, III, and IV, and Ritual, Part V, The Inner Sanctuary The Book of the Great Light; (Charleston, AM 5722, 5638, 5639); printed in New York, J.J. Little & Co. Printers, in 1867, 1877, 1878, and 1879 respectively.

The plates preceding each Degree, 4th through 32nd, are the earliest color depictions of the Southern Jurisdiction's regalia, taken from the early Liturgies, and generously provided with permission by Elizabeth A. W. McCarthy, desk top publishing specialist in the office of the Scottish Rite Journal. House of the Temple, 1733 Sixteenth St. NW, Washington DC 20009

A Matter of Character

Masonic authorities work hard at defining Freemasonry. We attempt to tell the world what we are, and are not; what Masons believe; what we do in lodge, the kinds of charities we support, our importance in the world, why men should join us; and even how to join. Every state and national Masonic organization offers printed and digital materials about Masonry. Essentially all have websites; and many have social media pages.

In spite of these best efforts, Freemasonry still endures its share of "not so informed" information, propagated by anti-masons, conspiracy theorists, and individuals who print hatred just because hatred sells. It seems that regardless of how hard we strive to explain our altruistic aims and motives, there will always be those who misunderstand the world's oldest and most respected fraternity.

But all of this really makes little difference. What does make a real difference to everyone—both Masons and the public at large—is the character of Masons. The character of Masons speaks more eloquently than all the books and pamphlets written about our fraternity. In the community where Masons are seen as men of high integrity, the fraternity stands in high repute. In the community where Masons do not have the respect of the public, the fraternity has little chance of becoming known and respected.

It is just that simple. The reputation of Freemasonry rests literally in the character of each Mason. It is in the power of every member to glorify or diminish the institution.

Most people will never read a word about Masonry or know of its philanthropies. The public's perception of the fraternity will never be well defined. The sole basis of judging it will be the character of the men who are known to be Masons. Masonry is to them what they see in the temperament of Masons.

One bad example can do a lot of harm. When one of us is caught up in some public scandal, or unethical business dealing, or an immoral act, the public takes it for granted that Masonry either condones such behavior, or is too weak to be of adequate influence by its teachings to prevent it. But the Mason who lives up to the teachings and obligations of Masonry will be a man above reproach—not only to his brethren; but also among his neighbors, his family, his friends, his business partners, and his community.

So, the reputation of the world's oldest fraternity really is up to each of us.

It would be wonderful to hear the merchant say, "I have been taken in by a good many scoundrel, but never have I had any trouble with a man who wore the square and compasses." Or to have the judge say, "Never in my experience as a judge have I had a case before me of two Masons going to law." Or, to hear non-masons say, "I frequently attend social gatherings of Masons and while I don't know anything about the inner side of Masonry, their exhibition of good mindedness and solid behavior impress me to think that their teachings must be good."

It would speak volumes about us if most people thought our most famous Masonic emblem, the letter G, stood for *Gentleman*. After all, every man who wears it is to be one.

You see, we are what other people say we are. The best argument for Masonry is a good man. Just as the best example of humanity is a good human being.

Foreword

by Chuck Dunning, KCCH

*"We are to hear and read and meditate,
that we may act well; and the action of Life is itself the great
field for spiritual improvement."*—Albert Pike

When Bob Davis and I struck up an acquaintance more than two decades ago, among the first building blocks of our emerging friendship was mutual love of the Scottish Rite degrees and Albert Pike's writings. We also shared an understanding that Masonry is about more than words, visual symbols, elaborate ceremonies, and fraternal fun. We agreed with the above quote from Pike, understanding that Masonry herself begs us to carefully study, deeply contemplate, and earnestly employ all the wisdom, strength, and beauty she offers. We also agreed it was essential for us to willingly allow her to catalyze significant changes in our lives, and thus learn and grow in ways we could not predict, to continue becoming different men than the ones who first knocked at her door. Neither of us has achieved anything like perfection in that work, and sometimes we are much farther from our ideals than we would care to admit. Nonetheless, both of us, each in our own ways, have experienced much wonder and joy in the process.

One of the great joys I have known is our work together with several other like-minded brethren in the Education Committee for the Guthrie Valley of the Scottish Rite. The voices and faces of those men arise in my mind as I read what is compiled in this book. It represents not only the philosophically, psychologically, and spiritually profound insights and questions that can come from brothers engaged in such work, but also the most practical realizations relevant to our social well-being and the impact we make on the world. If we are to maximize our potentials for beneficial change in ourselves and our relationships with others, then we must give careful attention and sincere effort in both realms—the heavenly and the earthly, the abstract and the concrete, the ideal and the actual.

We Masons often recite lofty ideas within our sacred spaces, work diligently at memorizing their words, and perhaps even expand our vocabulary in the process. Yet how often do we feel so genuinely inspired by them that we strive to reframe the lessons in our own words, elaborate upon them in terms of our own lived experiences, and form questions and intentions about how we might actually think and act differently? If you are like me, you have heard yourself make excuses like, "That's just who I am. I'll never change." That can be understandable, especially as an expression of exasperation with oneself. Even so, it may well be that nothing more un-Masonic could ever come from our mouths. Sadly, it is far too easy to be preoccupied by simply getting through the rat-race tasks of our everyday lives, entertaining ourselves with vanities and trivialities, assuming we have gone as deep as we need to go, and sometimes knowingly hiding from the challenge to learn and grow. These follies are sad because they block us from the joys of fulfilling more of our potentials for knowing and expressing wisdom, strength, and beauty.

With every turn of the page, this book offers its readers many opportunities to pick up the tools of change in their lives. As a compilation of work from several brothers, it likewise serves as a constant reminder that you are not alone in trying to make sense of what you have seen and heard in Masonry. In that vein, one of the best features in this book is the abundance of questions it presents for further thought. They are worthwhile not only in themselves, but as examples of the kinds of questions you can raise in your own mind and share with others. More importantly, every such question always points out a path of further contemplation, action, transformation, and joy.

Now let's get to work!

PREFACE

It has been one of the unique privileges in my life to serve as the General Secretary of the Valley of Guthrie, Orient of Oklahoma, Ancient & Accepted Scottish Rite of Freemasonry for the Southern Jurisdiction of the United States (a Valley is the geographic area that a particular Scottish Rite Body serves in a State). I presume it was a match made by divine intervention, as I did not prepare myself for a career in Freemasonry. I prepared myself to be in city planning and city management. I had known since I was a young lad that I wanted to be in a field of servant leadership, and I could think of no profession greater than city management to facilitate that aim and purpose in my life. I was fortunate to be in that profession for 14 years.

Besides, one didn't get paid to be a Freemason. It was not a thing one thought about as a career path. Like many men I knew, I was an active Freemason, and gave as much volunteer time as I could in supporting my local Blue Lodge and the activities of the Guthrie Scottish Rite, as that was the Scottish Rite Body situated the closest to my place of residence. I have always enjoyed the philosophy and symbolism in Freemasonry, and found the Scottish Rite to be the college course in Masonic teaching. It was something I loved and studied more than actually participated in.

One day out of the blue, I was visited by the President of the Guthrie Scottish Rite Foundation and the Chairman of the Guthrie Scottish Rite Board of Directors. These two fine gentlemen had been sent by the presiding officer of the Scottish Rite in Oklahoma to offer me employment as the

Secretary of the Guthrie Valley. I talked it over with my wife, and agreed to accept the position. That was in August 1986. I served in the position of Secretary for the Valley for 30 years, retiring in 2016. It was also a wonderful position of servant leadership.

It was indeed a remarkable privilege because Guthrie is one of the largest Scottish Rite Bodies in membership in the Southern Jurisdiction, second only to Dallas, Texas. Moreover, it has a national reputation for the Scottish Rite experience it offers men who advance in Masonic education beyond the instruction of the Symbolic Lodge. This is partly due to the fact that Guthrie is the location of one of the largest and most beautiful Scottish Rite Temples in the United States, and is often listed among the top three of Masonic edifices in America. It attracts attention. It is a great pilgrimage for men because it also houses a hotel, kitchen and dining rooms so that one can enjoy the building and the experience over the course of a weekend without leaving the building. More importantly, the Masonic experience in Guthrie is widely acknowledged to be among the most meaningful and valuable because Guthrie has always remained focused on the original purpose of the Rite—More Masonic Light, knowledge and insight in Masonry.

This happens because the Valley has a legacy of conferring all 29 Degrees (4° - 32°) of the Rite at least once each year. And it has been doing this since 1917. Such a venture requires more than 400 volunteers, which add greatly to the fellowship of men, as well as the teachings one receives.

In addition, Guthrie has an active Education Committee comprised of remarkably knowledgeable men. In addition to the degree presentations performed by the actors, along with the many volunteers involved in the theatre production of the degrees, the education committee conducts breakout sessions for both members and candidates, exploring specific ideas, themes, symbols, and teachings relating to the Scottish Rite.

The Valley also includes an Academy of Reflection where meditations and reflective programs are offered to those who desire to experience the contemplative aspects of the Scottish Rite.

Thus, the various interest groups served within the organization create an extraordinary fraternal experience on a scale that is seldom matched in other Valleys of the Scottish Rite.

All of this information is provided as a preface to the purpose of this book. It could not have been written without the many hours of conversation, insight, experience, knowledge, and individual contributions put forth by the Guthrie Valley's Education Committee to make Masonic knowledge and enlightenment the primary mission and goal of the Guthrie Scottish Rite.

As the Secretary of the Valley, I long had a concern that the archaic language, biblical settings, costuming, and pageantry of the degrees, as beautiful as these are, may, in presentation, create a kind of disconnect between the ancient settings of the teachings and the contemporary life of the men who experience them. After all, the lessons of the Scottish Rite represent the mythic journey of the hero. And, for men, this journey is nothing less than the journey to the mature masculine soul. It is a journey of awakening consciousness, of self-discovery, of all the trials and victories that are inherent in the experience of life itself. This is challenging enough in the best of circumstances. But, for men who are out in the real world, investing the majority of their time in occupations, raising families, giving service to their communities, and helping others along the way, precious little time is left for one to think about who he is, from whence he came, where he is going, and what has meaning to him beyond the usual activities of his life.

It seems a worthy purpose that we strive to present the teachings of Freemasonry in a way that will enable men to understand how these teachings actually apply to them in their contemporary life. This book is an effort to bridge the gap between the beautiful language, symbols, themes, quests, and philosophies offered in the degrees of the Scottish Rite; and how these profound ideas are to be understood and applied in today's world.

This book is divided into two sections. The first presents an overview of the foundational principles of the Scottish Rite, a brief historical timeline of its degree development, the traditional themes carried out by its instruction, and the mythic journey or quest element represented within each Body of the Rite.

The second section presents a contemporary interpretation of the essential teachings of each Degree of the Rite. It also offers the reader a set of questions that can be contemplated when thinking about the instruction received by each degree. It is hoped the reader will be better enabled to understand how the teachings of the Scottish Rite can be applied in the world today, just as they have been used by men of past centuries. The degree lessons are for individual study as well as group participation. The ideas and insights offered for each degree can be read in the lodge, chapter, council, or consistory, and the questions can be discussed by the group. It is hoped that every brother will take the teachings of the Rite into his heart. They truly represent the path to self-improvement, enlightenment, and happiness.

Acknowledgments

I am not the sole author of the words presented here. It is the combined work of the Education Committee of Guthrie. Each member of the committee regularly makes significant contributions to the emphasis placed on education, which, in part, defines the Guthrie experience. Their invaluable influence is conveyed in the insights and ideas they present to candidates and members at each Reunion. Over time, many of these contributions have been transferred to written or digital form and are now provided at each of the Guthrie gatherings. Without being certain at this point who has written what on any particular degree, I have included their wisdom, with permission, as a collective effort of the team.

I especially want to express my gratitude to the following committee members whose words are included in some significant way in the text:

Chuck Dunning, KCCH—Director of the Guthrie Education Committee, and founder of the Guthrie Academy of Reflection. He is a member of Haltom City-Riverside Lodge#1331 in Texas and is also a Class Director in the Valley of Fort Worth. He is the author of "Contemplative Freemasonry." His insights and contribution to the degrees of the Chapter of Rose Croix are especially significant in this work.

Kevin Main, KCCH—Member of the Guthrie Education Committee, who created many of the topics now addressed in the candidate education programs. His thoughts on the Degrees of Knighthood conferred by the Council of Kadosh are included in this work. He is a Past

THE JOURNEY OF THE ELU TO ENLIGHTENMENT

Master of Plano Lodge#768, Plano, Texas, and is on the Education and Service Committee of the Grand Lodge of Texas. He also serves as the chairman of the Reunion Directors and co-chairs the Education Committee in the Valley of Dallas.

Mark C. Phillips, 32°—An Adept in the Guthrie College of the Consistory, whose essays are among the most enlightening of all the work that has been completed by members of the College. His insight in the areas of commitment and adversity expressed in the lessons of the Lodge and Chapter Degrees are a part of this work. He is a Past Master of Newport Lodge No.85 in Newport, Oregon; is an officer of the Research Lodge of Oregon No. 198 in Portland, and an active member of the Valley of Portland.

I also express my deep personal regard for the work of the remaining members of the Guthrie Education Committee. These brothers do outstanding work, as well, and we are fortunate to have them. Thank you to brothers Clyde Schoolfield, Jason Marshall, Shane Pate, and Kyle Ferlemann.

But none of us has made more of a contribution here than Dr. Jim Tresner, 33°. G∴C∴, who served as the Director of Work for the Guthrie Valley for the 30 years I served as Secretary. He was the Grand Orator of the Grand Lodge of Oklahoma and an Honorary Past Grand Master. He was my Masonic mentor, and dear friend. He was a teacher and a communicator. He was the most brilliant Masonic scholar I have ever known. And he lived to share what he knew about Masonry with those he came in contact with. He dedicated his life to Freemasonry, and this book is dedicated to him. He is sorely missed.

To read this book is to know something more of Dr. Tresner's mind, and what had meaning to him as a man and Mason. He influenced the thinking and contributions each of us has made to this work. It has been compiled by us in his memory, in the hope that the reader will gain much insight in the journey and lessons of the Scottish Rite, and in your development as an enlightened man.

Robert G. Davis, 33°, G∴C∴
General Secretary Emeritus
Valley of Guthrie
Orient of Oklahoma

THE JOURNEY OF THE ELU TO ENLIGHTENMENT

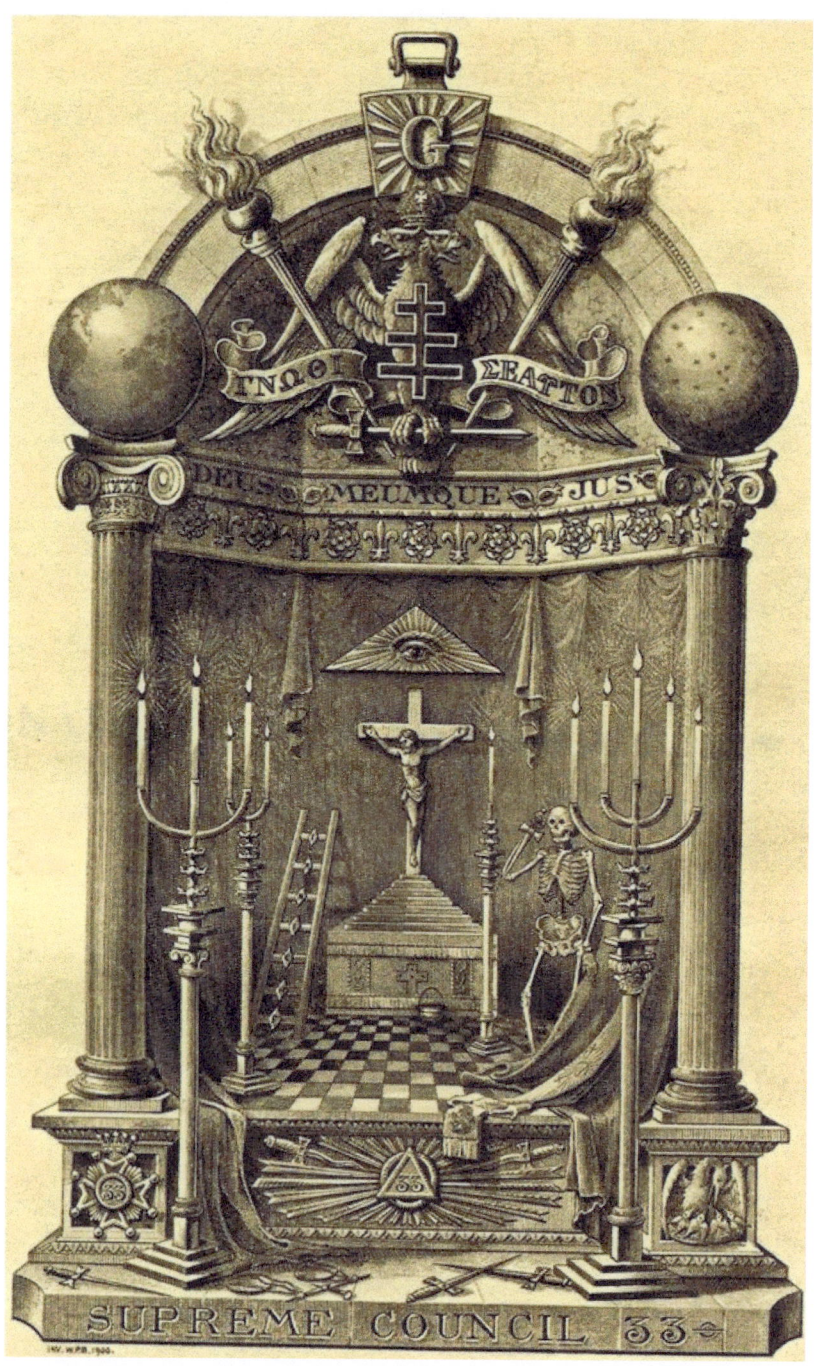

Introduction

The Degrees of the Scottish Rite are among the most dramatic and instructive in all of Freemasonry. They are meant to inspire us to pursue knowledge, gain wisdom, and live strong in life. Such motivation is the best path of practical living. The labors on this path are the Way of the Mysteries; of unveiling the mysteries of our own being. It is the true way of the craftsman.

The teachings of the Scottish Rite are a course in comparative religion, philosophy, ethics, history and mythology; all taught through the medium of allegory and symbols. These teachings add significantly to, and contribute a deeper understanding of the degrees of the Blue or Symbolic Lodge, within which we have all become initiated men and begun our journey to self and spiritual improvement. The goal of every Masonic Degree, of whatever Rite, is to inspire the individual pursuit of knowledge and meaning. The Scottish Rite focuses on the history of man's search for truth. We do not assert the accuracy of its legends or offer a single interpretation of the lessons of its Degrees. They are only presented as worthy of our consideration. For the search for truth lies within each man.

The story of the Scottish Rite is the story of man's excursion into life. Through its teachings, we learn of our struggles with pride, selfishness, intolerance, greed, envy, and passion. We learn that life is seen and viewed, approached, lived, and judged by moral and ethical measures. Life's ills

THE JOURNEY OF THE ELU TO ENLIGHTENMENT

and inequalities and injustices are seen and weighed with reference to their moral quality, their spiritual value. And the evils which define human weaknesses, are exposed.

Our teachings offer us ways to discover how a new and better world rises to those who become awakened through their own imagination and understanding. A world in which every man becomes a brother; and the essence of love and toleration becomes possible for every soul.

The structure of the Rite is naturally progressive, though the lessons taught and the virtues inculcated in one Degree are not superior to those of another. The Degrees are not strictly chronological, although their moral and intellectual teachings become progressively comprehensive. In the Scottish Rite, we learn from the past. We learn to build for the future. We build our own lives by applying the mortar of the past—the cement of brotherly love, equality, and truth—to our own practice and examples of living. And when we take to heart the beautiful lessons, the high principles, and the profound ideals which the Scottish Rite Degrees so completely and effectively present to us, our life is indeed transformed and improved.

But it is only when we have prepared our hearts and minds to receive, feel, and experience the lessons before us that we make real progress in Masonry. Each Degree in the Rite explores a specific set of ideas; provides a guidepost, or marker, which gives us personal insight about our own journey, or quest, in life.

The Degrees are administered through four Bodies-- the Lodge of Perfection, Chapter of Rose Croix, Council of Kadosh, and the Consistory. As in the Blue Lodge, these Bodies consist of elected and appointed leaders of the Rite, who meet at prescribed times to carry out the work of the Rite.

INTRODUCTION

The Lodge of Perfection consists of the Fourth through the Fourteenth Degrees. These are known as the "Ineffable Degrees" because these Degrees are focused on the rediscovery of the Ineffable name of God. By "ineffable" we mean "incapable of being expressed in ordinary language." These Degrees are so named because the Lodge of Perfection brings to conclusion the story commenced in the Blue Lodge, teaches the quest for light, and inspires the awakening of one's moral and intellectual nature. The quest of the Lodge of Perfection is self-discovery.

The Fifteenth through the Eighteenth Degrees are conferred in a Chapter of Rose Croix. The first two in this series focus on the legend of rebuilding Solomon's Temple. We are taught the value of liberty and learn we are the custodians of Freedom. The last two reveal the importance of religion and affirm the new commandment of Love. The quest is to make Love the guiding force in our life.

It is important to remember that Freemasonry cannot and will not advocate or teach a belief in the creeds or ideologies of any one religion. It does not presume to tell its members what to believe. All good Masons may receive the Scottish Rite Degrees. They are presented as drama, not as dogma, for the purpose of instruction. Its ritual, among other things, recounts man's search for truth and his attempt to find his place in the universe.

The Nineteenth through Thirtieth Degrees comprise the Council of Kadosh. "Kadosh" is a Hebrew word meaning "holy" and/or "consecrated." These Degrees are philosophical, mystical, and chivalric. They are designed to further explore the moral and ethical lessons taught in the Lodge of Perfection and Chapter Degrees. The quest is to find ways to strengthen the Light of Masonry in the matters and affairs of the world.

It should be noted that the chivalric Degrees lead us to a metaphor often misunderstood by both Masons and non-Masons alike. As the knights of the crusades sought the liberation of the Holy Land, we seek to liberate ourselves from the bonds of intolerance, prejudice, and ignorance. Thus, in some Degrees, we are styled "Knights." We believe that when man is unfettered from the chains of ignorance, he will naturally seek to work with his fellowmen in the great causes of humanity.

The last two Degrees are presented by a Consistory of Masters of the Royal Secret. The Thirty-First Degree reminds us of the ultimate task of man's self-examination. The Thirty-Second Degree teaches us that the search for perfection is ongoing. The quest of the Consistory is self-examination and empowerment.

The sources of the lessons and symbols of the Scottish Rite are many and varied. They derive from such sources as early Christian traditions, symbolic alchemy, and a special form of Jewish mysticism known as the Kabbalah. Contrary to popular belief, the Kabbalah is not a system of magic or divination, but is rather a branch of esoteric Jewish philosophy seeking to interpret passages from the Bible. For example, early students of the Kabbalah noticed that the phrase "And God Said…and it was so" occurred ten times in the first chapter of Genesis. They believed that as the light flows outward or emanates from the sun, so the energy of creation flowed from God by his Word and created the universe. Three of these emanations were called Wisdom, Strength and Beauty, the metaphorical supports of the Blue Lodge. The Lord's Prayer also mentions three: Kingdom, Power, and Glory. The Kabbalah and its connection to

INTRODUCTION

Masonic symbols are explored in the Degrees of the Rite. As well, other sources of Masonic symbolism are provided in the Degrees.

Symbols are employed in the teachings of Masonry for several reasons: first, metaphysical and spiritual concepts, such as descriptions of God, cannot be expressed readily in ordinary language; second, symbols can provide a metaphysical garment to present ideas on several levels, according to the fitness of the student to receive the knowledge; and third, symbols help us remember the instruction we have received. The great Masonic scholar of the nineteenth century, Albert Pike, called symbols "the soul of Masonry."

Since the Scottish Rite welcomes all good men of whatever faith, a distinction between Masonry and religion must be made. Religion, of necessity, asserts dogmatic authority, while Masonry simply counsels reflection on the great mysteries of the human condition. Masonry cannot—and never will—assert authority as to creeds, submit prophets for judgment, offer writings from God, or reveal divine truths beyond simple virtue and morality.

It is essential to remember that Freemasonry does not pretend to offer salvation of the soul. Each Brother must return to his Church, Mosque, Synagogue, or other place of worship to discover for himself the means of his salvation. Masonry is concerned with the here and now, and attempts to make this world a better place to live through each man's work in his own self-improvement.

The dramatic form of the Scottish Rite Degrees is a venue both entertaining and instructive. Our ultimate task is to learn the lessons of practical morality and ethics and the sublime teachings of religion and philosophy so that we may live them and teach others.

Our labor is to study, to reflect, to ask, and to learn. What a glorious thing this is for each man to experience. What timeless relevancy exists here! What a blessing life is when we know what we can become!

The Scottish Rite as a Vehicle for the Transformative Art

Those of us who are active in our communities and are known as Masons; or, who work in Masonic buildings which offer daily public tours get a chance to talk with a lot of non-Masons. We are finding there are a surprising number of younger men asking questions about Masonry. These men have generally already done a lot of website surfing and have formulated an opinion about us. In fact, we often discover in these conversations that men come into Masonry knowing more than many Masons know about it; they have gone to the trouble of reading through all the anti-Mason rhetoric that is out there, have sifted through the good and the bad, and have arrived at their own conclusions that Freemasonry is a venue for truth-seeking, a vehicle for self-development; a quest for the spiritual. There are secret associations to be discovered there, and these associations are not doctrinal, they have not been filtered by political and religious bias. Many young men are coming into our Order with these kinds of expectations of discovery and personal improvement.

As Scottish Rite Masons, it is essential that we understand we have the tools to serve the needs and expectations of this new generation of men; just as we have in past generations. Our purpose is tied directly to their expectations. After all, the Rite is the product of the four great movements in history, which were all tied to the structure of consciousness, and, what men who come into

Masonry are searching for is an awakened consciousness.

There have been very few reliable histories written which traces the origin and development of the Scottish Rite and its system of degrees. Since the Rite was originally a French institution, the first real historian of French Freemasonry was thought to be a Parisian Mason named Thory, who published in 1815 a treatise on the beginnings of the Higher Degrees. He was a devout patron of the higher degrees and is known to have distorted the facts at times to support his point of view. And those who followed him tended to do the same. And there were those historians who were opposed to the higher degrees and found it difficult to write an objective account of the same. A fellow named Rebold wrote a history of Freemasonry in Europe, but since he did not subscribe to the high degrees, was known to have a significant prejudice against the French system in particular. Then, there were a number of French historians who were avowed advocates of one particular jurisdiction of French Masonry over another, and found it difficult to keep their grievances against those systems out of their own historical accounts. Thus, the history of the first fifty years of the Scottish Rite is, in some cases, more an account of probabilities than of a reproduction of actual Orient or Supreme Council records.

Albert Pike, being aware of this, prepared a compilation of documents translated from French works in 1859 that gives us all that can be found in the works of French writers up to that year. Much of this effort was unpublished by Pike himself, although he gave it to the Supreme Council for its use. After several attempts by that body to complete the project, finally, in 1925, the Supreme Council authorized Grand Commander Cowles to prepare the material for publication. Cowles selected Charles Lobinger, 33°, G∴C∴, to undertake the writing, and his book was issued in 1931. His work has long been considered the definitive history of the Scottish Rite Degree system. The brief historical commentary provided here is taken from this important document; and, for the purpose of this study, represents an adequate overview of the origin and development of the Scottish Rite as a system of instruction foundational to one's understanding of what the Rite is designed to do for men of the fraternity.

The four great movements, which influenced Scottish Rite teachings, were the Renaissance, the Reformation, the French Revolution, and the Industrial/Social Revolution. The inspiration of the Renaissance began in Italy in the 14th century and lasted through the life of Michelangelo to 1534. It is important to Masonry because the inspiration of the Renaissance was the growth of knowledge and the rediscovery of classical learning, including the Hebrew Kabbala, which is the only spiritual system of which we have any knowledge that reconciles reason with faith, power with liberty, and science with mystery—ideas which we know are uniquely woven within the teachings of Freemasonry. It can even be theorized this is the reason we find 32 paths of wisdom in the Scottish Rite. The Kabbala had a considerable influence over 16th and 17th century theology, philosophy, science and medicine. And it was during this same period that the intellectual community began to profoundly influence free thought and the advancement of metaphysical ideas. It's indeed a curious thing to contemplate that the Kabbala has such a prominent intellectual base in the structural fabric of our degrees. Pike tells us "all Masonic associations owe to it their secrets and their symbols." Indeed, it can be posited that Speculative Masonry arose from the Operative Guilds after the Renaissance had brought to England the philosophy of the Kabbalah and the ideas, which grew from it.

The second movement, the Reformation, began in Germany in the 1500s and is equally important to Masonry because it redefined the concept of religious allegiance and doctrine brought about by Martin Luther. It was the Reformation that gave Freemasonry its freedom from ecclesiastical control and the prominence of the Bible in all its ritual and symbolic forms. In fact, had it not been for the Reformation, Freemasonry would likely have always been an appendage of the Church, as were the Guilds and as such as we find in the Catholic Knights of Malta.

Certainly, English Freemasonry was a product of the Reformation; so much so that many Masonic scholars now believe the higher degrees, which were invented in France shortly after Anderson's Constitutions of 1723, were created as a reaction against the theism of the early English Craft degrees. We know the theistic elements of craft Masonry were prominent up to the Union of 1813. And there is no question the degrees we practice today in the Scottish Rite are tied to the old French Masonic Rites. The third movement was born in the 17th century and encompassed the 18th century; and became known as the Age of Enlightenment. It blossomed in France as a result of concerns over political and civil liberties. In fact, the Scottish Rite may be more the product of the ideals promoted by the French Revolution than any other societal movement.

The fourth began in England in 1756 and moved

quickly to other western countries and was marked chiefly by the constant application of new inventions and methods of industry along with the condition of those who operated within them. One can find many centers of ethical thought in Masonry that were influenced by this movement. We need only to read Albert Pike's lectures in Morals & Dogma to discovery its influence on Scottish Rite instruction.

Now, the important thing to understand here is that all four of these movements influenced, and made possible the succeeding one. It was the rebirth of knowledge in the Renaissance that led the way to the Protestant Revolution. It was the spirit of freedom and equality generated in the Reformation, which greatly aided in promoting the French Revolution. And it was the political and civic upheaval of the Revolution, which, in turn, led to the industrial and social revolution.

There is little doubt that the system of Masonic teaching we have inherited took its form during the period midway between the Reformation and the French Revolution—again; we call this period the Enlightenment. Our founders enjoyed the benefits of the Renaissance and Reformation ideas; and we know they associated with many of the intellectuals and enlightenment thinkers who were actually preparing for the great political upheaval, which became the French Revolution.

There was a huge transformation that took place when Speculative Masonry moved from Great Britain to the Continent. The whole nature and spirit of our Order was changed. Masonry was suddenly at the center of Renaissance ideas. The Renaissance brought about new attitudes, which fundamentally affected human thought. Among these are three that resonate clearly with all thoughtful Masons—

(1) love of truth, (2) love of beauty, and (3) love of man. Love of truth was the thirst for knowledge and the pursuit of learning. Love of beauty was the revival of the fine arts, and the study of the classics. Out of these two ideas was born the third; the Love of man; that is, the improved perception of the dignity of man. This idea was brought forth in a special phase of thought known as humanism, which dignified man as a rational being and proclaimed that man counts as man, and not just a miserable sinner or a lost soul.

This was a profound statement—even culture shaking. All things could be valued in respect to their effect on human welfare. Suddenly, civilization, industry, education, religion, government, and society had to justify themselves on the basis of that test alone. Here then was the point of contact between the two great sources of Masonry—the Kabbala, which gave man a map of consciousness for exploring the nature of Deity and his relationship with the Divine; and Humanism, which embraced the value of the individual and his right to self-improvement through independent inquiry into the nature of truth and societal well-being.

Suddenly it became possible for men to think in terms that a brotherhood of man was possible, even when men were not of the same religion. This is again a fundamental Masonic idea. One result was that Humanism, with its Renaissance accompaniment of the love of Truth and love of Beauty, actually made the Scottish Rite and entitled it to bear the name of the University of Freemasonry.

The movements of the Renaissance and the Reformation released enormous amounts of spiritual energy, which came to fruition during the Enlightenment. They opened up the individual spiritual path, especially the inner way in which the physical man could be transcended into a closer relationship with Divinity. They allowed the deeper self to sort out the difference between illusion and reality. On the ethical level, they allowed individual moral conscience to take a critical stand against any form of governance or control regulating free conscience or choice. And they made possible a link between the moral and the spiritual aspect of the self, so that a path could be charted through virtues toward the ultimate goal of enlightenment and spiritual liberation.

These ideas are precisely where the teachings of Masonry are centered. They define for us what our central purpose and mission must be.

The experience of the candidate through the degrees of Masonry is a journey to higher awareness. It is designed to carry the man to a higher level of insight. Its power lies in its ability to integrate its lessons into the psyche of each individual; meeting him on the level of his own experience, and giving him an opportunity to be transformed by the path of his own life. This is profoundly serious work and admonishes us to be aware that everything we do in lodge or on stage, every word we speak, every move we make, is supposed to create an illusion that takes our candidate to another realm of consciousness—just as it did for us. Such illusions cannot happen except in special, sacred places, which are removed from the outside world. We call these places lodges, chapters, councils, and consistories. Our ancestors thought of them as private workshops for learning the secrets of Masonry.

The instruction of the Rite clearly facilitates this journey for our aspirant. The Rite is built on the clear understanding that men need to be engaged in a quest for self-improvement. For men, life needs to be seen as a journey. Men have to be initiated into manhood. And they have to be anointed by other men. The Rite facilitates this fundamental psychological need in men.

It's all about awakening the slumber of his consciousness. In the big picture, from an organizational perspective, there is no more important work to do in men's behalf. This writer can think of no other organization in the world, which exists principally for this purpose.

Thus, these liberating movements of the past have literally made it possible for us to write about the philosophy of the Scottish Rite today. And all that we now do is centered around three great ideologies of human progress which were born from these four eras of western civilization—the principles of enlightenment, freedom, and toleration. Before we begin our journey in instruction, it behooves us to explore the significance of these three great principles of personal and societal development.

WHAT IS ENLIGHTENMENT?

Any text designed to provide foundational material for understanding the Scottish Rite would not be complete if it did not include some thoughts on the subject of enlightenment. What is enlightenment? How is enlightenment significant to understanding Masonry? What is the meaning of enlightenment in the context of Masonic history and philosophy?

There are indeed two meanings of enlightenment in the overall rubric, which is Freemasonry. There is the societal meaning of Enlightenment, which, as previously mentioned, refers to an era of history encompassing the 17th and 18th Centuries, into which Freemasonry, as a social institution, was born. This form of enlightenment has often been styled the history of ideas. Its context is derived from the western world of ideas that places its values primarily in the pursuit of scientific, objectively verifiable knowledge, individual autonomy, social progress, and justice. From a social perspective, enlightenment is the fulfillment of an intellectual quest exemplified by confidence in the power of reason.

And then there is a second meaning of enlightenment in the context of eastern thought, which derives from the central theme that individuals are capable of attaining personal enlightenment as a goal of self-improvement and spiritual development—that there is such a thing as a mystically awakened mind. Enlightenment is the fulfillment of the human quest for perfect understanding.

Both meanings are important to an understanding of Freemasonry, for Masonry encompasses a perspective, or value system, that is clearly drawn from both the west and the east. Both share the image of light overcoming darkness. Indeed, the exploration and merging of these two pillars of enlightenment thought is one of the hallmarks by which we are able to claim a universality of ideas.

To have some basic understanding of the first meaning of enlightenment, we begin by briefly examining the social and political setting of the 18th Century, which ultimately enabled the ideas which had long been discussed only within the tyled recesses of the lodges of British Freemasonry, to be incorporated into the governing practices of continental Europe and the greater society itself. As we shall see, it was the model of the lodge that became a part of the governing structure of democracy. It is largely for this reason that Freemasonry is considered an Enlightenment institution.

In 1752, David Hume enumerated the ingredients of the 18th Century Enlightenment era: *"The cultivation of the age depended on a conjunction of freedom in politics and invention in industry. The same age which produces great philosophers and politicians, renowned generals and poets, usually abounds with skillful weavers and ship-carpenters. We cannot reasonably expect that a piece of woolen cloth will be brought to perfection in a nation, which is ignorant of astronomy, or where ethics are neglected. The spirit of the age affects all the arts; and the minds of men, being once roused from their lethargy and put into fermentation, turn themselves on all sides, and carry improvements into every art and science. With refinement comes sociability; and both export their benefits to public life. Thus, industry, knowledge, and humanity are linked together by an indissoluble chain."*

The advancement of knowledge meant the advancement of reason. Rationality and rationalistic philosophies of life was a characteristic product of the time. Philosophers were agreeing that if one had thoughts about the social order, these might as well be reasonable thoughts. It was a time when old rules were questioned and changed for the sake of reason.

The assumptions that had prevailed throughout the middle Ages were challenged. Could traditional authority be trusted? Could societal progress be guaranteed without respect for human dignity? Was the advancement of knowledge possible without freedom of will? It was a time for questioning the freedom of choice in human relationships.

For instance, a father's power over his children and the husband's power over his wife declined dramatically. The patriarchal family, which was the pattern of the 17th Century, gave way to the nuclear family—one that could enjoy intimacy and equality. Young girls could choose their partners. It became contemptible to force girls into an uncongenial connection for the sake of parental prestige or profit. The choice of a husband or wife concerned the happiness of the young couple themselves, rather than their parents. This was a revolutionary idea. Like many other elements of society, the age marked a time when the world of the family was changing in the direction of freedom.

The essence of the Enlightenment was that such change was possible largely because freedom became safeguarded by reason. Rational love, this idea that a sober and well-considered mutual esteem existed between man and woman, was elevated to a social ideal. In such an atmosphere, women and children secured new respect and new rights. Children were discovered as human beings in their own right. This was a stunning idea. During the middle Ages, adults had treated children as toys, strange animals, or small grownups. The precise age of the child was not known, and, if known, it was irrelevant. Children mattered not so much in the family, but in the economy--as labor, and in law, as links to family succession. Before the Enlightenment period, children were seen only as property, and their deaths were felt in very much the same way as one's cow might die. By the 18th Century, it became shocking for a child to die.

In fact, all segments of society benefited from the new humanity of the Enlightenment. It became less fashionable to make victims than to aid them. Even the laboring poor came to be regarded as human beings. While there were still tyrannies and prejudices, these produced no new persecutors or martyrs. Since humanitarians were convinced that knowledge produced humanity, they began to take instances of callousness as evidence not of innate cruelty, but of surviving ignorance. It was hard to think of the men of the 18th Century as being anything but optimists. Leading philosophers began seeing the advantages of the good of humanity over the interests of country. In fact, all over the West, in London as in Philadelphia, philosophers joined articulate businessmen in commending activity and in postponing immediate gratification for the sake of some higher and more enduring satisfaction. Virtue of action became a favorite text.

The lodge, the philosophical society, the scientific academy; all of these became the underpinning for the republican and democratic forms of government which evolved during the 18th Century. The approach the Masons took toward civil authority was through changing the attitude of the individual; to redirect his thinking inward toward self-reform, toward virtue and reason. In a 1744 defense of Freemasonry before the Parisian press, Freemasons argued that Freemasonry was a school of virtue. Masonic leaders publicly stated that the real work of the Freemason should mean that "in his presence, everything changes, all things in the universe are renewed and reformed, order is established, the rule and measure of things is understood, duty is followed, reason listened to, wisdom comprehended; and mortals, without changing their essence, could appear as new men."

The idea of finding one's morality through fraternity, and practicing ethics through sociability, was, of course, a real threat to those religious institutions that had traditionally been in charge of establishing the laws and rules of ethical and moral conduct. The ideals of the Middle Ages were sectarian, that is, they were not capable of being universalized. They involved little respect for the opinions of mankind. And this would become the classic organizational conflict between faith and reason, which, as we know, Freemasonry has since had to endure.

But, as for the state, the Freemasons assured secular

authorities that the role of the fraternity was to defend their fellow citizens, to avenge the injuries of the nation, and thus, extend the boundaries of the empire. The Freemasons advocated their agreement with the established policy that sages make the laws. Their position was that true Masons are heroic sages who believe in God and are faithful to the Prince. In other words, it was reasonable to expect that humankind could live in concord with a balance of moral and civic mandates. And central to this Masonic identity was the belief that merit, and not birth, formed the foundation for social and political order. Because of their ties to the aristocracy, the Masons were able to mirror the old order of things, while creating a form of civil society that would ultimately replace it.

Margaret Jacobs in her important 1991 work which looked at Freemasonry and politics in 18th Century Europe stated that the "constitutional principles and legislative assemblies of 1789 had their foundation and form in the practices and ideals of the Masonic lodges." Dr. Jacobs suggested that modern civil society was invented during the Enlightenment in these assemblies of sociability, and Freemasonry was the most aggressively civic of all. The European lodges had been organized around British constitutional principles, around elections, majority rule, and representative government. Along with this structure came the assumption that reform in society and government was possible through virtuous and self-disciplined leadership. The cultivation of virtue and reason, as practiced in the lodges was presumed to have meaning for civil society as a whole. And this theme became the spirit of the Enlightenment.

In addition, the 18th Century became known as the

century of philosophy. Instead of confining philosophy within the limits of a doctrinal structure, instead of tying it to unchallengeable ideas and deductions from those ideas, the Enlightenment wanted philosophy to move more freely by questioning, examination, and foresight; and through this immanent activity to discover the fundamental form of reality, that is, the form of all natural and spiritual being.

The philosophical ideal of the Enlightenment was to educate the masses—and to focus its instruction on prejudices and barbarities, in particular the wrongness of political and religious tyranny. The role of the enlightenment philosopher was to spread knowledge and set up a public standard of truth. Its principles were above board, freely accessible to all men, and not dependent upon only some revealed truth monopolized by a chosen race, class, or church.

In this context, philosophy was no longer separated from science, history, jurisprudence, and politics. It was the atmosphere in which all these things could exist and be effective together. Philosophy was no longer the isolated substance of the intellect. But was able to present its intellect in the character of its investigations and its cognitive methods. Accordingly, all the philosophical problems, which were inherited by the 18th Century, moved into new positions and underwent changes in meanings. They were transformed from fixed forms into active forces and imperatives. They gave the Scottish Rite its reason to be.

It was the use the Enlightenment made of philosophic thought, and the position and tasks it assigned to such thought that changed society's ideals and aspirations. And this became the central hallmark of Scottish Rite effort. Thought itself became a spontaneous activity; it not only analyzed and dissected ideas, but it actually facilitated the order of things. It conceived that ideals were necessary for the good of society.

The true nature of enlightenment thinking was the process by which it brought about a new order of things; where, through its doubting and seeking, tearing down and building up, it created an age in which reason and science were both venerated as man's highest faculty. The real philosophy of the Enlightenment was not the sum total of leading thinkers—men such as Montesquieu, Diderot, Voltaire, Kant, and Hume--but in the overall form and manner of intellectual activity in general.

The 18th Century was engaged in a critical examination of the source and limits of reason. It analyzed the extent that we can solve problems, using reason and knowledge. It questioned whether all knowledge derived from experience, or was grounded in experience. It questioned if understanding contained certain properties that could always be defined.

Kant, for example, raised the question whether our concepts of understanding are based on the organizations we are in, or how we go about describing things. He argued that knowledge had to be based on constants. It's not about how many things we can know; but if there is an experience, a form of understanding that transcends time and space.

He suggested there are two classes of things we can know about—those that are always true; that is, they are true by definition (A bachelor is always an unmarried man, for instance). Or, since every experience we have will be within a context of space and time, then every knowledge claim we make will match up with some pure category of understanding. If this is true, then synthetic propositions will either take place in time, or their truth will be known *a priori*.

This was an important idea in the context of Masonic teaching. That we have the freedom to act does not need to be proven—it needs only to be thinkable. The idea of freedom is a thinkable idea; if one believes he is acting as a free agent; then that is sufficient for moral judgments to be possible. Morality exists insofar as we are able to choose freely from alternative courses of action. Actions have moral weight when chosen rather than compelled. There must be freedom of choice if moral judgments can be made at all; if we are to be charged with wrongdoing or praised for worthy actions. The men of the Enlightenment established the ideals of tolerance, free thought, and rational consent.

There are, in fact, categorical imperatives that are governed by the "laws of freedom." There are principles of moral authority, which take precedence over hypothetical laws. One is not a moral being just because he is a human being. What constitutes a moral being is one who has the power of reason. It is by the virtue of our autonomy as reasonable beings that there can be morality.

If we are prepared to do wrong just because the consequences are negligible, then we are not moral beings. Man is never a means to an end, but always an end unto himself. He cannot suspend moral precepts whenever they are not serviceable to him. We cannot use another person simply by claiming we have a right to do so. To use another person as a means or a tool is to cancel the very moral autonomy on which "right" and "wrong" become possible. Enslaving another is thus a formal rejection of freedom as a moral imperative. Because, if moral freedom can be denied here; then it can be denied here, there, and everywhere.

Lying also refutes moral imperative. If you lie to another to get him to do something he would not otherwise do if he knew the truth, you deprive him of his standing as a moral being. You can never justify something on moral grounds just because it makes you feel good, or makes you happy.

Kant's moral theories tried to save us from conditional morality, and gave the Scottish Rite the basis for its focus on the study of principles and situational ethics. We work from the enlightenment understanding that the power of reason is not just the sum of facts and ideas that have always been with us; but that reason is an acquisition. It is not an inheritance. The mind is not a treasury where all truth is stored, but rather the intellectual force, which guides the discovery and determination of truth. Thus, truth is a quest in which knowledge and principles and ideas become an energy or force, which can be fully comprehensible to the individual and his society.

This conviction lead to Lessing's famous saying that the real power of reason is to be found not in the possession, but in the acquisition, of truth. The age of the Enlightenment did more than any other century of Western history to combat the powers that encourage ignorance bigotry, and tyranny; and to give men a better world to live in. Today, we may consider ourselves more enlightened—or at least we have a chance of being so. And this is the basis of all Masonic thought and philosophy. We are all on a quest. We use our experience, our senses and sciences, our powers and passions, our knowledge and insight—all in the search and discovery of truth. This was the imperative of the Enlightenment and the heritage from which we came.

There is a second meaning to enlightenment, to which I referred at the beginning of this lecture. It is a meaning, which also had its roots in Enlightenment Era thought. The lust for knowledge, which theological dogmatism had long outlawed and branded as intellectual pride, was called a necessary quality of the soul in the 18th Century. Montesquieu even attempted to provide a theoretical justification for the presence of an innate thirst for knowledge within the human soul itself. He said; *"our soul is made for thinking, for perceiving; and such a thing must have a curiosity, for just as all things form a chain in which every idea precedes one idea and follows another, so one cannot want to see the one without desiring to see the other."*

He was actually repeating a much older body of thought here. The quest for knowledge about human nature and the purpose of human existence belonged to a general body of thought referred to as the Mysteries. The core of the Mysteries rested on one crucial idea—that man exists in two parallel worlds at the same time—the physical, material, sensual world, a world with edges—and a vast, limitless, eternal, non-material world not available to ordinary perception, but which is still equally a part of his universe. In Masonry, we often refer to this duality as the material and spiritual nature of man. The Mysteries were the schools, which provided the gateway to these non-material realms and the knowledge of the natural laws operating in them. The exploration, defense, reinforcement, and consolidation of knowledge as both an intellectual and sacred path became the cardinal aim of 18th century culture.

The logic of clear and precise ideas and their examination leads to the logic of individuality, which leads to the principle of identity, and from the principle of identity we are led to the principle of infinity, then from continuity to harmony. In these fundamental progressions of ideas lay the great tasks which eighteenth century thought had to accomplish.

Like the enlightenment of ideas, like the cosmos themselves, each individual is in the process of becoming—always growing, changing, developing, and evolving to higher and higher states that will ever more beautifully express the perfection of the source of existence. Enlightenment is the realization of the truth of being. The word "Enlightenment" is translated from the Sanskrit word "Bodhi," denoting awakening, wisdom, and awareness. From a Masonic perspective, we think of it as the quest for light, or perfection—a spiritual journey we make into ourselves; and within which we discover and live out that truth. It is the matter of the eye seeing itself. And the path by which this is accomplished is Initiation—a ritual experience wherein we may discover moral awareness, responsibility, and self-knowledge. It is also essential to our understanding of initiation that it has a philosophical, psychological, and human dimension.

Philosophically, enlightenment means comprehending the unity of all dualities, the harmonious composite of all opposites; the oneness of endless diversity. In psychological terms, it means transcendence of all sense of limitation. In human terms, it means understanding that the journey is in the teaching, that the path and the destination are ultimately one. In theological terms, it means comprehending the union of God and Man; or, rather, of God and humanity.

We live the great mystery of life, and our task is to unfold and understand that mystery so that we may discover our true nature and our identity with the Divine. For it is in living with such identity that we find the source of all happiness, all goodness, all beauty, all truth.

The degrees of the Scottish Rite lay out the way for understanding the mystery of our being. The Rite is the real spiritual matrix of our craft. It facilitates the candidate's symbolic journey of transforming disbelief into real light. And his brothers partake in the mystery with him to assist in his transformation.

We need also to understand that enlightenment is ineffable. It can't be described. It is beyond words, images, and concepts. It cannot be grasped by intellect, logic, or analysis. It has to be experienced to be known. We are taught in Masonry that symbols conceal as much as they reveal, that the language of our degrees are only about truth—they are not truth itself. So, while we may learn a great deal about enlightenment principles and ideas, reading about it is no substitute for the practice of a spiritual discipline, or sacred tradition of some kind. It matters not how much effort we put into seeking enlightenment, it can never be achieved. It can only be discovered and experienced.

We are reminded in the very early lectures of Freemasonry of the scriptural passage, *"Seek and you shall find. Knock and it shall be opened unto you."* This means that there is a universal intelligence that will provide everything you need every step of the way. Its entire purpose is simply to awaken you to your true nature. Enlightenment, or the kingdom of heaven, is your birthright.

The mission of the Scottish Rite is that its lessons will direct you to the path of enlightenment. It invites you to become a Knight of the East and West. Your journey is to spread those basic principles that enable all people to live fraternally together by laying aside animosities and differences. This requires a change in consciousness. The

THE JOURNEY OF THE ELU TO ENLIGHTENMENT

Scottish Rite offers guideposts for this journey; a journey to nothing less than a change of consciousness. For, as we change how we think, we also change our state of mind. And as we are able to journey into ourselves, we also ascend Jacob's ladder into higher realms of mind. We do not change reality, but we change our perception of reality, which is the goal of enlightenment.

John White, in his wonderful book, "What Is Enlightenment?" informs us that the difference before and after enlightenment is in us—not reality. The limitation is also in us—our consciousness. And when that limitation is transcended by the journey we make, we perceive our world differently and therefore relate to it in new ways. Our sense of identity changes. We are brought into the realm of infinity. We experience the cosmos as unified and intimately one with our own essential being, rather than experiencing ourselves as a separate, isolated physical form apart from all the rest of existence.

Enlightenment, then, to both the 18th Century intellectual mind, and the 21st Century seeker of Truth, is liberation. It is freedom. Our goal as members of the brotherhood of man under the fatherhood of God is to strive to free ourselves and to free others. For as long as one person is not free, no one is free. Therefore, we must become one with each other.

This is our great work in the Scottish Rite. We are to study the degrees of the Rite with a consciousness that, as we learn its lessons, we learn how to live. When we live in service to humanity, then the true goals of the Enlightenment—Liberty, Equality, and Fraternity—are achieved within us and in the world. Only a transformed consciousness can transform the world. This is the lofty ambition of Scottish Rite Masonry.

IV

WHAT IS FREEDOM?

The concept of Freedom is the second fundamental teaching of the Scottish Rite. Grand Commander Pike wrote; "It is not enough for a people to gain its liberty. It must secure it." His point is that Freedom is never free. It depends on a moral condition. Freemasonry's task is to address the moral sphere within which freedom or liberty can exist. Both words are typically used to mean the same thing.

One could well argue that the Scottish Rite was created during the Enlightenment era to provide an instructional guide for teaching the criteria upon which a people can be free. Pike begins addressing the meaning of freedom as early as the Fellowcraft degree. He admonishes us that we owe it to ourselves to be free. We owe it to our country to seek to give her freedom, and to maintain her in it. We encounter freedom in Pike's lectures throughout the degrees.

But exactly what is freedom? And what are the different

associations between freedom and other virtues, say, for instance, freedom and justice, or freedom and the law, or freedom and equality? Are men truly free when their actions are regulated by law? Does freedom mean that one can do whatever he wishes, or whatever he has the power to do, whenever he desires to do it? And when he cannot, is he less free? Do considerations of justice draw a line between freedom and license? Can there be freedom apart from equality? Does it make a difference to freedom whether or not laws are just? Do all men have a right to be free?

Indeed, the traditional issues of freedom seem to be stated in these kinds of questions. This chapter addresses the several distinct ideas of freedom in the context of the Scottish Rite's great motto of liberty, equality, and fraternity.

Hegel wrote that the "history of the world is none other than the progress of the consciousness of Freedom." This would appear to have validity in the sense that one would seem to have little effect on human progress unless he is given the power to exercise some degree of choice over his own outcome, and the outcome of others. Other historians, however, would disagree. Some see man as free to work out his own destiny, and look upon the great crises of civilization as turning points in which freemen, or men having free will, exercise a free choice for better or worse. Tolstoy felt that events of history are inevitable, and therefore our perception of the degree of freedom we have depends on how we observe and react to each event as it happens. His suggestion was that, in every action we examine we see a certain measure of freedom and a certain measure of inevitability. We therefore have more or less freedom depending solely on how inevitable a course of action is.

WHAT IS FREEDOM

There is some truth to both Hegel's idea that freedom is a matter of conscience; and Tolstoy's suggestion that we work out how free we are within the context of how and where we live. Our external environment, at least to some extent, determines the level of freedom we have. There is a vigilance associated with liberty. And there is no doubt that freedom can be lost as well by non-users as by miss-users. As a starting point to how we might think about freedom, we need to first look at the meaning of the word "Freedom."

It is an English word adapted to speaking of freedom from certain restraints or undesirable conditions, as well as of freedom to act in accordance with some desire, or to exercise a certain privilege. The real question here seems to be a metaphysical one. Can any finite thing be absolutely free? The traditional answer is 'No.' Neither people, nor states, have infinite power. While states and even Grand Lodges might argue they are sovereign, such autonomy is incompatible with living under human law or government. To be totally independent would make one an anarchist; or one who is free from law and government. We can safely say that such a natural province does not exist in any civilized country in the world today. So, the natural freedom of man is not realistic; or really applicable to human progress in our time.

Pike suggests that there is but a single principle, and that is the sovereignty of man over himself. This sovereignty is called liberty. But Pike also points out that where two or more people choose to associate together, a degree of this liberty or freedom is lost to each; that is, we abdicate a portion of our individual freedom to the common right or good of all. Actually, the situation is even more basic than Pike suggests. In fact, every human being is born at a certain point in time, and into a certain environment in which he has no control. He grows up in the social culture of his environment. He is taught a certain religious belief system and he develops under the influence of a certain world outlook beyond his control. That same person, because he is born of a certain family also inherits at least some of the good and bad attributes, skills, habits, and even illnesses from his family. Again, certain physical and mental characteristics are passed from generation to generation by heredity, and are beyond one's own will. Therefore, the will of man is not entirely free. He is, at least to an extent, the prisoner of the factors that emanate from his own heredity and environment.

But Pike's point is that everyone who lives within a family unit, or in a community or nation, whether he wills it or not, makes a contribution to the joint sovereignty of all members within the group or community. It is this giving up of a portion of our own sovereignty that led to the great Enlightenment motto of Liberty, Equality, and Fraternity. So, sovereignty can be thought of as liberty. The degree of concession which each makes to the good of all can be thought of as equality. The protection each of us gives to all others in our society is fraternity. Pike makes the remarkable observation that freedom is the summit, and equality is the base of this arrangement. This maxim suggests two things—that it is only when people have equal rights that they are the most free. And freedom is not an absolute.

It might be said the only natural right of man is the liberty each man has to use his own power for his own preservation, that is to say, the preservation of his own life and property. However, this freedom or natural right of man belongs to man only in a state of nature, or in a state of emergency. As has been pointed out, when we leave nature and enter a community, or state, or nation, we exchange this natural liberty for a civil liberty.

The degrees of Masonry primarily address this idea of civil liberty, with its many ramifications in ethics, law, justice, economic, and social well-being. If men do not have free will in an absolute sense, that is, if their will is, in reality, a synthesis of sociological, psychological, economical, legal, and historical factors, then it is important that they at least have the freedom to think about choosing between alternatives which can provide them the best life possible.

Learning how to think about making the best possible choices in our adventure of life is the task of the Scottish Rite Mason. Because when reason is employed in directing the actions we take, then choosing between good and bad actions becomes an act of freedom itself. Kant said that reason is in itself the pure will, and that will is in its very essence free. Since this appears to be a contradiction of what we have previously discussed, let's look at the idea of civil liberty a bit deeper.

So, what is civil liberty in the context of Masonry? According to Masonic philosophy (if there is such a thing), we insist on a civic guarantee that we are free to do what the law does not prohibit; and we are free to make our own choices in matters that the law does not address, provided that our choices do not negatively impact others. Our civic duty is to see to it that the laws we produce for ourselves through our elected representatives, i.e., the laws of our government, will produce only the limitations and the licenses as we would also agree to have if there were no laws at all. In other words, in a free society, the degree of freedom that we enjoy is not absolute because it is necessarily constrained by the legislative power that has been established by consent. But once the constraints in the public good have been established, then it is a freedom for each individual to follow his own will in all matters not prescribed by the laws of the country in which he lives.

Masonry then associates freedom with virtue and morality. The Masonic imperative is that we use our freedom properly only when we act virtuously; we misuse it when we act viciously. We are free only when we are not slaves to our own vices. We are free only when we practice morality; when we are focused on living moral lives. We are free only when society itself does not tyrannize us individually with its collective dictates of opinion.

Augustine said that the distinction between freedom and license, in fact, applies to every free act. His position was that, since there is no good act that is not prescribed by the moral law, the whole of freedom consists in doing what that moral law commands. Of course, this definition does not take into account problems such as political liberty and ethics, especially when the spheres of law and liberty are separate from, or opposed to each other. To break the law may be criminal license, but to obey it is not to be free. It may be that the sphere of freedom indeed increases as the stringency of the law decreases, but freedom is not tied only to law.

Freemasonry takes a broader point of view. It teaches that freedom is, in fact, not absolute. But man can still be free enough; meaning that he is free enough to exercise free will so long as laws are just and men are virtuous. If a law is just, then a man is not compelled to do what he would freely have done even if the law did not exist. Only the unjust is coerced or constrained by good laws. However, the Scottish Rite also instructs us that freedom can be abridged by law; and by society itself.

This is precisely the problem of a good man living under unjust laws. Montesquieu held the same opinion. He argued that governments and laws interfere with liberty when they command or prohibit acts contrary to the free choice of a good man. John Mill, in his classic treatise on liberty, also adds that society can and does execute its own mandates independently of law; and if it issues wrong mandates instead of right; or any mandates at all in things which it ought not to meddle, it practices a form of social tyranny that can be more formidable than many kinds of political oppression. This is the classic challenge of all those who have historically not chosen to conform to the ideas of the masses, and have been socially castigated for it.

Protection, then, against the tyranny of government is not enough to meet the standard of freedom. There needs also to be protection against prevailing opinion and feeling when that opinion and attitude becomes tyrannical. Likewise, there needs to be a protection against the tendency of society to impose its own ideas and practices as rules of conduct on those who may dissent from them when such imposition fetters the development of, or prevents the formation of any individuality not in harmony with its ways.

Society does not have a right to compel all individuals to fashion themselves upon the model of its own. This is the fundamental problem with cultural or political correctness, or right-wing populism. Assigning meaning to ourselves and then having the freedom to articulate what is important to us without fear of punishment or cultural reprimand is an essential criterion for the expression of free will. But whenever a society dictates that only certain ideas, words, expressions, and behaviors are acceptable, and any idea which is not endorsed by the majority should, in fact, be forbidden by law; or worse, the notion that those who do not adhere to the socially accepted norm be punished, is an encroachment on freedom. The obvious problem with such a declaration is that there is no legal authority sanctioning what behaviors are to be adopted and which are to be condemned. The dynamics are the same in almost all right-wing populist causes. The members are, for the most part, not groups who conspire to bring down government and democracy. Instead, they are often our own neighbors and business associates; self-appointed average people motivated by a combination of material and ideological grievances and aspirations to coerce people into their way of thinking.

It is not the intent that this be a political essay. Rather, the point being made here is that there is a limit to the legitimate interference of collective opinion with individual independence. To find that limit, and to maintain it against encroachment, is as indispensable to a good condition of human affairs, as protection against political despotism.

The degrees of the Scottish Rite seek a resolution to this fundamental issue in human freedom. Freedom from government or social coercion is also freedom for the maximum development of individuality. We have just as much right to be as different from others as our personal inclinations, talents, and tastes enable us to be, so long as we do not attempt to deprive others of their efforts to obtain the same individuality, or violate the moral sphere in our own efforts to be free. This freedom to be different is one of the principle ingredients of human happiness. In fact, it is indispensable to the welfare of society.

And this takes us to the next point. The Rite teaches us that freedom is intrinsically tied to reason. This was the view of Plato. The theory is that whenever a man is governed by reason, he is free, for he does the will of no one but himself, and does those things only which he knows are of greatest importance in his life, and which he therefore desires above all things. Kant adds that will is the capability of reason to be practical. What he is saying here is that our ability to make choices and direct action independently of our sensuous impulses represents practical reason, and that kind of will is in its very essence free.

Freemasonry makes this point very early on. We have to learn to subdue, or set aside, our passions if we are to improve ourselves, and make any real progress in life. This concept of subduing our passions has everything to do with freedom. The man who acts under the influence of only his passions or sentiments acts in terms of inadequate ideas. He is in bondage because he is not his own master. He follows the worse of alternative choices, even when he knows better, and can see there are better options before him. His judgment may be shadowed by error and ignorance, by fortune, or passion; but he is not free because he is not looking out after what is of greatest importance in his life—his own well-being and ultimate happiness.

And the same is often true when we act only with feelings and sentiment. Mill observed that people are accustomed to believe that their feelings are better than reason. But the practical result of being led only by feeling or sentiment is that, in each person's mind, his feelings represents everyone else's; and since everyone else's feelings should duplicate his, they will naturally always act the way he would like them to act. The obvious problem with this position is that it does not account for one's freedom to judge independently, or to apply one's own critical thinking skills to the problem at hand. In such a case, there is no objective way to ensure that prejudice, superstition, envy, jealousy, fear, or self-interest has not formed the basis for reason.

But the Scottish Rite suggests that when pure reason rules, man acts both with adequate knowledge and in the light of truth. He is free because he is doing the will of no one but himself, and he does those things he knows are of greatest importance to his life because he has reasoned the possible results of his alternative judgments in a matter. Herein is the whole rationale between ignorance and Masonic light.

The bottom line of Masonic virtue is that the freedom of enduring importance in the world is the freedom to acquire and attain knowledge. For it is in the acquisition of knowledge that we also acquire reason. And knowledge is not just the fruit of man's own experience. One does not have to have been to Australia, for example, to know where Australia is, to know its principal towns and its many particularities. Knowledge is not obtained only through experimentation. It is also obtained through a thinking process.

The main manifestation of intelligence is reflection, that is, the faculty of being able to reach the unknown with the help of what is already known. This faculty is called wisdom. So, if intelligence is "land," wisdom is the "building" built on this land; and the principal influential factor in this construction is the desire of man to build it; in other words, the desire of man to use his will in that direction. We are applying to our behaviors what Dewey so aptly said, that reason is the "freedom of observation and of judgment exercised in behalf of purposes that are intrinsically worthwhile." Thus, we are indeed led by passion, but guided by reason, which results in wisdom.

Applying this duality between reason and sentiment, then, to our spiritual lives, a virtuous man is morally and spiritually free when human reason triumphs in its conflict with passion. We are moral agents of our own spirituality. We are spiritual beings who can either gain or lose our freedom according to whether we submit to the guidance of reason or follow our passions or sentiments.

Now, in the context of spirituality, we need also to be clear on where reason stops and faith begins, since faith is so often based on sentiment, as well. Pike said a man's faith is as much his own as his reason is his own. His freedom consists as much in his faith being free as in his will being uncontrolled by others. No man or body of men should be authorized to decide what other men should believe. Every religion and truth should be judged of by reason. However, it should be pointed out that Masonry does not teach that spiritual freedom can be attained by reason alone. Rather, it instructs us that ultimate spiritual freedom is a freedom acquired not of this world, but of divine, or supernatural grace. And grace is not the province of man. Spiritual freedom is the independence of the soul. It is the undisturbed possession of truth.

However, Masonry does teach that a man, as a breathing, eating, and walking being on earth, is capable of reaching a high level of spiritual freedom by practicing the acquired virtues—by reasoning that he has a future and thus his actions can have consequences. We are the most free when we live virtuous lives. Virtue is the truest liberty. Freedom of thought and conscience is not entirely utopian. Men become daily more free because the freedom of man lies in his reasoning power. We cannot see salvation by virtue alone, but we will certainly have less for which to be embarrassed when we are judged by the "Great I Am" if we have led virtuous lives. That requires the acquisition of knowledge and wisdom; and thus, reason.

We can order our own life as we please only when we have taken the effort to become more valuable to ourselves and to others. That is the essence of freedom and free will. At any time, we are enabled to live according to the whole light of knowledge that is within each of us. The raising of the Master Hiram is a resurrection to freedom of thought and action. The Master Hiram becomes the symbol of human liberty—liberty of the soul and of the body—liberty of the intellect and of the conscience—freedom from error and prejudice; from vice and passion, as well as from spiritual and temporal subjugation.

Herein lies the freedom of man—as we receive more light, we possess more liberty. The object of Freemasonry is the transformation of man and people to that life of liberty that God intended. We need only to prepare ourselves to be fit for freedom. It is indeed true that not every man can be free.

By means of the morality of Masonry, we advance toward its philosophy; and every degree that we take and come to understand is a step toward civil, moral, and spiritual freedom.

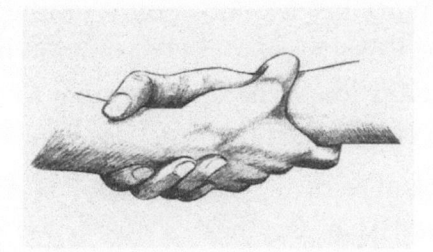

What Is Toleration?

*May Brotherly Love Prevail and
Every Moral and Social Virtue Cement Us*

Every Freemason will recognize the above declaration as the epilogue of the closing prayer given at almost every Masonic lodge meeting. It was penned by William Preston in 1772.

It is an admonition for toleration.

Frederico Mayor, in an address dedicating the Beit-Hashoah Museum for Tolerance in Los Angeles in 1993 said; *"...our ability to value each and every person is the ethical basis for peace, security and intercultural dialogue."* Albert Pike stated it even more poignantly in the 10° by declaring that without toleration *"we are mere hollow images of true Masons, mere sounding brass and tinkling cymbals."* The fact is that a peaceful future depends on everyday acts of kindness and respect. It is a lesson every Freemason knows well.

Among all the teachings Masonry imparts to its members, none is more important than championing the ideal of toleration. Thus, it can well be argued that toleration is the third great principle of Scottish Rite philosophy. As we begin our awesome journey to become Masters of the Royal Secret, it behooves us to have an open mind about toleration in the same way that we have viewed the requisites of enlightenment and freedom.

In the book of lectures for the Symbolic Lodge, we read; "By the exercise of Brotherly Love we are taught to regard the whole human species as one family; the high and low, the rich and poor; who, as created by one Almighty Parent, and inhabitants of the same planet, are to aid, support and protect each other. On this principle, Masonry unites men of every country, sect and opinion, and conciliates true friendship among those who might otherwise have remained at a perpetual distance."

That is a lofty ideal indeed. And it would seem to work well so long as we don't encounter someone, or some group, who, in our view, is obviously evil to the core. The exercise of brotherly love does not mean that, as a result, there can be nothing to which we might disagree. We tolerate when we object to something but nevertheless refrain from impeding it. Religious faiths, for example, are conflicting as well as different in that they present rival bodies of belief. As an adherent of one faith, we may have good reason to disagree with and to disapprove of other faiths. Religious tolerance requires of us not to prevent, or to seek to prevent the practice of other faiths even though we have reason to disagree with and disapprove of them. We tolerate when we refrain from impeding that to which we object. If we do not object, we have no reason to tolerate.

Toleration is therefore not a response to every difference. Others may possess preferences or pursue forms of life different from our own, and that should not bother us. If we accept that others have different life styles than we do, we simply respond to our differences by being nonchalant toward them. Again, we have no occasion to tolerate them. On the other hand, when cultures conflict rather than merely differ, as they sometimes do on matters of values, we may well find ourselves presented with questions of toleration. What ought to be a matter for toleration can be controversial simply because people have different views on what we can reasonably disapprove of or dislike.

Hence, there is a certain 'paradox to toleration." It is easy, for instance, for a "good man" to profess that to tolerate someone or something means simply to accept them or it. In the view of the good man's point of view, rather than putting up with something to which they take exception, tolerant people simply take no exception. They are open-minded and accepting of others, even when the beliefs and practices of others differ from their own. However, there is an obvious practical problem with rejoicing in all differences. In doing so, we remove disapproval and dislike from the idea of toleration. How can it be good or right not to prevent a wrong; especially a preventable wrong?

What is important to understand about toleration is it's combining of two sorts of reason; reason to disapprove or dislike with reason to refrain from impeding what we disapprove of or dislike. What sort of reason, then, can be a reason for toleration?

Fortunately, there are many different reasons why we might, or should, opt for toleration rather than intolerance.

As an employee, we have reason to tolerate a superior's objectionable conduct if we want to gain his support in seeking a promotion. We have reason to tolerate the shortcomings of other countries if we want to retain them as allies. We have reason to tolerate an opposing view of a spouse in the interest of sustaining a relationship. We have reason to tolerate a loss of some freedom for the greater good of living together in a community.

In Masonry, we are more concerned with moral reasons for toleration; that is, to the moral status possessed by persons and to the respect and equal respect that we owe one another as persons. People, by virtue of being people, are entitled to pursue their preferred forms of life and others are duty-bound not to prevent them from doing so. Thus, a person has a right to the toleration of others and others have a duty to respond accordingly. As Masons, we all represent the brotherhood of man. To be a part of such a brotherhood means that we accept the general idea that people should possess equal liberty to live as they choose, and this liberty should be mutual and reciprocal.

Toleration is an important ethical theme and we must give much credence to its application because it deals with one of the most challenging aspects of public policy in relationship to society as a whole. One of the central questions is how should a society provide for the differences exhibited by its population? Should it view them with indifference, or seek to diminish them in the interest of social unity, or view them as positive goods that it should facilitate or promote?

The answer is not simple because the differences themselves are so diverse. How do we respond to different languages? How do we respond to different religions? Or other beliefs? How do we think about the differences that exist due to inequalities in the economic well-being or social status of citizens? And how do differences make a difference in other places or countries, with traditional cultures much different than our own? Can someone who is genuinely committed to a particular form of life readily accept that other forms, to which he feels no similar allegiance, are no less good? The records of history certainly suggest we are not so good at responding to these kinds of questions. We are not tolerant, *a priori*, of life conditions that are entirely different from our own. In fact, it would appear that we hold to intolerance more than we embrace acceptance. Indeed, the history of much of the world is a saga of deep ethnic divisions, regional conflicts, religious zealotry, and economic hostilities among peoples. Intolerance, jealousy and greed have fragmented almost every country in the world.

Still, this does not mean that good men and women should drop out of the battle for virtuous ideals. If ever there was a time to embrace what is good in humanity, we are living in that time. America was created in the light of virtue; but it seems our pluralism has either lost the vision, or insists on redefining it.

There was a time when people came to America seeking asylum from such human suffering and strife. The altruistic nature of democracy has made the United States a multi-cultural society. Now the same divisions that have caused so much suffering and loss in the rest of the world are becoming manifest in the freest country on earth. We are becoming a nation filled with mistrust and animosity.

The natural reaction to diversity is to isolate ourselves in our own culture. It's a kind of "out of sight, out of mind" mentality. It is easy to believe that we can't get hurt if we stay within our own group. We can't get into trouble if we don't participate. Undeniably, as Freemasons, we receive much personal joy from being together in the tiled spaces of our lodge, free from the strife of the world, protected by the contract of love we pledge to each other; without regard for geographic or political or cultural boundaries.

But that peace of mind, that collective will to love each other, that feeling of trust and security we share, that identity we have as brothers does not come from without us. It comes from within. It happens because we integrate the lessons we learn in our lodges, chapters, councils, and consistories into our own psyche. We become what we have been taught. We choose to live the tenets of our Order. We choose to improve ourselves in Masonry. We make a conscious choice that we are going to be special men; that we are going to distinguish ourselves from the rest of the community. And that happens when we practice the brotherhood of man out in the world as well as in our tiled recesses. Everyone benefits when they have direct access to real examples of moral and social virtue in and around them every day. That is the impact Freemasonry was designed to have on the world.

With people now migrating to America in record numbers, steady and ubiquitous examples of moral and civic virtue are more important than ever. We must now acknowledge that everyone who has perceived themselves as 21st century American-born citizens is rapidly becoming a minority. This perception is strong across every culture. National unity will never be possible if we feel threatened by every group outside our own. We cannot remain an island of brotherhood amid tyranny, intolerance and hatred.

WHAT IS TOLERATION

Our own way of life is being threatened. We all intuitively know that the time has come for all Americans to make a little sacrifice and effort toward a greater cause. As Masons, we are obligated to fight against tyranny wherever and whenever it exists. It is our obligation to stop the bully and the brute. The question is where do we begin?

Since (as the saying goes) you can't teach an old dog new tricks, it seems the only chance we have of achieving and maintaining a sense of national unity at home is to develop a healthy learning environment among our children that will give them a full cross-cultural understanding. And such understanding will not just happen. To communicate and learn from one culture to another takes entire families out of their comfort zone. To achieve a reconciliation of idealistic, ethnic, religious and cultural differences between the old ways and the new will require an extraordinary feat of will and learning. In most cases, toleration itself will have to be learned and practiced.

That is where we as fraternal men come in. In fact, the Scottish Rite was made for such a mission. If the Rite is indeed a great power, it is so because influence is power; and will is power. The teachings of the Rite answer these kinds of questions: What kind of society might we have if we were to achieve a culture of peace? How much would such a culture manifest itself in our family lives, communities, state and national politics and international relations? What relationship exists between tolerance and peace? Can human rights be realized without a social commitment to tolerance? Is there a significant relationship between human rights and democracy? What are our own personal and community concerns about the issue of tolerance? How do our concerns relate to tolerance on a global scale? How can we contribute to promoting a tolerant world?

If our own history is a guide, Freemasonry gains civic and social relevance when it stands up for what it stands for. There can be much value in sharing our values with the cross-cultural world in which we live. We may not have the numbers to be a national voice all at once. But we still have a voice. We can at least take the lead in diagnosing the kinds of intolerance that hinders the world; and then pledge, individually and corporately, to do whatever is necessary in educating the next generation of adults that tolerance is indeed the most reasonable means to peace in the world.

As an example of how this might be pursued, the ideal of our exercise of brotherly love, as was introduced at the beginning of this essay, may actually have force within humanity's ability and willingness to recognize peace as a shared good. We know, for instance, that most ways of life have an interest in peace; all, or nearly all ways of life have interests that make peaceful coexistence worth pursuing. People's interest in peace consists not only in their being spared of suffering and bloodshed, but also in their enjoying the many positive goods for which peace is a practical precondition.

Freemasonry's concept of the just society as one that remains neutral between people's different comprehensive doctrines and conceptions of the good is the best model of the politically tolerant society. The Scottish Rite teaches that it is not neutrality that gives rise to toleration, but that toleration makes the case for neutrality. How is this brought about? It can only occur by establishing a government in which citizens may not use any of the instruments of political power either to promote or to disadvantage a particular doctrine or conception of the good. A neutral state is always the offspring of an unusually thorough commitment to toleration. This means that it is up to each of us as citizens to construct the arrangements under which we live.

The task of the Scottish Rite is to teach its adherents to distinguish between citizens as architects of the government in which the role they play is not engaged in tolerating everyone, from the citizens as members of the society practicing in accordance with the role they stand in a tolerant relation to one another. This requires, above all else, that we be tolerant men.

The journey we take through the philosophies presented to us as Scottish Rite men in regard to moral behavior, principles and situational ethics, through the reconciling influences of the ancient mysteries' traditions, through the lessons of civic virtues and the history of ideas, we become aware of the conflicts of want and beliefs; what is true and false, right or wrong, prudent and imprudent, ethical and unethical. We learn how the conflicts we encounter can be provided for. We learn that beliefs are capable of being correct or incorrect, or more or less correct; and people do not necessarily have an interest in holding and acting on their beliefs merely because those beliefs are their own. People are indeed capable of moral change. They have a more inherent interest in holding and acting on correct beliefs.

As long as we as a people living together in a pluralistic world continue to differ and disagree, sincerely and reasonably, it is hard to see how we can do better than take seriously the case for toleration. Without it, we will reach too easily for the words; "I have a right to persecute you because I am right and you are wrong."

THE JOURNEY OF THE ELU TO ENLIGHTENMENT

It seems like such a worthy mission to stand on what we stand for in the brotherhood of men--enlightenment, freedom, and toleration--thus it is important that we know the value of these three great principles. It seems a good way to begin this present review of the teachings of the Scottish Rite.

The Six Major Themes
of the Scottish Rite

The work of the Scottish Rite is to inspire and teach man that he must improve, refine and perfect himself. He must become a fit and worthy recipient of the Royal Secret, with all the requisite knowledge that such a responsibility demands. The degrees of the Rite constitute a journey towards ever broadening horizons of knowledge. They teach a nobler virtue, honor and truth, and of one's duty to direct one's life toward those ends in all we think, speak and do. Each Degree, or Body of Degrees, has a general theme, or central idea, upon which its instruction is centered.

Keeping in mind that, though each degree of the Rite has a central theme, no degree teaches only a single lesson, and no symbol has a single meaning; here are the six major themes presented in the Scottish Rite.

The Perfect Elu Tradition

A brother becomes an Elu in the first degree of Masonry when he receives the Apprentice's prayer. Hands are laid upon his head and he is anointed as one of the "elected" or "elite" entering the Brotherhood of Man. He has been selected by his peers because they see his potential to rise among the best to become the small elite of enlightened minds. But even though he is chosen, he may not become enlightened. God has made men with different intellectual and spiritual motivations and capacities. The Elu Principle avows that, from the ranks of men who desire to improve themselves in Masonry, some will take on the pursuits and occupations of the Initiate's life. These will become the Perfect Elus, the continuators of Creation who will receive the highest levels of knowledge and insight. These will become the gifted and enlightened men.

From this lofty principle arises one of the first questions that must be explored in the Degrees of the Lodge of Perfection. What is required of us to become Perfect Elus? How do we rise above our own circumstances? Indeed, what are our circumstances? What are the hidden lessons taught in the Elu of the Nine and Elu of the Fifteen that address these significant questions?

Well, to get there, we must first begin with the journey we have undertaken to qualify ourselves to be Elus to begin with.

Almost every Mason knows that the Degrees of Masonry represent a journey of a man's life. We know, for instance, that it is often said that the Entered Apprentice Degree represents the journey of youth; the passage a young man takes as he begins to consciously weigh the differences between right and wrong, knowledge and ignorance, good and evil, and starts to mold the character he will fashion for himself, using the influences of his life as his guide. He has, in a real sense, been initiated by the circumstances of his life; for good or bad. Freemasonry provides him a stable image for life building, and admonishes him to start over if his first attempt didn't go so well.

Likewise, we think of the passage of the Fellowcraft as one where the initiate takes stock of his progress in life; a kind of review of what he knows, and doesn't know, what has worked for him, and what still remains to be done. He makes an accounting of what he has learned from his experience, his upbringing, friends and acquaintances, education, culture and community. If he is like most men, he reaches a point where he has studied just about everything in his life but himself. He becomes consciously aware that life is not just about outward appearances, tasks, money, and relationships. He feels a hunger for additional meaning. Masonry informs him that, to feel complete, he ultimately has to affirm himself. This requires a different kind of journey all together.

In Masonry, we think of this more intimate and deeply engaging step in the journey to manhood an important awakening for each man. In ritual terms, it is called "passing the outer door of the temple." And it occurs immediately after we have made the ascent of winding stairs, given the password and token to the Junior Warden, and told by our spirit guide that we are at that moment arriving at the inner temple of Freemasonry. And that inner work is nothing less than the arduous journey of discovering who we are.

Regrettably, this is a stage of the journey that a majority of the male population in the world will never choose to take. Never mind that the consequences of not knowing oneself are staggering. But the journey to mature masculinity doesn't stop for the rest of us just because some guys choose to exit the train. For the man who sincerely sees Freemasonry as a transformative art, where he really decides to consciously work on himself; then everything it suggests to him, and instructs him from this point forward in his life, has to do with his awakening consciousness. And that awakening begins when he correctly interprets the meaning of the drama section of the Master Mason Degree.

It can well be imagined that most men have the same thought when they experience the Master Mason Degree for the first time. It is easy to interpret the Hiram story as the hero's quest; but it is also easy to misinterpret who the ruffians are in our drama. We see them only as the bad guys who murdered a good man of great integrity, and left such a void in the construction of God's temple that his death made him a martyred hero. The lesson was obvious enough. A good man was unjustly murdered by selfishness and greed; the bad guys were ultimately caught and brought to justice. And we all went back to being comfortable that the bad guys always lose and the good guys always win in the end.

Regrettably, in many Grand Jurisdictions, the story of the ruffians is very brief and only anecdotal. We spend just enough time on the ruffians to convince the observer that they are the bad guys, they get what is coming to them; and then we focus on our hero, the good man Hiram Abiff, unjustly murdered for doing no harm to anyone.

It is indeed the old "good vs evil" story. Good wins. Evil is punished. And then all is right with the world. We can go back to sleep, comfortable that our fairy tale ended just like all of the others we ever read. Our hero sets out on a great cause, he runs into opposition; he continues with his cause, even knowing that he is at risk. He gets killed because of his commitment to the cause, and we commemorate his death because we are inspired to follow his honor.

But wait a minute. If that is all we learn, we haven't learned anything we didn't already know. If that were all we learn, our ritual drama would be entertaining, but predictable. There must be more to our story than that?

THE SIX MAJOR THEMES OF THE SCOTTISH RITE

The question we must ask is what does the role of these ruffians mean to our own life?

It is important that we understand that the ruffians are a part of every man; they are aspects of our personality for which we should be the least proud, or at least the most concerned. They are the shadow side of our being, the ignorance, the short sidedness, the selfishness, the prejudice; the baggage that we have been carrying with us all along, but not yet fully recognized, let alone overcome.

The Scottish Rite knows this aspect of a man's journey well. The point of awakening consciousness is precisely where the Scottish Rite joins each man's journey. We receive him into the Rite immediately following his apparent resurrection from the baggage of his life. And this is the reason the ruffians are not brought to justice until the 9th and 10th Degrees. Remember the Scottish Rite is a system of 33 Degrees, and contains its own Apprentice, Fellowcraft, and Master Mason rituals.

The authors of the Rite knew that we wouldn't wake up to the worst aspects of our being on our own. We all need a guided path to self-improvement. The experience of the aspirant through the degrees of the Rite is intended to be his journey to a higher awareness. It is a progressive system of awakening consciousness. Its power lies in its ability to integrate its lessons into the psyche of each individual, meeting him on the level of his own experience, and giving him an opportunity to be transformed by the path of his own life. The ascent to perfection is an ascent of consciousness.

Thus, the journey of the Elu is to first discover the inner work he must do on himself if he is going to become an enlightened one. Each of the Degrees of the Lodge of Perfection show him a different aspect of his man circumstances. To elevate his status and affirm himself, he must overcome his ruffians within. The Lodge of Perfection degrees instruct us on what we should look for in identifying our personal ruffians.

Since these are subtly hidden within the allegories themselves, they are articulated here so they will not be overlooked.

In the 4°, it is the mystery of our own being that has not yet been revealed to us. Our inadequate understanding of things, our ignorance and short-sidedness, our passions and prejudices, selfish motives, and lazy approaches to learning.

In the 5°, our ruffians are our selfish interests, idleness and selfishness, our non-committal approach toward the interest, happiness, and welfare of others, our unearned privileges, our lack of concern for equity and fairness—our self-serving motives.

In the 6°, we encounter our hasty judgments; judgments made solely on appearances, our inability to separate perception from reality, our me-first attitude; our prejudices and fears.

In the 7°, the ruffian elements are the decisions we make based on the merest of pretense; or made on the basis of an inflated self-righteousness; our injustice toward those who are different than us; our hastiness to condemn; failure to decide when decisions are required; or our reluctance to judge for fear of being wrong.

In the 8°, our failure to learn or apply the techniques required for us to elevate our consciousness to higher ideals, our unwillingness to change and progress; or our willingness to advance in Masonry without study or applying ourselves; our laziness in actually learning the various meanings of

Truth in philosophy, education, religion, and politics; our latent tendency just to let life be what it will be.

Then, in the 9°- 10°, we face our biggest foes: ignorance, ambition and fanaticism. Pike informs us that ignorance is our "J-m," the greatest enemy of human freedom; ambition, which breeds tyranny, our "J-o;" and fanaticism, which springs from intolerance and persecution, our "J-a."

So, the largest challenge we face in our journey to mature masculinity is to figure out what is required for us to overcome our ruffians within. We cannot affirm ourselves in our own skin until we have accomplished this task. In the 9°, Pike informs us to stop daydreaming and get moving. The essence of a meaningful life, whether in Masonry, or elsewhere, is to act and to be committed. Commitment is the clarion call of the Ninth Degree. It is the inner state of being obligated or emotionally impelled to participate fully in a cause. And in Freemasonry this cause is our own transformation to a higher state of being.

To fulfill our purpose as Masons means that we will actively implement our values and beliefs in specific ways to improve ourselves and help others do the same. True Masonry is not speculative or theoretical or sentimental; but experimental and practical. Masonry is action, and not inertness. It requires its initiates to work. Making personal commitments is an intrinsic part of our life's identity, whereby we accept something or someone as being of ultimate importance to us. Being committed requires more than merely having an opinion or understanding. Taking a stand for our own self-improvement and the interest of others requires being committed to actively striving for what makes life truly important and meaningful. Commitment implies a search for the right answers in life, which entails asking the right questions.

As an anecdotal story, Colonel and Brother William Barret Travis asked the right questions at the Alamo. He did not ask his volunteers if they wanted to see Texas become an independent State. That would have been merely a request for their opinion. Instead, he asked them if they were willing to cross a line that he drew in the sand with his sword that would signal their intent to go against a numerically superior foe and likely suffer a merciless death—all in their struggle to secure Texas' independence. That was asking them if they would commit themselves to support a belief that they claimed was supremely important. The story goes that all but one did cross the line. The solitary holdout reportedly fled before the final assault commenced, thus surviving to tell the story.

We must ask ourselves what is the right set of questions that spurs our commitment? Pike believes that these must come from our principles. Principles are the rules of action that shape and control our conduct. Most men have sentiments, but not principles. Pike suggests that it is our principles that are permanent and controlling impressions of goodness and virtue. The question we must all ask is how do we form principles? They must be based on values we select before we act. It is our principles that define what we do, and they are defined by who we are.

Parenthetically, the 10° addresses tyranny and intolerance in religion; particularly the form of fanaticism that is so insidious that it undercuts opportunities for anyone to gain true spirituality. In the Masonic degrees, deprivation of spirituality is represented by interruption of temple building and by the loss of the Grand Master's word. Rather than employ violence to eradicate fanaticism, as was the mission of the Elus of the Fifteen, today's Freemasons are called to stop religious fanaticism with the more effective and peaceful strategy known as religious tolerance.

We recognize that religious faith is uniquely personal and impervious to criticism because the content and extent of our faith in any one moment reflects only a transitory stage in our spiritual maturity. Tolerance means that we respect others' ability to improve themselves by letting them discover the truth about something by themselves. Spiritual enlightenment comes from incremental stages of voluntary and personal self-development, as one voila moment builds upon another. It is impossible to have those voila moments if we are emotionally straightjacketed into a non-negotiable ecclesiastical absolutism.

Freemasonry teaches us a supremely important insight about spiritual truth: that we believe in Deity is more important than the particulars of what we believe about Deity. The fact that we believe indicates our good character and integrity. That we believe should be a common and shared experience among all of us. It is the result of our most sincere introspection and deliberate acceptance of truth.

What we believe is less important, but what is important is that we acknowledge another man's beliefs are as worthy of our respect as his other Masonic values. *You must remember that it is not by your plumbline that you judge him, but by his. And it is his square and his level, not yours, by which you are to determine his actions. His opinions may differ from yours politically or religiously, but they are his tools, not yours.* The bottom line is that the only proven method of overcoming religious spite is to tolerate it by establishing a common ground in which all may agree. This is the Tenth Degree's lesson.

THE JOURNEY OF THE ELU TO ENLIGHTENMENT

All this brings us to the hidden meaning and instruction of the Elus.

In the Elu of the Nine, Solomon and his court, along with King Hiram, who has come to Jerusalem for the funeral of the Master Hiram, are fearful that the murderers of Hiram may have escaped. Although search is being made, they have not yet been captured. A shepherd from Joppa comes with news that he may have seen one of the murderers in the mountains east of Joppa some 40 miles away from Jerusalem. Solomon selects nine of his court officials by lot, so as not to make any invidious distinctions, and these nine Brethren, afterwards known as the Nine Elus, are sent to capture the miscreant. A battle ensues in which the murderer is killed and his head is brought back to Jerusalem for identification. Solomon awards them into a new Hebrew and Phoenician Order of Nobility that is committed to principles of education, freedom, enlightenment and patriotism that we have previously discussed.

The Tenth Degree then continues the story of the Ninth Degree. In the Elu of the Fifteen, although one of the murderers of the Master Hiram has now been dealt with, the other two are still at large. One of the Elu of the Nine returns to the court of Solomon with word that they may be hiding in the land of Gath. Solomon appoints six additional Elus to accompany the original nine to Gath to try to capture the criminals. They are captured and returned to Jerusalem. Solomon also awards the Elus with the Order of Nobility.

Now here is where it gets interesting. By calling each new knight an Elu, Pike wants us to appreciate the fact that commitment is not merely a human venture. Elu is a French word that connotes the Biblical principle of "spiritual election." It is important that we pick up on the fact that the Elect of the Nine and the Elect of the Fifteen were selected and rewarded by Solomon, who was Deity's anointed representative on Earth. Solomon was the first king of Israel born to a reigning king. King David was inspired to rise from his deathbed to order that the prophet Nathan anoint Solomon, King of Israel even while David still lived.

The inference here is that, just as the Elect of the Nine and Fifteen were selected by Deity's anointed representative by no invidious distinction, means that we too can join the ranks of the elect today by simply accepting, and implementing God's invitation for us to become more than we already are. And we accept God's invitation by living better lives here on earth, so that our eternal reward is magnified.

The Biblical term "elect of God" had to be familiar to Pike when he conferred the title "Elect of the Nine" at the conclusion of the 9°, because Elect of God refers to a Judeo-Christian concept that all of us are Deity's spiritual children. We are invited to partake in all that Deity possesses through legal entitlement as His co-heirs.

Like all the other Old Testament covenants, the Abrahamic covenant represented a divine election that was bestowed upon the Israelites, whereby they were guaranteed eternal salvation if they committed to keep certain obligations. Individuals who entered into this sacred covenant were assured divine assistance during times of hardship. Even in their post-exile distress, God promised them that their divinely guaranteed benefits were not eternally lost and eventually would be restored.

So here is the hidden knowledge of these two Degrees.

Spiritual election is not restricted to a special few; neither is it an automatically inherited right. It is available to everyone, and is a divine gift. But God confers such blessings upon those who demonstrate commitment to obeying the Divine Law. And they can make their election sure by doing what God commands them to do, which includes being kind and caring to others.

It appears Pike may have been conversant with this concept since he arranged in his portrayal of the Ninth Degree for King Solomon to select the "elect of the nine" by lot in order to prevent criticism of invidious distinction. His care to show the limitless possibilities of spiritual blessings available to every Perfect Elu coincides with the Biblical message that anyone can become a spiritual heir to Deity.

Now, here is the crux: Whether the conditional gifts associated with spiritual election become operative for a particular person depends upon that person's commitment to live by divine principles. Similarly, the Elect of the Nine are designated conditionally as elect when they commit to apprehend Hiram's murderer. They are rewarded afterwards with the conferral of knighthood to confirm that they indeed possess the virtues that they exhibit through their commitment.

The lesson to understand here is that Divine election does not confer greatness according to the world's standards. Rather, it works through a deeply abiding relationship between the Creator and his Created. It is this divine relationship between God and Man that gradually transforms the man into a divinely ordained template of virtue and integrity. So it is with the elect of the Nine. We join the ranks of the elect, are permitted to advance through the higher Scottish Rite Degrees, and are slated to become a Perfect Elu, but only as we commit to actually and faithfully implement the Masonic virtues we are taught in our lives. Like the knights of old, we are morally impelled to rise above our circumstances through a committed, interrelated program of virtue and achievement. It is not how long we live that is important, but how we use the time allotted to us. Pike would have us make the most of our knightly existence by being committed to a great cause. In one of his most powerful observations in the lecture of this Degree, he writes:

> "A useless life is short, if it lasts a century; but that of Alexander the Great was long as the life of an oak, though he died at thirty-two. We may do much in a few years, and we may do nothing in a lifetime. If we but eat and drink and sleep, and let everything go on around us as it pleases, or if we live but to amass wealth or gain office or wear titles, we might as well not have lived at all; and we have not the right to expect immortality."

So, you see, honest and conscious commitment is an essential to a well-lived life, as it is to eternal bliss. To become a Perfect Elu, we must combine and integrate worthy virtue in dedicating our lives to self-improvement and altruistic efforts that benefit others. Our commitment to freedom, education, enlightenment, patriotism, and pure religion will have positive eternal effects that are proffered to us by a grateful Deity as co-heirs of His celestial glory and exaltation.

And that is the teaching of the Elu principle in Freemasonry.

THE JOURNEY OF THE ELU TO ENLIGHTENMENT

Royal Arch, or Sacred Vault Tradition

There are three main Royal Arch degrees in Freemasonry—the Royal Arch of Jesiah, worked in Ireland; the Royal Arch of Zerubbabel, worked in England and in all Chapters of the York Rite; and the Royal Arch of Solomon, worked in the Scottish Rite Lodge of Perfection. All have as their principle aim the discovery of the Lost Word. The Royal Arch Tradition is among the most significant themes in all of Masonry.

One of the great mysteries of life is that no man can know the principle of his own life. No single element of life has an intrinsic, essential reality of its own. The power and action of will, movement, of thought, memory and dreams are all mysteries. Yet we have a natural impulse to seek the unknown, to seek God in the mystery of our own being. The Royal Arch Tradition maintains that a man must gain access to the knowledge of the divine truth only by seeking ever deeper within his inmost self, his soul. In Masonry, the crypt or vault is an inward symbol reminding us that it is the internal and not the external qualifications that make a Mason. A man's soul is his spiritual dimension of the universe, the inmost part of his being where alone he may feel and realize the nature of God and find peace within himself.

We are informed that the most sacred treasures of Freemasonry are hidden in darkness; concealed from view by those who are not prepared to receive them. Indeed, one of the three great Bodies of the York Rite is styled "Cryptic" Masonry. This word comes from a Greek word meaning "to hide." It is a concealed place, a subterranean vault. We are given a hint in several of the degrees of Freemasonry that the sacred treasure may be found in an underground vault. It would seem we are led to believe that we may find the Lost Word by looking within.

Yet, we also find various ascending themes in the degrees of Masonry. In the Entered Apprentice Degree, we encounter a ladder leading upward from the ground floor of the temple; whose principal rungs are faith, hope and charity. In the Fellowcraft Degree, the ascension takes the form of a set of winding stairs, at the summit of which the candidate, in his newfound glory, beholds himself as a mirror image of his own divine nature. What does it mean, then, that we must both ascend and descend to search for the most divine nature of our soul?

In Freemasonry, we are thus confronted with a metaphor that represents one of the foundational symbolic images in the study of spirituality. Its fundamental meaning is one of self-awareness and transcendence. The metaphor is most often represented by a ladder or stairs. In Masonic symbolism, both descents and horizontal movements into a cave, vault, or tunnel represent moving downward into the personae of one's own mind and unconsciousness. The purpose of this movement, whether ascending or descending, is for the aspirant to discover his own true nature and his connection with nature, or the universe, or the Divine. It is no less than the hero's quest. In mythology, the quest of the hero can almost always be understood as a descent into one's own mind to discover his true nature and identity. In the degrees of the Blue Lodge, this descent is represented by the circumambulations about the lodge.

The thing to be gained on this journey into oneself is insight, not just knowledge. That is why it is a personal quest. Knowledge can be gained from books or from a teacher, but

THE JOURNEY OF THE ELU TO ENLIGHTENMENT

insight must be the result of the individual's confrontation and exploration of his own thoughts, feelings, experiences and understandings. Real knowledge of yourself cannot be given you by someone else. You must go deep inside yourself to discover the meaning of your existence.

Ascending is represented by movement upwards on a ladder or stairs, or by a horizontal movement as in emerging from a cave or tunnel. It symbolizes changes in levels of consciousness, increasing awareness, and ultimately a knowing of the Deity in a way which can only be experienced within oneself. It is transcendent, ineffable and individual. It is sometimes known as the mystic experience. Most spiritual traditions teach that the insight of the self-journey is necessary before the experience of transcendence is possible. The winding stairs lead to the Middle Chamber, which may be understood to represent insight, intuition, revelation and gnosis. It is another representation of the Sanctum Sanctorum or the Holy of Holies in King Solomon's temple—man confronting his own identity with God.

In Masonry, the Royal Arch, or Sacred Vault tradition, represents this deeply engaging and hidden symbol of Man's highest aspiration, reminding us once more that it is the internal and not the external qualifications that make a Mason. A man's soul is his spiritual dimension of the universe, the inmost part of his being where alone he may feel and realize the nature of God and find peace within himself. The goal is to be able to say, with Judas Maccabaeus "I feel the Deity within."

The Royal Arch raises Masonry higher on Jacob's ladder of awareness and awakening toward communion with the True and Living God, and the eventual transcendental integration in the life hereafter of the human creature with his Divine Creator. This is the greatest quest we will ever take.

Rose Croix Tradition

Among the easiest of emblems to interpret, the rose and cross is one of the great combination symbols of Freemasonry, second perhaps only to the square and compasses. To the Christian Mason, the cross refers to Jesus Christ. But in a broader sense, it symbolizes self-sacrifice for the sake and redemption of mankind. It represents the integration of opposites within the material and spiritual nature of our being, and is one of the primary symbols of our consciousness. The rose, being among the most beautiful of flowers, symbolizes perfection, and represents hope in a new awakening, renewal, and a resurrection of life. The two together (Rose Croix) symbolize faith and hope in immortality won through sorrow and sacrifice. The Rose Croix Tradition informs us that the world is what it is, and we should focus on how to deal with it so that good and the law of love may prevail. This requires a constant fight within our self, and in society.

The duality of darkness and light is once again powerfully exemplified in the Degrees of the Chapter. The allegory presented is that every man in every age must come face to face with adversity. We can all relate to the problem of adversity in our lives, even if we do not understand it and want to avoid it. Adversity if as ubiquitous as work. But it is also the springboard of achievement. We are called on as men and Freemasons to act responsibly whenever we are subjected to it. Instead of complaining to others when

THE JOURNEY OF THE ELU TO ENLIGHTENMENT

adversity strikes, we use it as a catalyst for improvement. It is our way par excellence to define ourselves and to endure our world. The trials which are presented to us in so many of the degrees we witness in our heroic journey would mean little unless we learn that the importance of undergoing them allows us to obtain light, wages, and the ineffable Word. Embracing adversity is an essential requisite if we ever hope to embrace the ultimate Masonic prize—an intimate knowledge of, and oneness with, Deity.

Thus, there are two consistent motifs throughout the Blue Lodge and the Lodge of Perfection. One is adversity, battling the shadow side of our personality, which also serves as a catalyst to self-improvement so long as we stay active and move toward our ultimate goal. The other motif is the majestic temple itself, which is analogous to a permanent, immovable jewel and source of Masonic Light.

We encounter adversity again in the Chapter degrees, dealing with a set of trials to determine our resolve to acquire knowledge and commit ourselves to a higher truth. We are sorely tempted to prove that honesty is a fallible human quality. We are reminded again that when we are engaged in the work of building our lives and rebuilding the world into a more must and equitable place, there will always be adversity, temptations, and distractions to pull us away from our path.

Notwithstanding, the Rose Croix tradition marks a turning point in Scottish Rite philosophy because it is here that we move from temple rich imagery to temple free desperation. It is the first time since the candidate passed between the pillars in the Second Degree that no temple is featured somehow in a Masonic degree. Throughout our degrees, the temple motif seemed eternal. The tabernacle had stood in the desert for 400 years and Solomon's Temple stood in Jerusalem for 400 years after that. We had the reassuring presence of the Temple, wherein resided the instructing Shekinah of Deity, and all the other ornamentations and symbols associated with that grand edifice. The temple was our story, and what we learned and then lost in both the Blue Lodge and the Lodge of Perfection was in direct proportion to the existence and subsequent destruction of the Temple. Everything we had learned and gained in our pilgrimage to perfection had once again evaporated. The ineffable Word has again been lost. This is only possible if there is no longer a Sanctum Sanctorum or Chief Priest to pronounce aloud the sacred name of Deity. And it could be possible only by the incurable absence of the Temple.

In the ceremonies of the Chapter, a third temple, successor to both the Temple of Solomon and the Temple of Zerubbabel, is imagined—the spiritual temple within each man—the building of which is the ultimate objective of Freemasonry. It is only when the Mason reaches the 18° that he faces inescapably the mystic experience, and he is induced to apply this experience to his own spiritual development. The Rose and Cross replace the three pillars of the old Temple with the three theological virtues. Faith in God and mankind, which is Wisdom; Hope in the victory of good over evil gives Strength; and Charity towards all living creatures through respect of life, tolerance and selflessness is Beauty. Such are the safest paths through adversity. We are instructed to follow these virtues as the highest form of human expression:

1. Religion founded on love and toleration.
2. Philosophy, which springs from faith in one God

and hope for a future life.
3. Morality, which embodies the wisdom of all ages.
4. A political creed, which rests on the three pillars of liberty, equality and fraternity.
5. The raising of the Mason's mind to a higher level of mystical consciousness.
6. The fulfillment of the moral foundation, which makes this mystical assent possible.
7. The intimate realization of Love, the New Law.

The Rose Croix Tradition affirms that the first step for the reformation of the world must be the reformation of the spirit within each human being. By this means only will we arrive at a solution to one of the great enigmas of nature and the manifested world.

Ancient Mysteries Tradition

The Ancient Mysteries tradition is one of those timeless checks and balances, which remind us that our concept of Deity must be felt within because it cannot be wholly conceived intellectually. A society's concept of God and the universe changes over time with its scientific development. The objective of the Mysteries was to cause a change in the initiate's condition of mind wherein he could feel the common core, or universal truth, in all religious traditions. The methodology Masonry employs to treat topics that cannot be known or explained is to mystically inspire a feeling about these higher principles through the use and expression of symbolic images, emblems, and hieroglyphs. This was the way of the Mysteries. Rather than a prescribed routine of creed, the Mysteries invited their initiates to seek, feel, compare and judge in order to awaken the mind and develop its creativity.

The general doctrine of the Mysteries was that one single religion could not convey the true nature of an unknown God. Faith alone does not a Truth make. Instead, logic, reason and faith were the essential ingredients of true religion, and all three of these elements were required for one to approach a balanced understanding of the nature of God. Logic and Reason were necessary for the attainment of virtue; but could only go so far in validating the existence of God. To go beyond that—to truly commune with the Godhead—required faith.

But the problem with faith alone was that one could never be sure that what he experienced was real. Pike warns us that, since we are governed far more by what we believe than what we know, we need some form of offsetting weapon to protect ourselves from the over-zealous emotionalism of belief. Logic and reason, then, serve to place a check on emotion.

The teaching was that it is in this balance between Faith and Reason that true religion is to be found. The Ancient Mysteries Tradition affirms that the gap often created by the insufficiency of popular religions and dogmas can be filled by reason and virtue. There exists an essential unity of belief regarding the nature of God among all religions, past and present.

The Scottish Rite places much attention on the Ancient Mysteries tradition. The Degrees of the 22nd through the 27th explore these traditions. Elements of these mysteries are interwoven within many other degrees of the Rite, as well. Pike spent a great deal of time on this topic because he believed the authors of continental Freemasonry in Europe used the ancient mysteries tradition as a template for structuring the form of Masonry as an Art of Initiation. He posited the methods used in the Mysteries were the best available to spur man's intellect, and the lessons of the Mysteries were also very similar to the great truths taught by Masonry. Pike suggests the three things, which were unique about the mysteries, are that they all had remarkably uniform ceremonies; the theme was the death and resurrection of a deity. And what was taught in the mysteries concerned the universe, the completion and perfection of all instruction; wherein things were seen as they were, and nature and her works were made known. This was important because it was free from dogmatism and tyranny, which gave the early instructors of mankind an opportunity to adopt her lessons and impart them through her.

The associations between Freemasonry and the Mysteries are stunning. To state only a few examples, all of the Mystery Religions had more than one stage of initiation, or level of membership. In fact, the majority had three. The idea was that as the initiate passed from one stage to another, he gained more understanding and insight. The levels of membership were progressive in nature. And the initiate could not advance until he had demonstrated some understanding of the material presented at each level. The initiation was considered a kind of 'death' in which the novice arose through rebirth or spiritual resurrection. We find this same association in the craft degrees of Freemasonry.

There were other associations of which we are familiar. To be accepted into a mystery religion, one must be considered a person of good repute and character and had to profess a belief in God. Vows of secrecy were demanded and these could not be communicated to those who were not initiates. Ritual purification, such as baptism or anointing, was required of all novices and there was a waiting period before one could advance to the next level of membership. Candidates were blindfolded, left in a chamber for contemplation, endured trials involving the elements, and were received into a sacred drama illustrating the trials and victories of the god of one's particular mystery tradition.

Finally, education involving the study of mathematics and astronomy, knowledge of the processes of alchemy, the nature of morals, allegory, and myth were included. The Mysteries were very much about the history of man's thought.

Pike also believed the ancient mysteries formed the basis for studies in comparative religion. His treatise on the lectures of the degrees of the Rite was the first published work on comparative religion in America. Pike knew every man had to personally confront his faith before he could truly be free.

The Mysteries represented for the initiated mind the center and focus of philosophy and theology. They are worthy of our attention because they epitomized what is most certainly one of the momentous eras in the evolution of the Western religious tradition—the moment when religion ceased to be a national institution and became a matter of personal conviction. If we want to know what our ancient brethren thought, believed and held sacred, our best avenue is through the Mysteries.

Knighthood Tradition

Every man needs to possess at least some knightly energy. Being a knight is one of the essential archetypes of manhood. The virtues of knighthood are rooted in every man as archetypal patterns of thought and feelings, which can be accessed through initiation, that is, via a change in one's state of mind. We literally organize our world, our sense of self, by our thoughts and words. When we access the knightly aspects of our being, we are manifesting in our own lives the qualities of the good and wholesome knight; the knight in his fullness.

There are two historical roots to chivalry; and each contains lessons, which are said to be imbedded in the soul of every thoughtful man. One is the chivalry of virtue, which arose from the 13th century conventions of chivalry that directed men to honor, serve and do nothing to displease ladies and maidens. This is the stuff of Arthurian myth, but it created the concept that men were capable of being noble; that nobility in manhood is an acquired trait.

Virtuous chivalry also has a warrior dimension that is played out dramatically in the knighthood degrees of the Scottish Rite. Men have conceived, constructed and protected great civilizations. They have fought endless wars, built magnificent waterways and trade routes; have created and sustained empires, which have lasted for centuries. And they have done all of these things through the warrior energy, which enables them to live life to the fullest. Being aware that life is finite and death is but a single breath away, gives great clarity of mind. This awareness moves the knight to an outpouring of life energy wherein he knows that every act counts and every deed is done as if it were his last. Such a man always engages life and never withdraws from it. The Knight of Saint Andrew or Knight Kadosh is called upon to use his energy and loyalty to some worthwhile endeavor—a cause, a people, a task, a nation; even a God. His goal is always larger than himself because his energy, endurance, perseverance, and loyalty are to a greater good beyond his own personal gain. And, in the Scottish Rite, he is also called upon to destroy in the cause of the greater good. He abolishes corruption, tyranny, oppression, injustice, ignorance, and fanaticism. And, by the very act of destroying, he is also building a spiritual temple to humankind. All knights in Masonry, of whatever degree, carry a sword in one hand and a trowel in the other.

The other root of chivalry is spiritual and religious and began when the Roman Emperor Constantine I had a vision of the cross in a battle with his archenemy Maxentius. This established the first Christian Order of Knighthood and modified the ideal of chivalry to include the glorification and moral development of its members through both military and devotional activities. Thus, the Warrior-Monk tradition was born.

Freemasonry draws on the Knighthood tradition, which dates back to the Crusades. There are few stories in human history that have been repeated more often in written works than the saga of the Christian Crusades. From the time Helena, mother of Constantine, made it fashionable for followers of Christ to go to the Holy Land to visit those places that scripture sanctified, there has always been a deep urging to make a pilgrimage to sacred places. Such journeys of devotedness have sustained courage and heightened one's devotion to their faith for generations after generations.

Pilgrimages have a deep symbolic significance in both Religion and Freemasonry. The journey is often a long voyage where one loses the sense of his secular ways by seeking upon earth the traces of a consoling and helpful divinity. Sometimes it is a memorial to some holy personage, a martyr or apostle; in others, a sacred relic such as a remnant of a temple that has long been archived to the memories of a glorious past. But in all cases, the intent is to give us hope that our own lives can also become a miracle. Because these journeys tended to be wrought with peril, one of the great merits in the eyes of the faithful, next to the pilgrimage itself, was to devote oneself to the service of pilgrims. This formed the basis for the knightly orders; or the birth of the knighthood tradition.

In the higher degrees of Masonry, the interest in sharing something of our own history with the glorious past of the Templars is attributed to Chevalier Ramsay, who put forth the chivalric origin theory of Masonry in an oration he delivered in 1736. Ramsay made no actual reference to the Templars, but his oration excited the imagination of men; or, more specifically, their interest in the chivalric virtues of manhood. The result was the development of knighthood ideals as one of the central themes of the higher Degrees. It is not important whether we can trace a lineage to some actual order of medieval knighthood. What is important is that the soul of these original orders is worthy of emulation through their ideals, aspirations, traditions, and secrets.

Knights of chivalry were expected to be the most gallant and virtuous of men. Such men dedicated themselves to the defense of right in the world. Their basic ideals were family unity, moral education, courage, honor and courtesy. A Mason is first and foremost a moralist, a philosopher, a symbolist and spiritualist; but he is also a soldier of honor, loyalty, duty and truth; actively engaged in the warfare of life. The Knighthood Tradition declares that the fight for the very best virtues against ignorance, tyranny and fanaticism is a constant engagement. Life is a battle for good and to fight that battle heroically and well is the great purpose of man's existence. We all progress upward toward perfection through the same life struggle. Our goal is to live up to the promise of the Elus. This is the essence of true Masonic Knighthood.

SECRET TRADITION

The Secret Tradition in Freemasonry is as old as the fraternity itself and has layered meanings. Freemasonry is the world's oldest and largest secret society. At the most basic level, its ceremonies demand secrecy from its members and its members expect to keep their promises not to discuss with the outside world their experiences within its tyled spaces. Yet, Freemasonry does not insist upon secrecy because it has anything to hide from the world. The secrecy relates, at the first level, to the ways in which one member may know another in a global fraternity of men. Considering the obligations one member has to another, even if he does not personally know that other member, it is appropriate to have ways of recognizing those to whom those joint obligations are assumed. At the most basic level, then, every fraternal society has its secret handshakes, signs, and passwords.

Likewise, every Degree in the Scottish Rite has its signs, tokens, and words. In many Degrees, there are three or four such words—passwords, sacred words, words of engagement, covered words, creative words, true words, etc. These are often given in Hebrew, Egyptian, Sanskrit, Phoenician, or Chaldean languages; and are generally associated with a character in a Degree, the theme of the Degree, or Body of Degrees; a host of angels, attributes of deity, or simply virtues portrayed in the degree. In America, these are rarely given or explained in degree exemplifications since the total collection of degrees are generally conferred over the course of a few days or weekends. It would be less than useless to expect candidates to remember over twenty-nine secret words at one setting; let alone recite them once every few months in order to get into a lodge, chapter or council meeting. The secret words of the Rite are more often explained in education programs that are held between reunions of a Valley.

At a higher level, it is a useful lesson in self-development to have obligations of silence. A man must learn above all things to be secret, which, is, to keep the secrets entrusted to him by others. Only in that way can he be a true friend to others, or a true husband to his wife. It is important for any friend not to let slip something told to him in confidence that would give pain and distress to the one who has trusted them. If a man cannot be trusted to keep confidential those things his friends and family confide in him, he cannot be trusted in anything. Secrecy is the first step in developing self-discipline and self-control. Each of us values deeply the friend in whom we can confide. In the sure knowledge that what we tell him will go no further. Freemasonry teaches that each man should strive to be such a friend.

At yet a higher level, it can be stated that there is no essential secret in Freemasonry since it is, above all, an aptitude and a state of mind. It is a virtual secret to the uninitiated much like literacy is to an illiterate. Secrecy in Masonry is synonymous with mystery. A mystery is a reality, which has not yet been fully understood. The secrets of Freemasonry cannot be revealed because they are insights and understandings which take place in the hearts and minds of Masons, and so literally cannot be told or communicated to another any more than one can exactly communicate to another what salt tastes like.

This means that those who possess its secrets are inevitably changed by it. Their status shifts in some way as the mysteries are revealed through the progression of the ritual teachings, which are made known to them. Thus, at this level, secrecy is essential for effective rites of passage. The existence of the group is not the secret. The secret is the ways and means by which members become transformed by their experience. The secret is the process of initiation itself.

At the highest level, the Secret Tradition comprises that which is hidden within the allegories, hieroglyphic instruction, and symbols portrayed in the Degrees of the fraternity itself. It deals with the loss and recovery of a certain treasure of secret life, which becomes the subject matter of the tradition. The form involves a great symbolical quest whose guideposts are imbedded in the ritual language; but not evident to anyone who is not consciously or subconsciously seeking a path to enlightenment. Emblematical Freemasonry is very deeply concealed from the uninstructed for the reason that it can so easily be misunderstood by those who are not adept in the study of hidden knowledge. It can only be known by communication of a Master, or through some channel of secret instruction, or by the act of God in illumination.

The mystery of the Word in Masonry is the testimony of a secret kept in reserve, which corresponds to the state of man; that is, to the human condition. The quest is a way of going back to the fall of man in order to approach the divine in the universe again, realizing that which was lost was never really lost, but remains concealed, by necessity, within the very structure of the universe.

Masonic legends and symbolism are chiefly concerned with the mystery of a building; not a physical building, but a certain holy house, which is spiritualized and erected in the hearts, and not by the hands, of men. The mystery of this great endeavor can only be revealed by reconstructing a temple to God on the physical plane, in which those initiated into the mystery itself are the living stones of this spiritualized temple. It is a temple in which man himself is the architect, the builder, and the building material. The legend of this master builder is a macrocosmic legend that applies to the world at large. It is a concealment of the divine in creation. It is also a legend of the microcosm, of the individual; the concealment of the divine in man. Thus, the Secret Tradition is the manifestation of the divine in the universe to the higher part of our consciousness; and it is the integration of our higher consciousness in that which is Divine in the universe.

The bottom line for the thoughtful man is that he desires, as the major goal of his life and as a Master of the Royal Secret, to unravel the mysteries of his own being.

The Secret Tradition represents the quest for equilibrium in the universe, the harmony and unity of the whole, and its application to our personal lives. This is the ultimate quest of mankind, and teaches us above all else to reverence ourselves as divine immortal souls and to respect others as such, since we all share the same divine nature, intelligence and ordeals. This requires LOVE, which is the true word of a Master Mason, the Royal Secret and Holy Doctrine of every true brotherhood.

VII

THE QUESTS, OR THEMATIC JOURNEYS OF THE SCOTTISH RITE

One of my favorite stories in the Grail tradition is the legend of Alexander. In the German version of the story, Alexander comes to a mountain with two thousand five hundred sapphire steps leading to its summit. He climbs the mountain and finds a city adored with gold and silver, in the center of which is a temple of gold. It is called the "House of the Sun."

Alexander goes to the middle of the temple and comes upon a bed, whereon lies a beautiful old man of great size and strength, clothed in silk. The man is asleep. In the room is a transparent golden crown hanging from a golden chain; and a precious stone from which light flows out across the temple. Also hanging from the ceiling is a golden cage, with a large bird inside. The bird, in a human-sounding voice, calls out to Alexander and says: *"Alexander, desist henceforth from setting thyself up against the gods. Turn back home and do not, through recklessness, hasten thy passage to the heavenly bodies."* Alexander does not waken the old man, but sets off to retrace his steps.

And thus we find the human in search of himself, on a quest to reconcile the opposites within, so that he may become transformed in the consciousness of God.

Across every mythology the world has ever known, this is the story of the Hero's quest. It is the search for the Holy Grail. It is the journey of the Master Mason for the

THE JOURNEY OF THE ELU TO ENLIGHTENMENT

Lost Word. And it is the quest in the Scottish Rite for the Royal Secret. This chapter explores the quest aspect of the journey through the degrees of the Scottish Rite. It is hoped that it will provide the reader a concise understanding of the importance of the Scottish Rite and its practicality in contemporary society.

Each Body of the Rite allegorically explains a different element in the quest tradition. The experience of the candidate through the degrees of the Rite is supposed to be a journey to a higher awareness. It is designed to carry the man to a higher level of insight. It is a progressive system of awakening consciousness. Again, its power lies in its ability to integrate its lessons into the psyche of each individual; meeting him on the level of his own experience, and giving him an opportunity to be transformed by the path of his own life.

The Rite is built on the clear understanding that men need to be engaged in a quest for self-improvement. For men, life needs to be seen as a journey. Men have to be initiated into manhood. The Rite facilitates this fundamental psychological need in men. It is all about awakening the slumber of his consciousness.

QUEST OF THE LODGE OF PERFECTION

The quest of the Lodge of Perfection is a quest for self-discovery. It is a quest for more Light in Masonry and the Awakening of our own Spirituality. The foundation for the degrees of Perfection rests in the understanding that, in Masonry, the lodge is a representation of the world and our journey through the degrees represents our journey through life. We have prepared well for our Scottish Rite journey through the Craft Degrees. As an Entered Apprentice, we learned the importance of our outward relationship with others and the institutions of our society. As a Fellowcraft, we were taught that it takes a combination of intellect, experience, intuition, feeling, emotion, and education to make real progress in life. We discover our dual nature; that there is a spirit within us, which can lead us to self-improvement. As a Master Mason we turn inward, and come face to face with our own worst enemy—our ego; and then we are given the opportunity to transcend our passions and our prejudices, and become true to who we are.

It is at this point that we are ready for the Scottish Rite experience. As previously mentioned, to a large extent, the degrees of the Lodge of Perfection relate to the shadow side of our own existence—our ruffians within. We have prepared ourselves through our own efforts to advance to a higher awareness that is to be found in the degrees of the Rite. And, like the craft degrees, it is a progressive system of morality, veiled in allegory. Our first task is to overcome ourselves.

The quest of the Lodge of Perfection, then, is to come as close to Perfect Truth as we are able in this life. Masonry is above all a philosophical society. God has arranged his great purposes that each man has a work to do, a duty to perform, a part to play in the gradual enlightenment of the world. The completion of our first quest of the Scottish Rite—the quest for Spiritual Awakening—is made in an underground room, a cube, wherein we are instructed in the final mysteries of the Lodge. We have prepared ourselves to then purify and strengthen that spark, once awakened, and to make it the guiding force of our life.

This guiding force is nothing less than our own

empowerment as men. We are capable of remarkable performance when we know that we are more than just an accident of nature, more than animal, more than chance, more than chemistry, more than sociology—that our essential nature is the direct result of the workings of divine will. This newly discovered insight, this uniquely beautiful mystery within us enables the possibility that we may secure for others a balance of love, faith, and reason essential to universal harmony and a better world for all. Once armed with virtue, the quest of the Chapter of Rose Croix is to decide what we do with our own empowerment.

Quest of the Chapter of Rose Croix

In the Lodge of Perfection, we are on a quest for More Light in Masonry, and the awakening of our own spirituality. We discover we have unfinished business with ourselves and we chase down the ruffians within so we can work out our new potential. At the conclusion of this first series of Scottish Rite Degrees, we journey into our own being, uncover the truth in the caverns of our own consciousness, and discover that divinity is embedded within us and therefore assures us that the quest for perfection is indeed attainable.

In the Chapter of Rose Croix, the quest is to purify this new light of discovery and knowledge and make it the guiding force in our life. We leave the physical temple tradition in Masonry and begin the divine work of building our own temple to God. We are the architect, the builder, and the building material of our own life. We are building a temple of freedom for our soul, as well as a heritage that enables our soul to impact favorably the lives of others. In the Rose Croix Degrees, we learn of principles ethics and, having discovered who we are, how this new energy will play out in our life. It requires moral fiber. We have to be able to conquer temptation to be truly free. We are the custodian of our own freedom.

QUEST OF THE COUNCIL OF KADOSH

In the Lodge of Perfection, we are on a quest for More Light in Masonry, and the awakening of our own spirituality. In the Chapter of Rose Croix, the quest is to purify this new light of discovery and knowledge and make it the guiding force in our life.

In the Council of Kadosh, the quest is to express that strengthened spark in the matters and affairs of the world. Albert Pike informs us; *"the true Mason labors for the benefit of those who come after him, and for the advancement and improvement of his society and culture, in particular, and the human race at large. All men live forever in the good they have done for Mankind. This is an instinctive impulse, which tends to prove the immortality of the human soul. His influences that survive him make Man immortal. It is the dead that govern, as the thoughts of the past are the laws of the present and the future."*

Pike tells us frequently that Masonry is work. It is that work which we are called upon to do. It is by the virtue of our efforts, our expanding awareness, knowledge, love and personal growth that we are enabled to make a difference in the world.

In the Council of Kadosh, we also explore the Ancient Mysteries Tradition. The ancient Mysteries were a series of increasing purifications of the body and mind, and increasing awareness of one's spiritual identity. It was a journey, a process of self-discovery. The sole purpose of the Mysteries was to explore the nature of God, Man and the Universe and their interrelationships. They came to be because they were the best tools devised by man in his perennial quest for a higher knowledge of the Truth hidden behind appearances in the universe and in him. They filled the gap created by the insufficiency of the popular public religion and worship to satisfy the deeper thoughts and aspirations of Mans' mind.

It is of great importance that we keep our ideas of God as pure and elevated as possible. Gods constructed in our own worst images tend to condone our own worst actions. It is then even easier to make a god of money, of social status, of power, or of ego. As a Mason, your concept of God should constantly evolve to higher and nobler planes. Beware of literalism. It is impossible for a limited human being to truly conceive the unlimited. We must, of necessity, make do with concepts of God, which fall far short of Him. Still, we can and must conceive of the best; our standard must be higher than ourselves. In the process of living out your quest by actions in the real world, follow duty; not desire.

Finally, in our quest to purify the discovery of our spiritual nature and apply it to the affairs of the world, we make a journey through the knighthood tradition. Knighthood is one of the archetypes of manhood. In the Scottish Rite, we investigate the chivalric traditions of the past. We are reminded there are new and higher battles that Masons must wage within themselves and with society in the journey to mature masculinity.

As previously stated, a Mason is a moralist, a philosopher, a symbolist and a spiritualist. He is also a soldier of honor, loyalty, duty and truth. But truth is always his first duty. It does indeed require knightly heroism to stick to fixed and pure spiritual values in a world of political, economic, and practical realities in which everything tends to become debatable and relative.

The world is in great need of men who say, "I will do the right thing because it is right. I will not do that which I believe to be wrong, even though it is convenient, advantageous, or popular. I will not convince myself that it doesn't matter, or that it's 'only a little wrong', or that since everyone does it, then it must be right." As a Knight Kadosh, you are obligated to be such a man.

Quest of the Consistory

The final quest represented in the fourth Body of the Scottish Rite is the quest for perfection through Self-Examination and Empowerment. One of my favorite films in the epic western genre was a 1990 classic produced and directed by Kevin Costner. It was titled Dances With Wolves. It is a story intended to represent two cultures in collision—the good/evil duality that prevails in the human condition. It is a story about heroism, of values and order; loyalty to tradition, harmony, unity and fraternity; about hatred, intolerance, greed for power and tyranny.

But the film also offers the added dimension of examining a man's search for himself that mirrors his search for the frontier; that mythic place of freedom, peace and ultimate escape from tyranny—the Eden of harmony he craves for his surroundings and his place in the world. In many respects this movie illustrates the final quest represented in the fourth Body of the Scottish Rite; every man's personal quest for perfection through his examination of self, and the empowerment he gains as a result of knowing who he is; what has meaning to him, and the duties he owes his gender and his society.

The instruction of the Rite is virtually over; yet two tasks still remain. We have to look back once again to the third Degree of Craft Masonry. One can never take the ruffians for granted. To be a man of the world, we must constantly re-examine our perceptions and understanding of Truth. We must be ever vigilant over our thoughts and actions if we hope to succeed in our last quest in this life: to Know Thyself, that is, to affirm the character we truly are in the drama of our existence.

We should be harder on ourselves at this point in our journey than any outside critic for the reason that no one can defeat us now except ourselves. We now have the tools to judge ourselves and others according to the Masonic wisdom we have already been taught in the previous degrees. These degrees have presented the virtues and wisdom for which men should strive. They have taught, above all, how to escape from the apparent contradictions of elements and forces in Man and in the world so that we can effectively merge together into the unity of the whole, and participate in the universal harmony and order of things.

Immortality demands that we convert our knowledge and faith into actual self-improvement. Our spiritual improvement will then reflect on society. The lives of great men teach us that we, too, can and must make a difference in the world. We must carefully examine our own motives and avoid self-deception at all costs. Unless we are without sin (and no one is) we have no right to complain of the sins of others. To judge other people is to give both them and God a right to judge us. The whole teaching of the Rite is aimed at getting us, as men, to focus on reaching a state of mind to be "one in oneself." This is the highest level of realization we can attain in our efforts to transcend our human condition. It is the culmination of the human quest. In the 31°, the candidate, like all heroes of the great mythic cycles, goes through a deep purification process represented by the most searching questions into his own character and life. The ultimate objective is to become the best one can be, and seek the best way to serve others in the world. Such is the only path to Masonic Light. In such a place, what is right stands, and what is wrong ultimately falls. We were created with this moral sense, which makes us the instrument of God's principles. To live as a reflection of God's wisdom, power and benevolence is the true Mason's duty.

In the 32° the lessons of all the preceding degrees of the Rite are summarized into a single coherent "Holy Doctrine" which represents the basis of all knowledge and wisdom. The Scottish Rite is the custodian of the fundamental truths and symbols which have been and remain common to all major cultures throughout the ages.

The candidate, a Knight Kadosh, is presented as a brother of high morality, a lover of knowledge, a seeker of wisdom interested in the great truths of philosophy and religion and the symbols of Masonry, and willing to become a benefactor of mankind. He is taught that only knowledge, philosophy, and doctrines that bear fruit in wholesome action for all are of real value. This is the whole of the chivalric tenet of Masonry and the culmination of the quest of a Knight Kadosh.

Freemasonry has taught us that there are no essential secrets in life. There is only the mystery of that which we do not yet know; a reality that has yet to be understood. The major quest of our lives, as Masters of the Royal Secret, is to continue to search for these mysteries. We all progress upwards toward perfection through the same life struggle. Our journey demands moral strength, humility and caution. Our search teaches us, above all, to reverence ourselves as divine immortal souls and to respect others in the same light. Since we all share the same divine nature, intelligence and ordeals, all we can do is love.

VIII

HISTORICAL TIMELINE OF THE HIGH DEGREES

Brother Arturo de Hoyos, 33°, G∴C∴, Grand Archivist of the Supreme Council of the Ancient and Accepted Scottish Rite, S.J., has written extensively on the history and evolution of the Degrees, which have become known as the High Degrees of the Masonic system of instruction. There is no need to repeat here, that which has already been written. I recommend Brother de Hoyos' *The Scottish Rite Ritual Monitor and Guide* to anyone interested in a more thorough construction of the ritual time line of Freemasonry. While this present work is focused on an interpretation of the principal lessons of the Degrees of the Scottish Rite, a chronological time line is presented here in brief to acquaint those who may have a curiosity about the age and evolution of the Degrees now practiced in the Southern Jurisdiction, USA.

1598 William Schaw, Master of the Work appointed by King James VI, writes the statutes or rules governing the activities of operative masons.

1599 Schaw issues his second statute or rules forming the organization of lodges and creates the hierarchy of officers.

1620 The London Mason's Company, formed during the Middle Ages to regulate stonemasons, is known to have admitted non-operative masons into the guild lodge still remaining in the company's possession as early as 1620, wherein men were accepted into the lodge and then made Masons.

1630 The Mason's Word is known to have existed in Scotland.

1696 The Edinburgh Register House MS, gives the earliest description of Masonic ritual, consisting of two Degrees, Apprentice and Fellowcraft.

1711 The Trinity College Dublin MS recognizes Master Masons as possessing their own unique secrets.

1717 The era of Speculative Masonry is formally ushered in when four London Lodges assembled at the Goose and Gridiron Ale House and established the Grand Lodge of England.

1725 The first record of the conferral of a Master Mason Degree on Brother Charles Cotton on May 12, eight years after the organization of the premier Grand Lodge. The Master Mason Degree became known as the first of the high degrees.

1730 The story of Hiram's death and burial appears in print for the first time in Samuel Prichard's exposé, Masonry Dissected.

1732 Loge L'Anglose, founded in Bordeaux, France, and chartered by the English Grand Lodge, formed an offshoot Lodge known as Loge LeFrancaise. This Lodge had a passion for conferring the so-called Scots, or Haute Grades, or higher Degrees.

1733 Scots, or Scotch Mason's Lodge appears in London; the name given refers to a type of Masonry practiced, rather than referring to native Scotsmen.

1735 Scotch Master Mason Degree was being conferred in England on Master Masons, and consisted of three officers. By 1734-35, two additional degrees, styled "excellent mason" and 'grand mason" were invented. These were the ancestors of the Scottish Rite and originated in France.

1743 A French Lodge, Loge Parfait Harmonie, is founded.

HISTORICAL TIMELINE OF THE HIGH DEGREES

Brother Etienne (Stephen) Morin was a charter member of this Lodge.

1744 The book, "Le Perfait Macon" was published, which revealed the secrets of the Scottish Masons. The theme it describes remained the ritual basis for the 15° and 16° of today's Rite. Bordeaux and Paris become the stronghold of higher degrees.

1761 The French Grand Lodge of Paris, 'Grand and Sovereign Lodge of St. John of Jerusalem,' granted a patent to Stephan Morin as Grand Inspector empowering him to establish perfect and sublime Masonry in all parts of the world.

1763 Morin creates, compiles, and delivers a 25-Degree system known as the "Order of the Royal Secret" through deputies he appoints in the Western Hemisphere. By 1791, this 25 Degree system is working in Jamaica, New Orleans, New York, and along the Eastern seaboard.

1801 The first Supreme Council of the higher Degrees in the world was established in Charleston, South Carolina. This Council compiled and added 8 Degrees to the 25 Degree system it inherited, and the "Supreme Council of the 33rd Degree for the United States of America" as we know it today was born.

1804 This system of Ineffable and Sublime Degrees was subsequently denoted the "Scottish Rite" in an agreement signed between the Supreme Council of France and the Grand Orient of France.

MORIN'S ORDER OF THE ROYAL SECRET

By 1763, Stephen Morin created and began promulgating this Masonic Rite of 25 Degrees, which he called the "Order of the Royal Secret," or "Order of Princes of the Royal Secret." This Order included many of the most popular degrees worked at that time. The 25 degrees of his Rite were divided into seven classes:

1st class
1°   Entered Apprentice
2°   Fellow Craft
3°   Master

2nd class
4°   Secret Master
5°   Perfect Master
6°   Perfect Master by Curiosity, or Intimate Secretary
7°   Provost & Judge, or Irish Master
8°   Intendent of the Building, or Master of Israel, or Scotch Master of the three J.J.J.

3rd class
9°   Chapter of Master Elected of Nine
10° Illustrious Elect of 15
11° A Chapter called Sublime Knights Elected

4th class
12° Grand Master Architect
13° Royal Arch
14° Perfection. The Ultimate of Symbolic Masonry

5th class
15° Council of Knights of the East or Sword
16° Grand Council of the Illustrious & most valiant Princes of Jerusalem
17° Knights of the East & West
18° Knights of the white Eagle or Pelican, known by the name of perfect Mason, or knight of the Rose Croix

HISTORICAL TIMELINE OF THE HIGH DEGREES

6th class

19° Sublime Scotch Masonry, called by the name of Grand Pontif
20° Venerable Grand Master of all Symbolic lodges, Sovereign Princes of Masonry, or Master ad vitam
21° Prussian Knight or Noachite, In Two Degrees—otherwise Called, The Masonic Key
22° Knights of the Royal Axe—or the Grand Patriarchs By the Name of Princes of Libanon

7th class

23° The Key of Masonry. Philosophical Lodge of the Knights of Eagle, or Sun
24° Chapter of Grand Inspector of Lodges, Grand Elected Knights of Kadosh, Now by the Title of Knights of the white & black Eagle
25° The Royal Secret, or the Knights of St. Andrews, and the Faithful guardians of the Sacred Treasure

THE REMAINING EIGHT DEGREES OF THE RITE

The remaining eight degrees which comprise the total of the Ancient & Accepted Rite practiced today in the Southern Jurisdiction were not created by the 1801 Supreme Council. They were compiled from older rituals worked between 1750 and 1765. The first four, from the 23° to the 26°, are independent and form a coherent group. They originated from the "Scottish Trinitarian Order" (Ordre des EcossaisTrinitaires) founded in Paris in 1756. A French Brother, Jean-Baptist Thomas Pirlet, spread the rituals of this Order as they were practiced in 1765 by the Chapter of the Globe of Holy Trinity" in Lyons, France. Pirlet had been a member of the "Council of Emperors of the East and West," which acted as a Sublime Scottish Mother Lodge between 1758 and 1782 and was involved in increasing the number of degrees as well as selecting and aggregating independent degrees within a new Rite of Perfection, also called the Rite of Heredom. Pirlet left the Council in 1762 to found his own "Council of Emperors of the East" to make a different selection of degrees with priority given to the Scottish Trinitarian Order.

The 23°, Chief of the Tabernacle, and the 24°, Prince of the Tabernacle, the first and second Degrees in the group respectively introduced the candidate, the future Levite, to the lower ancient mysteries of the Hebrews, with the Ark of Alliance and other ancient cultures. This corresponded to the Entered Apprentice and Fellowcraft levels. The 25°, Knight of the Brazen Serpent, or third Degree in the series, presented the higher ancient mysteries with Moses' covenant with his people in the desert so that the candidate might become a priest in the Holy of Holies. This represented the Master Degree. The 26°, Prince of Mercy, or fourth Degree, introduced the candidate to the most profound Christian Mysteries, such as the essence of God, material Creation by an immaterial Deity, Trinity, and the Incarnation, Nativity, Passion and Resurrection of Jesus, which implemented the ultimate objective of the Ancient Law through its mutation into the New Law of love and mercy.

Although the Christian mystery of Trinity is a major topic, it is not this Trinity that was the root of the "Trinitarian" appellation: It was the triple alliance of God with Mankind, symbolized by the Great Light of the Delta, including Abraham's sacrifice and bond with his people through circumcision; Moses' bond with his people in the desert through the Brazen Serpent; and Jesus' blood shed to redeem Mankind. The 27°, Knight Commander of the Temple, produced later in Lyons in 1762, reinforced the basic teachings of the other four degrees, and was the first of the chivalric degrees. It was developed by Louis Claude Henri de Montmain, who conferred it as a detached degree in Charleston from 1798 to 1802. It was considered the crowning point of Masonry.

The final grouping consisted of the 29°, Scottish Knight of St. Andrew or Patriarch of the Crusades, added by the Council of Emperors of the East and West about 1766; the 31°, Grand Inspector Inquisitor, established by the Council of Emperors of the East and West in 1758; and the 33°, Sovereign Grand Inspector General, created by the Supreme Council in 1801 from rituals dating to around 1761.

Having outlined the historical basis of the degrees of which we are the present descendants, we will now move to exploring the essential philosophical lessons of the 29 Degrees now practiced in the Southern Jurisdiction.

The explanations and interpretations offered for each of the Degrees are based on the rituals of the Rite, which were revised by Albert Pike in 1857 and published as his "Magnum Opus" or "Great Work," and now in the public domain; but the words presented here is the collective work of the Guthrie Valley Education Committee.

THE JOURNEY OF THE ELU TO ENLIGHTENMENT

THE INEFFABLE DEGREES

IX

Lodge of Perfection

Much has already been introduced to the reader in regard to the Lodge of Perfection, the first Body of instruction of the Scottish Rite. The explanation of the Elu Principle has revealed much about the journey of discovery the candidate will take in this first quest of the Rite. He is fully engaged in trying to sort out what he is going to do with his life once he was thrown off the circumstances that have conditioned him in his youth, and determines that he must take on the mantle of manhood with all the challenges and responsibilities which go along with that profound task.

Maturity calls on every man to leave the dependency of his youth; the protection his family and community have given him, the support and advice he has received from those who are older, the imprinting of attitudes, behavior, and social norms his culture and society have bestowed upon him before he could be trusted with the independence of adulthood. His responses to life have been well established by those who have surrounded him, for better or worse. As he moves into manhood, much of the patterning of his youth must be altered. He literally has to flip a new switch inside himself that will produce for him a wholly different set of response systems he will use as an adult which did not apply in his youth.

This is no easy transformation to achieve under the best of circumstances, and the extension of the period of dependency in our own time into the middle or late twenties, makes this challenge even more threatening than ever. If the crossing of the critical threshold of adulthood doesn't go so well, the results can be tragic. We have all seen enough failures and human disappointments to know that setting off on a new life without a rudder too often results in a dangerous and unsafe landing as an adult; wrought with insecurity, dismay, despair, futility, and regret.

Unless healthy response mechanisms can be implanted early on in this stage of life's transition, it is too easy for the young adult male to use his old childish response patterns as an excuse for his failures. He will invariably attribute his troubles either to his parents or to a parent substitute, his community, his country, even his world; rather than assign them to himself. It is easy for him to develop an attitude that only if the conditions of his life had been different, his elders less indifferent to his needs, his society less oppressive, or the universe otherwise arranged differently, he would not be in his situation.

Yet, the first requirement of adulthood is to establish in the individual the fact that he constitutes his own life and being. He can no longer blame his circumstances on his failings. He must develop a response system that will give him a grounding that enables him to move forward in life in a positive and productive manner. This process begins with a new discovery of who he is, from whence he came, and how to move forward with honesty, hope, and commitment that he can and will make it in spite of himself.

The teachings of the Lodge of Perfection provide him a facilitated path on his search of Light, of understanding, and an awakening to the best that is within him. And he has brothers along the way to help him when he needs encouragement.

LODGE OF PERFECTION

Our metaphor of instruction is the building of King Solomon's Temple. Since the building of the Temple is a symbol for the building of a happy, enjoyable, rewarding, and spiritually productive life, the candidate sets off on a quest, which is of earth-shaping importance to him. It is nothing less than his journey to mature masculinity. When it works, and most of us know many brothers for whom it has worked, our new brother of the Mystic Tie will emerge from this journey as something more than when he started. What he will find is what he has always longed for—his sense of personal identity in the world in which he lives.

THE JOURNEY OF THE ELU TO ENLIGHTENMENT

FOURTH DEGREE.

4°
SECRET MASTER

*"Woe unto those who aspire to that for
which they are unfitted."*
"Woe unto those who take up a burden they cannot bear."
*"Woe unto those who assume duties lightly
and afterward neglects them."*

The 4°, Secret Master, takes place in a lodge of sorrow, following the assassination of Hiram. The altar is covered with black cloth, strewn with silver tears. The apron and cordon are white, edged in black. White symbolizes purity, life, and light; black, darkness, mourning and death. They symbolize the loss of the Master and the True Word. More significantly, they represent the dialectic contest in the universe and in the soul of man, between light and darkness, good and evil, truth and error, reality and illusion. The candidate is reminded of the importance of duty and secrecy.

As stated previously in discussing the Elu Principle, to a large extent, the degrees of the Lodge of Perfection relate to the shadow side of our own existence—our ruffians within. We have prepared ourselves through our own efforts to advance to a higher awareness that is to be found in the degrees of the Rite. And, like the craft degrees, it is a progressive system of morality, veiled in allegory. Our first task is to overcome ourselves.

This Degree begins our quest for self-development, independence of thought, and the ability to live freely, profitably and creatively. In the Rite, the task is to engage the candidate's intellect directly, and, in so doing, encourage his introspection, which can arouse his emotions enough to develop additional insights about himself. This idea is revealed to the Secret Master in his journey to the Holy of Holies, only to find that he cannot enter without possessing the Key of Intellect, or Key to the Mysteries.

In Masonry, whenever a key is used, it has the same symbolism as the Egyptian ankh, from which the key is derived. It is the means by which the gate of immortality may be opened. But the gate can only be accessed when the right insights or secrets are known. The Secret Master is a passenger on this journey. He is given the key but he cannot yet gain access. There is something missing (as symbolized by the death of Hiram), and the missing element is the unfinished business he has with himself. The mystery is the mystery of his own being that has not yet been revealed to him. In the process of living, he must discover himself, overcome himself, move beyond his inadequate understanding of things; his ignorance and short-sidedness, his passions and prejudices; his selfish motives and lazy approaches to learning.

These are the ruffians we all have to overcome. A man must be comfortable in his own skin and affirm himself and his value as a human being. He must also know how to represent himself to others so he can be affirmed by them. There is an established path to self-esteem. As Masons, we have taken a pledge to be on it.

One of the principle teachings introduced in this Degree is the importance of secrecy. Masonry does not insist upon secrecy because we have anything to hide from the world. Considering the number of books by well-qualified Masonic writers available in almost any library, or online, it is nonsensical to insist that it is a "secret order." Far from being secret, Masonry takes every opportunity to tell the world what we believe and what we oppose.

But it is a useful lesson in self-development to have obligations of silence. For most of us, talk and discussion are natural. We discuss the weather, the fortunes of people in the media, our own hopes, fears, and dreams. All that is well; but just as the small child must learn that there are times when he may talk and times when he must listen, so we, as adults, must learn to guard our tongues. The Mason must be constantly on guard, else he may let slip something told to him in confidence, and give pain and distress to one who has trusted him. Each of us values deeply the friend in whom we can confide, in the sure knowledge that what we tell him will go no further. Each of us should strive to be such a friend.

The lessons of duty in this Degree are also most significant. Our world encourages us not to perform duty. Television, social and print media suggest that a life of self-indulgence is the right goal. "Do what you want to do when you want to do it." On the surface, it is an attractive path. We are told to "do that which is convenient, that which "feels good,' that which gets you ahead." But the Mason knows that his own growth and development, as well as the well being of his family, the state and nation, come about from the performance of duty—doing what is needed and right in spite of the fact that it is inconvenient, or unpopular.

"Duty is with us always, inflexible as fate."
"In health or sickness, in prosperity or adversity, duty is with us always, exacting as necessity."
"It rises with us in the morning, and watches by our pillow at night. In the roar of the city, and in the loneliness of the desert, duty is with us always, imperative as destiny."

It is important to understand that duty is a matter of conscience. Good men obey the law not because some external sanction might be forced upon them if they didn't. They obey the law because it is morally right to do so. For those whom the law binds in conscience, the sense of a law's moral authority is, for them, a sense of duty from which the dictates of their conscience flow. We share this understanding whenever, having made a promise or contracted a debt; we feel an obligation to discharge it even if no superior commands the act. The obligation is always to another individual, that is, to another human being who happens to be our equal in the eyes of God. It is the honest and just man who acknowledges his obligations in life because he understands the source of the obligation is virtue itself. His duty in the matter is an aspect of the virtue of justice; that is, a just man's acknowledgment of the debt he owes to others; or his recognition that he is under some obligation to avoid injuring others and to serve the common good.

Fidelity is a duty that inspires us to be faithful to our family and friends; true to the promises we make, to the pledges we give, and to the vows we assume. Fidelity is a virtue that can be achieved only by those who aspire to that for which they are fitted; take up a burden they can bear; and assume duties seriously and without negligence.

Like the light you bear, which yet you cannot see, truth and the Lost Word, which are light, are within the reach of every man that lives, would he but open his eyes and see. The broad highway of duty, straight as an arrow, leads directly to them.

In the old rituals, the candidate encounters an urn, which contains his own intellectual treasures, his moral conscience; and he discovers that what he learns will be his alone, that there is a quest, and that knowledge is there for him if he chooses to seek it.

Yet another lesson of profound importance in this Degree is that every man should be a friend of knowledge. Pike points out that the work of the Scottish Rite is to inspire and teach men that they must improve, refine, and perfect themselves. We must become fit and worthy recipients of the Royal Secret, with the requisite knowledge that such a responsibility demands. The degrees of the Rite constitute a journey of knowledge. The Rite is a great tapestry of knowledge, where moral, ethical, philosophical, political, religious, and mythical thought are interwoven to create a great body of teachings and lessons. Pike informs us that knowledge is the most genuine and real of human treasures; for it is Light.

Yet, it is an elusive pursuit. First, there is the challenge; how do we know what knowledge is? What can we know?

What are we capable of knowing? Who can claim to possess enough of it? And somehow, we have to formulate some basis of understanding that knowledge must be distinguished from belief and opinion, from ignorance and error, from truth and probability. It is not enough to claim one has the truth. Knowledge consists in seeing the reason why a thing is true.

A proposition, which is neither self-evident nor demonstrable, yields only an opinion; and is not knowledge. Even when a thing happens to be true, the opinion is often qualified by some degree of doubt or limitation. It is only when the mind has adequate grounds for its judgment; when it knows that it knows and why, does it have the certainty of knowledge.

We know too well the world is filled with un-truths and circumstances where appeals to emotion and personal belief are more influential in shaping public opinion than are objective facts. The dangers of false claims to knowledge are as great in our own time as they were to the ancients. Socrates said that ignorance is remedial. If one is ignorant, he can be taught. But the far greater threat comes from those who think they already know the truth, and then are impetuous enough to act on falsehood.

There is an important distinction to be made concerning deviations from truth. We can acknowledge that we sometimes make mistakes and say things that are untrue without meaning to do so. In that case, one is uttering a falsehood rather than a lie, for the mistake is not intentional. But what we have to guard against is willful ignorance, which is when we do not really know whether something is true, but we say it anyway without bothering to take the time to find out if our information is correct. Even that may be forgivable in that we can be blamed for only being lazy for not seeking out the truth. But what is not acceptable is when we tell a falsehood with the intent to deceive. We know what we are saying is not true, but we say it anyway. That is an outright lie.

And every lie has an audience. We may not feel we are uttering a falsehood when no one is listening, but when our intent is to manipulate someone into believing something we know to be untrue, we have graduated from a mere misinterpretation of facts into intentional falsehood.

In Freemasonry, we are engaged in the pursuit of knowledge. We have already been taught in our ascent through the winding stairs that the knowledge we possess comes from what our senses have taught us, what we have learned from our schooling, our family, and the culture in which we were raised. We know that knowledge also comes from intuition and insight, contemplation and study. The first and great philosophical conclusion of Masonic teaching is that the essential requisite of knowledge is education; not only as the basic requirement for the individual search for truth, but also to build an enlightened citizenry, which is the primary ingredient of a well-regulated and just society.

Finally, in this degree, we are urged to contemplate the nature of Deity, and the many attributes of the Divine, which we can take into ourselves--Wisdom to conceive, Strength to create, and Beauty to regulate our lives. We learn that we must take up and integrate into ourselves the virtues of confidentiality toward our fellows, obedience to the performance of duty (doing what is needed and right), and fidelity to our ourselves, our family and our country—all being prerequisites to a free mind, and essential to the quest for perfection.

THE JOURNEY OF THE ELU TO ENLIGHTENMENT

QUESTIONS FOR CONTEMPLATION AS A SECRET MASTER

1. How do we decide how much confidentiality we owe to others?
2. What is the difference between truth and fact?
3. What is the nature of secrecy as a virtue? As a social force?
4. What duties do you owe to yourself? To your family? To your community? To your country?
5. What is the difference between duty and labor?
6. What can we individually do to advance the cause of progress?
7. What are some barriers that prevent us from making progress in life?

LODGE OF PERFECTION

FIFTH DEGREE.

5°
Perfect Master

*"Death is the portion of every man and every woman.
This day is mine and yours, but we know not
what shall be on the morrow."*

In the 5°, Perfect Master, our quester encounters the death of a hero and he contemplates how often his own life is shaped by what he learns from the examples of others. He also faces the awesome reality that others watch him and learn from the examples he sets. It is therefore essential that he live as if his own death was just moments away; that what he says and how he acts impacts into eternity.

It is both natural and good that we should love and enjoy life, but it is an error to forget that death can happen quickly and unexpectedly. Our duties to life compel us to remember that death is always just moments away.

However, we should not consider this as a fearful

thought—for death can never be fearful to the Mason who understands the immortality of the soul—but as a reminder not to postpone important matters. Almost all of us have been in that saddest of all positions; having lost a friend or loved one without having said all of the kind and loving things we now wish we had said. How often we think of times we wish we had said, "I love you," or 'I'm sorry," or "You did well," or "Thank you." Words which cannot now be uttered this side of eternity.

The awareness of death is a powerful incentive to live well; not motivated by fear but by love and gratitude. The Mason who remembers that his heart may stop in the next five minutes is unlikely to hurt others, for he knows he may never have the chance to make amends. The Mason who realizes that he may never see a friend again will probably find some way to express his friendship. The Mason who knows that his next moment may be his last, and who wishes his children to remember him as a kind and loving father is likely to be a kind and loving father.

It is easier for the Mason who has accepted death—who has spiritually and emotionally died and risen again—to be a Perfect Master. Those who, in war, accident, or medical emergency, have been very near indeed to the borders of eternity and have returned, report almost without exception that is it now easier to live well, since they know it is possible for them not to live at all.

Thus, the profound warning in this Degree is that death is a portion of every man. There is no defense against time. We won't get the chance when we are dead to do what we could have done with our life while we lived. We are already dead to all those months and years which we have already lived, and we shall never live them over again. It is important that we not waste our precious time in trivial activities.

The other weighty lesson of the Perfect Master is that we have a vital charge ahead of us—to live respected and die regretted. In this Degree, the Master Hiram is mourned because of the work he accomplished in life, and the honesty and integrity with which he carried it out. The world seldom mourns the passing of a man who does nothing, who has made no contribution to the happiness or welfare of others, or who has lived for himself alone. It is not our ambition to be mourned after our deaths. It is our ambition to have lived in such a way that others are glad that we lived.

The fight we must make with ourselves is to be consciously aware of what we are here to do. Honesty and sincerity and good faith require purity of intent, truthfulness, faithfulness to commitments, and charity. Our battle is to overcome our self-serving motives. That is the ruffian in this Degree. A Mason must avoid that which deceives equally with that which is false.

The Degree also teaches that it is important to properly bury and decently mourn the dead. They are entitled to that show of respect. Our brotherly task is to raise up the eminent virtues of the deceased, letting any selfish thought die in our hearts, forgiving any mistakes or errors they have committed, and pledging to make reparations for any wrongs or injuries they may have caused to others during their life. When we mourn, we should not forget that we are mourning our own grief, our own sense of loss. For the dead have moved to a world and existence, which we believe, as Masons, is a far better and happier state.

Finally, the Perfect Master is admonished to take control of his life. Until it became necessary to consult professionals to assist in settling estate matters, every candidate in this Degree had to execute his last will and testament before he could proceed. The lesson is obvious. We cannot experience a sense of control over our lives until we are able to take responsibility for our actions. Our first duty in this regard is to our family. We have a duty to bring responsibility and accountability to the care of our family, our work, our relationships, our behavior, and the choices we make in life. We are to give the best we can to all of our life commitments. We must strive to do all we can to ensure that those whose lives depend on us are not lessened because we have lived. Our weapon is self-forgetfulness and altruism, the prevailing care in us for the welfare of others. This requires both industry and honesty. Our faithfulness in the performance of our duties is the best way to express our responsibility and debt to our posterity as well as our predecessors.

In his journey as a Perfect Master, the Brother encounters a monument of white and black marble, surmounted by an urn traversed by a sword and adorned with acacia. The urn of knowledge becomes the urn of self-examination. The sword proclaims his unrelenting enmity toward his own ignorance, falsehood, and egotism (his ruffians within). The acacia, symbol of immortality, reminds him that his quest is in the direction of a more virtuous life. His world is flanked in this degree by sixteen virtues, each worthy of consideration:

Strength	agility	cleanliness
grace	Resistance	felicity
neatness	beauty	Courage
precision	decency	health
energy	adroitness	sobriety
richness		

THE JOURNEY OF THE ELU TO ENLIGHTENMENT

In striving toward virtue, our quest becomes a journey of responsibility and accountability. We are admonished to think about the merits outlined here, as these constitute the qualities of a reliable man. We cannot arrive at the *sanctum sanctorum* but by purity of manners, righteousness of heart, and the secrets of the mind.

There are interesting esoteric considerations in this Degree which should also not be overlooked. In the 14th Degree, a question is asked relating to the Fifth Degree; "Are you a Perfect Mason?" The answer is; "I have seen the three circles enclosing the square upon the two crossed columns." The Fifth Degree solves the problem of "squaring the circle," which was set in the previous degree. In symbolic terms, squaring the circle means to leave the finite earthly realm, represented by the square, and reach the divine realm, represented by the circle, without beginning nor end; that is, to leave the material world of the body and reach the spiritual world; to leave the manifested creation and reach the Creator, the primordial Cause; to leave duality and reach the Original Unity, the One, the Aleph, from which the whole universe is projected.

The three red, blue and orange circles depicted on the apron are a metaphor for God's power, wisdom and beneficence. These enclose the cube symbolizing the finite universe, or God's manifested creation. The whole symbol represents God's protection over his creation. But the cube also symbolizes Solomon's Temple, Hiram's own creation within God's creation. The candidate, representing Hiram, is placed in the coffin, along with the square, compasses, gavel and rule, emblems of the virtue and authority of Hiram. In addition, the apron, cordon, and jewel; vestments of his rank and esteem, are laid upon his heart. A sprig of acacia is placed within the coffin as an emblem of life and rebirth; and the body is entombed.

Astonishingly, then, the candidate is resurrected from the coffin, and placed at the altar that he may be made a Perfect Master. The meaning of resurrection becomes the most important teaching of the Degree; and it involves a hidden construct of duality.

Resurrection involves two time periods; the period before the resurrection and the period after resurrection. But there are also two types of resurrection. There is the spiritual resurrection that occurs while a person is living; and the final resurrection, which occurs at death where the soul ascends to another place. Both resurrections are essential to the Mason's quest for the True Word.

The two resurrections involve four time periods (the square of 2); the time before the spiritual resurrection and the time after; the time before the final resurrection and the time after. Four is also the dominant number in the Degree. There are 4 raps in the battery, 16 columns in the lodge arranged in groups of four, or 16 candles arranged in groups of 4 candles placed in each corner of the lodge; the candidate makes four perambulations before his ascent to the altar. The four candles placed in all four cardinal points of the lodge symbolize that total resurrection takes place in all corners of the world.

The candidate portrays Hiram, and is symbolically raised from the grave to pay respect to the man that was Hiram Abif. The lesson taught is that the candidate dies in sin, but is revived in virtue. But the hidden meaning is that Hiram Abif is immortal; he is raised from the grave in every newly raised Master Mason.

Every man has the opportunity to be raised by the

virtues of his own life. Just as the emblems on the apron allude to God's protection over his creation; the spiritual resurrection of every Mason supports life in that it protects him by pointing his will toward the light of the good rather than the darkness of the bad. Each Mason has the power to overcome himself and become a "son of the spirit," a "son of Hiram," and a "son of God." It is extraordinary to contemplate that every Master Mason can experience a spiritual resurrection. The world is filled with people who will never have this insight. The result is that they will too often live a miserable life, or die too early.

Pike writes that "Death is dreadful to the man whose all is extinguished with his life; but not to him whose glory and whose influences can never die." Our spiritual resurrection provides the means by which we are able to reconcile the need for virtue and improvement with the certainty of death. It is the first resurrection that prepares every Mason for death.

Every day, new life is born and old lives pass on. At some point everyone who is born will die. Death is no different than the days which have already passed in our present life. We can remember the days gone by as we remember dear ones who have passed on; we can become the kind of men, living and dead, we have respected most from our past. But we cannot go back except for the memories we have. We can only move forward. So let us strive to live respected and die regretted.

We can now understand and interpret the symbol of the two crossed columns, which are also depicted on the apron of the Perfect Master. For man to reach his inmost divine nature, the Holy of Holies shown him in the preceding degree, he must enter the portico (columns) of his inner temple (the cube). This portico is formed by the pillars of Jachin and Boaz standing in the west where Hiram's body was found. The columns symbolize the strength and beauty of the soul required for the ultimate journey. After the passage, the columns are crossed to crucify the ego of the earthly body and bar any possible return to the material world. Man's higher self is free to begin its ascent toward the divine from whom he was originally projected.

Questions for Contemplation as a Perfect Master

1. How important is it to study the lives of those who have gone before us, and keep their memories alive in the hearts of every generation?

2. How can ordinary people make a difference in the future?

3. How can we do things which outlive us?

4. How does the Scottish Rite teach us to view death?

5. What are we supposed to do with the materials that were deposited in the coffin with the candidate? What ways can these be used to facilitate the teachings of this Degree?

6. What are ways that men can be the best role models to their family? To their employer or business? To their community? To their relationships with others?

7. What does it mean to be responsible to ourselves? To our actions? To our outcomes?

8. How do we create the experiences that will define our life in positive ways?

THE JOURNEY OF THE ELU TO ENLIGHTENMENT

SIXTH DEGREE.

6°
Intimate Secretary

"As all that the earth produces is created for the use of man, so men are created for the sake of men, that they may mutually do good to one another."

In the 6°, Confidential Secretary, the lodge represents King Solomon's audience chamber. Solomon had promised to give King Hiram certain cities in return for his aid in building the Temple. Hiram arrives in Jerusalem before the cities have been restored and, not knowing of the restoration plans, rashly concludes that Solomon intends to keep his promise in letter but not in spirit. He enters Solomon's chambers in a fit of anger. The candidate, a servant of Solomon, sees Hiram, does not know him, and, fearing for Solomon's safety, hides where he can give help if needed. When discovered, he is wrongly accused of being an eavesdropper. Solomon, by investigating the matter, brings the truth to light and restores the candidate to Hiram's good opinion and favor.

In this Degree, the quest is to go beyond the surface of things. There is one compelling lesson—*reality is too often what we perceive it to be; and not what is really real*. First impressions can be wrong. Most of the problems we have in life are the result of judging hastily from appearances. Most of the disagreements we have are the result of ignorance and misunderstanding. We are prone to judge people whom we do not know, or who are different from us, or who are on a different side of an issue with us. We almost always judge people with a jaundiced attitude of self-interest. We judge their motives based on the merest of pretense; too quickly, and often wrongly.

We live in a world that questions authority, morals, institutions, values, and even life purpose. We have, at the click of a mouse, access to a weighted defense of our present point of view. We often have little compassion or tolerance for those who have different opinions, who live in different cultures, or share different lifestyles from us. Fear and prejudice are the ruffians we encounter in this degree.

All Masonry is a struggle to overcome the "animal" within ourselves and to live at a more highly developed moral level. One of the most important parts of that struggle is to move from the natural selfish "me-first," attitude of the young child (and undeveloped adult) to the "you-first" attitude of the mature, nurturing, compassionate person

We may (wrongly) envy the men who, through selfishness, have amassed great wealth or power, but we do not admire them. We do not hold them up as great examples of others to follow. We do admire the woman who gives up a life of ease to help the poorest of the poor in India, the medical doctor who gives up a lucrative practice to take medicine to the remote areas of Africa, the businessman who gives almost all of his free time to teaching illiterate adults in the United States to read.

Universally, the people who do such things insist that they gain much more than they give up. It may not be possible or practical for all of us to give our lives to such a cause, but each of us can make meaningful contributions.

To have restored friendship between two people who, through misunderstanding, have come to anger may seem to be a small thing, but it is not small to those two friends. To have turned aside an angry word which, if spoken, might have resulted in the division of a congregation or an institution, may be the single most important act of a man's life.

Since we cannot know in advance which acts will be of overwhelming importance, and which will only bring comfort into some human life, it is wise not to neglect any opportunity to do good or bring peace. If you had ten one-dollar bills, and knew that one of them, when invested, would bring a return of a thousand dollars, but you did not know which one of them would bring the return, you would likely invest all ten to make sure the chance was not missed. Just so, given ten opportunities to do good, it is well to take all ten—not in the intent of benefiting yourself, but in the knowledge that you can benefit others.

We have a duty and obligation to others, both inside and outside the fraternity, to make life better and less contentious. We have an absolute obligation to care about others and to work for their interests.

The major moral lessons taught in this Degree are that we should be slow in judgment, to keep a balanced mind and self-control, to take the time to gather facts, and corroborate appearances before taking action. Zeal without discretion is fanaticism. The fanatic is ruled by his passions rather than his reason; he is led by emotion rather than judgment. Being a wise man requires taking the time to distinguish the difference between appearances and reality. In this Degree, King Hiram was wrong, as he judged hastily from appearances. However, he eventually behaves with brotherly generosity. King Solomon is right, as he keeps his dignified calm and self-control, avoids making Hiram lose face and helps him to recover his dignity. As for Zabud, who becomes the Intimate Secretary, he embodies that selfless duty faithfully and enthusiastically owed to those we serve and love. He embraces curiosity as a stimulus for human intelligence to search for truth.

Solomon's actions point out that a Mason's duty is to be a peacemaker and preserve harmony, avoiding violence and argument. When our brethren are in disagreement, we should not take sides and incite more argument. Let us instead seek that common ground which unites men of reason, and respects honest differences of opinion. This requires a benevolent heart. We are to be forgiving by nature, and generous in our judgments of others; never condemning or chiding, even if one is right and others are wrong. It is enough that we focus on our own faults rather than giving negative judgments to others.

Generosity as a Masonic virtue is more than charity. It is a commitment also of time and talent, sacrifice and dedication. The man who is owed gratitude keeps the scales in his favor. As men, we were created to care for and nourish one another and thus we are counseled to be zealous in the practice of that truly Masonic tenet--Brotherly Love.

So, here we are to look for Truth, and the task is to find it by developing faithfulness and care of others. Life is a series of covenants we make in which our performance means everything. Since we cannot know in advance which acts will be of overwhelming importance and which will only bring convenience to some aspect of human life, it is our duty to always perform with the best of intentions.

The essence of Scottish Rite teaching is healthy thinking. There is a purpose in life beyond gain and comfort. Our challenge is to work on developing our thinking in ways that will overcome our own prejudices and fears. This is the first step toward making things real.

Questions for Contemplation as an Intimate Secretary

1. How do we fairly and impartially judge a person, or his actions, without living in his shoes?
2. How might we develop a discipline not to judge others on appearances only?
3. How do we know when we have enough knowledge to form an effective appraisal of a situation?
4. Think about the stories in the media, which deal with judgments of people and situations. How do the conclusions of this Degree have application to daily life?
5. What is the difference between cunning and wisdom?
6. How do we balance keeping our word in spirit, as well as by letter?
7. What is the difference between anger and outrage? What are some circumstances in which outrage is morally justified?
8. What is the role of the peacemaker? How does one serve as a peacemaker in the midst of anger, outrage, false perceptions, hasty judgments, and human biases?
9. How do we pursue a healthy mind?

LODGE OF PERFECTION

SEVENTH DEGREE.

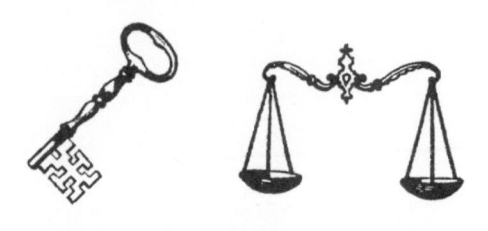

7°
PROVOST & JUDGE

"It is a grave responsibility to decide between man and man, where incorrect decision is injustice"

The 7°, Provost and Judge, takes place in a lodge representing King Solomon's tribunal chamber. It is said that King Solomon created a tribunal of seven Provosts and Judges after Hiram's death, to enforce the law among the workmen and to administer justice to both Hebrew and Phoenician alike. Adoniram was appointed chief of the Provosts and Judges and, as such, received a key to the ebony box holding the records of the tribunal. During the ceremony, Zabud addresses a dispute between Hebrew and Phoenician workers regarding attendance of the Passover feast. He rejects the pleas of two plaintiffs trying to influence his judgment. The candidate also represents Zabud as he aspires to assume the heavy burden of Provost and Judge. The principle teaching of the degree is to learn what justice should be and the qualities it demands.

One of the hardest things to do in life is to find the proper balance between alternative choices of action. Every major religion and philosophy has its equivalent "Judge not, lest ye be judged." In spite of that, most of us sit in judgment every day, listening to gossip and passing judgments upon people as if we were in full possession of all facts and had deep and intimate knowledge of the hearts and motives of those we judge. And yet, we bitterly resent it when someone presumes to judge us, or our actions and motives. When we judge others, we are putting ourselves at risk, both intellectually and spiritually.

Justice is an abstract concept, but it is also very real. There are many folk expressions which surround the idea of justice: "Cheaters never prosper; the mills of the gods grind slowly, but they grind exceeding fine; as ye sow, so shall ye reap." At times we are tempted to discount these, but they are expressions of a great truth.

Cheaters do not prosper. The cheat, the criminal, the unjust may appear to thrive and do very well indeed. And yet, always there is payment, and the very fact that one such is riding the crest of the wave is almost a guarantee that he is about to be engulfed. The inflexible law of Karma applies in all cases in the sense that wrong and injustice, once done, can never be undone. They are irrevocable and contain their own retributive penalty according to the basic universal law of cause and effect. An offence to others is therefore an offence to our own soul. No penitence or pardon will erase what is inscribed in the tablets of universal nature. Repentance can purify the wrong doer's heart and amend his future, but it cannot erase the past. It is a prodigious misfortune of life that the most profound lessons we learn are the result of our greatest sins. Yet, we know the law, just as we know that fire burns. If, for any reason, we put our hand on a burner, it is not the burner which punishes us; it is our own will that inflicts upon ourselves the consequences of the law. Man is his own sovereign by nature and, as such, he is the responsible master of his own fate.

If we had to pick a contemporary example of how polarized groups think today on matters of justice, we could hardly do better than choose the arguments presented by the Spirits of Retribution and Inaction in this Degree. On one side, we have Retribution arguing that normal men would do nothing to correct an unjust situation if it weren't for those brave souls who loudly insist that punishment for wrong doing must be not only tough enough to match the crime, but also severe enough to afterward cause men to live in fear of committing a crime. On the other side, we have the Spirit of Inaction, warning that it is always wrong to convict an innocent man. It is therefore better to wait, to bide the time, to let the passions of the moment wane before taking a chance on acting wrongly to condemn an innocent man. And, even when the accused is guilty, it is always better to deliberate calmly, at length and unhurried to be sure that the punishment never exceeds the crime.

We are rescued by the Spirit of Justice, who reminds us that men must indeed act, but not on the basis of a half-truth. It is wrong to consider actions of others on the basis of inflated self-righteousness. It is equally wrong to delay action to the point that justice is denied those who suffer. There is a balance between action and patience, severity and mercy, protection and punishment. Justice is not a matter of taking revenge; nor is it a matter of allowing evil to continue. Rather it is a matter of purity of motives. We should not rule by pride of opinion. We are admonished to be just when judging other men's motives.

Finally, we are reminded that every act we do (or fail to do) reverberates to larger and larger consequences. If we do an injury to another, that injury is permanent, and permanent for us as well. It is not that God sits in heaven as some sort of celestial score-keeper, eagerly marking down against our names each fault we commit; but that the moral sense is like any other—it is developed or damaged by our actions.

When we do good, it is easier to do good again. The very act strengthens the spirit. When we do ill, that act weakens our spirit. There simply is no such thing as doing wrong today and making up for it tomorrow.

Thus, in this Degree, our journey of discovery takes on the virtues of Justice, Equity, Impartiality, and Uprightness. As Masons, we must be concerned with injustice at all levels. We must, of course, protest against injustice when we find it in the world. But even more importantly, we must avoid doing injustice ourselves. To believe a slander against another is injustice. To pass on that slander or rumor is great injustice. To keep silent when we could save another pain by speaking is injustice. To look down upon someone because they have been less fortunate is injustice.

These and many more are easy to commit. It is not easy to be a just man, to constantly review our own actions and carefully make the better choice. But it is the path of the Mason, and the path you have chosen.

In thinking about the nature of justice, and making judgments of others, we are admonished to reflect on the words of Pike:

> There is scarcely one of us who has not, at some time in his life, been on the edge of the commission of a

crime. Every one of us can look back, and shuddering see the time when our feet stood upon the slippery crags that overhung the abyss of guilt; and when, if temptation had been a little more urgent, or a little longer continued, if poverty had pressed us a little harder, or a little more wine had further disturbed our intellect, dethroned our judgment, and aroused our passions, our feet would have slipped, and we should have fallen, never to rise again"

Justice is the equation of right and duty between man and man, or between the individual and society. The quest of the Provost and Judge is to find that equation, that balance in which we may know what justice means, how it is to be attained and realized, dispensed, and established for the impartial benefit of the whole. The role of judge is one of the most difficult any man may be called upon to perform. It is essential that a judge be a man or woman of absolute integrity. It is even more important that he/she be a person of uncompromising self-examination and self-honesty. It is better for a nation to have a corrupt president and a corrupt legislature than for it to have one corrupt judge. And this consideration is not only for Masons who are judges, but for all Masons. For any of us may be called to serve upon a jury, and, when so serving, we are in the role of judges, determining facts between people and making decisions as to guilt or innocence which have great consequence.

When you think about this Degree, try to remember the ebony box. It represents your heart, which is the repository of all your motives, the records of your inner tribunal, the plans of the inner temple you are building for yourself—your future moral life. How you build and respond to your own life can be a symbol of knowledge and wisdom, the principle of which is contained in your heart, waiting to be kindled by the revelation that awaits you in your transformation from Man to Initiate.

The pocket is said to hold the key to the ebony box and/or the records of King Solomon's tribunal and/or the plans of the Temple, when they are carried by the individual judge or builder in the field of life. Like the ebony box, this is a metaphor meaning that judgments, opinions and decisions of our "inner tribunal," our reason and affectability, are in the same place, within our heart, with our plans to build our own private temple. As such, they affect the person we are. Each thought of ours, each action, dream, virtue or vice, become a part of our life, no matter how tightly we keep them locked up in our inmost being, our ebony box.

Thus, let us be careful not to base our judgment on external appearances, as we are more easily predisposed to condemn others and forgive ourselves. We may not possess the virtue that others credit us with, just as others may be more courageous than we are, in their fight against evil, since we will never know the motives and suffering that are hidden in their inmost being—the ebony box.

The lessons learned here should instill loving kindness, charity, gentleness, pity, pardon and even grief for the fallen man, as he is eventually the victim of his own passions, propensities and circumstances just as we could be at any time. How we build and respond to our own life can be a symbol of knowledge and wisdom, the principle of which is contained within our heart. A good and true heart is the key to becoming transformed from a man to an initiate.

The Journey of the Elu to Enlightenment

Questions for Contemplation as a Provost & Judge

1. How should we react to a person who is accused of a wrongdoing before his matter is decided by a court of law? Does it make a difference if the person is also a Brother?

2. Is it okay to do lawful things that you feel are wrong, or unlawful things you feel are right? How do the boundaries between right and wrong differ from those between legal and illegal? How are they the same?

3. What do the Spirits of Retribution and Inaction represent in Masonry? How does justice act as a synthesis between the two?

4. What is required of the nature of human administered justice?

5. Would jury trials be better served by a panel of judges rather than a panel of peers? Would public policy decisions be better made not by elected officials but by representative panels of citizens, chosen at random?

6. How do we know that crime and injustice do not pay when inhumanity, wickedness, partiality and vice seem to be prevalent and strong?

7. How can we improve on how we think and act in matters involving our own personal judgments toward other people and circumstances?

8. How do we, as ordinary people, act as peacemakers in disputes between friends, amongst family, neighborhoods, and even people we have never met?

LODGE OF PERFECTION

EIGHTH DEGREE.

8°
INTENDANT OF THE BUILDING

"He knows much, who is conscious of his ignorance"

The 8°, Intendant of the Building, conveys that King Solomon, concerned with the completion of the Temple after the death of Hiram, and, in particular, the construction of the Secret Vault in which the sacred treasures must be kept, undertook to hire five young students whom Hiram had mentored to replace him in the event of his death. As each were taught a specialized area of knowledge, Solomon appointed each as an Intendant of the Building. The five lights in the East represent the five chosen Intendents of the Building. "Building" in the title of this Degree, refers not to the noun but to the verb—the process of building the Temple

Gareb, the chief artificer in gold and silver, symbolizes

all virtues adorning the character of a Mason. Zelec, the chief of stonemasons, symbolizes the strength and solidity of a Mason's character. Satolkin, chief of the carpenters, symbolizes the qualities that make work honorable. Yehu-Aber, the chief in bronze, symbolizes usefulness, charity and devotion to Masonry; and Adoniram, the superintendent, symbolizes the unifying of these virtues and qualities into one human perfect work, as necessary to complete the human temple.

One of the key concepts presented in this Degree is that no one can advance in Masonry who has not studied the lessons he has already learned. It does not mean that we require proficiency tests before the person is permitted to take the next degree—but that real advancement in Masonry, that is, real self-development, is progressive.

Until a musician learns how to read notes, sheet music does him little good. He can be surrounded by the finest, the most beautiful music in the world in manuscript form, and it would be useless to him. In the same way, we are surrounded by symbols and teachings of the Degrees, but until we have thought about them, studied them, discussed them, we cannot be said to know them or have mastered them.

The first philosophical theme of this degree is the essential importance of education; not only as the basic requirement for the individual search for truth, but also to build up an enlightened citizenry, which is the primary requisite of a well-regulated and just society. As Masons, we also acknowledge that the discovery of the Divine Truth, that is, the essential reality and unity of our Selves, the "treasures of our Sacred Vault," our soul, the higher truths of our being, demands an unceasing learning process.

THE JOURNEY OF THE ELU TO ENLIGHTENMENT

Progress comes from knowledge; as knowledge is power.

However, education is not only learning and keeping knowledge to oneself, but also teaching, instructing, enlightening others; that is, the transmission of knowledge and skill from one generation to the next. Hiram Abif taught his art to his five disciples so that they could reflect on his knowledge and develop their own positive, creative approach to life. The hope of every generation is to learn, to reflect on one's learning, and to develop a positive, creative approach to life, and, thus, to pass one's knowledge on to future generations, preserved and enriched.

We each have something original to offer mankind. Every one of us brings our knowledge and experience to the community, making the search for Truth and Wisdom a cooperative effort, the source of great works. It is therefore a moral duty to teach as much as to learn.

The 8th Degree is also one of the most political degrees in the Rite. The completion of the Temple in Society implies a political system based on freedom, justice and democracy, as well as an economic order based on capital and labor, politically kept in appropriate equilibrium, as these constitute the foundation of a genuine republic. Such is the political message of this Degree; just as an independent judiciary was that of the seventh Degree, and an enlightened and moral citizenry was of the fourth, fifth, and sixth Degrees. A citizenry enlightened by education, will produce a collective will of a people governed by the common good.

A Masonic lodge offers such a model for humanity.

As Masons, we have a genuine duty to study the principles of order, to determine what the laws of order are to man, to moral conduct, to right thinking, and to the acquisition of knowledge. The successful building of our spiritual Temple requires mastery of many kinds of information and insight from many sources. Our immortal life does not begin at death, but begins here in the present. We are already living in the first phase of our immortality. Our quest is a matter of taking one step at a time, and to learn at each step. It is important to remember that, while we may attain higher degrees, the genuine degrees are the ones which we personally labor to earn, and thus, deserve.

There is no real progress in life without studying the various meanings of truth, not just moral truth alone; but political, philosophical, and religious truth, so far as it concerns the great principles of each. Education, like Masonry, never forces us to learn. That decision is ours alone. The ruffian in this Degree is our latent tendency just to let life be what it will be.

It is easy to have an "eat, drink, and be merry, for tomorrow we die" approach to life. Masonry rejects this approach, of course, on the grounds that Masons believe the soul is immortal and so life is not "all there is." It further rejects this approach because it is selfish, leading man to live for his own pleasures and desires, and caring little about the ease and happiness of others.

It is also easy to see only the "woe is me" side of life; that life is nothing but a snare and a delusion, an insignificant period of suffering and sorrow. Masonry also rejects this approach for several reasons. First of all, it is essentially ungrateful. It suggests that God has condemned us to this life as a punishment. Masons believe that God has gifted us with this life as a wonderful opportunity to learn, to experience, to grow and develop. Second, a "woe is me" approach is selfish, leading us to overlook the good we might do and the benefits we might bring to others by encouraging us to think only of our own benefits.

In the place of these positions on the nature of life, Masonry adopts the "life is a gift of God" approach. And it is a gift we are expected to use wisely. The goal is to live in such a way as to be of use to others and a benefit to ourselves. Masonry adopts this approach as being the most in tune with the obligations of man to God. When a father gives a gift to his child, inherent in that giving is the assumption that the child will not use the gift to injure himself or others. The giving expresses the confidence of the giver in the receiver. The same is true in the gift of life. It is assumed that we will use it wisely and with benefit, investing ourselves in the process of making the world better.

Life is unique in another way. It is enriched by the sharing and interaction with others. It is as if life were a musical instrument. Solo work of great beauty, strength, and power can be performed, but it is only when all the instruments are united in an orchestra that all the possible timbres, sounds, and textures can be experienced. In just that way, a man may build a beautiful life, but its full richness, depth, and beauty can be experienced only when he interacts with the lives of others.

A major part of that interaction comes from the awareness and acceptance of responsibility for those around us. And the more advanced we are in any area of life, the stronger those responsibilities become.

A man may achieve great wealth, but if he hoards that wealth we call him a miser, and he dies a pitiable and lonely death, lamented by none. That same man, using that wealth freely and generously for the benefit of others does not impoverish himself. He still has enough for his own needs and desires. But he does good in the world, and we praise him in our hearts, and do not begrudge him his wealth.

A man may achieve great learning in some area, but if he hoards that knowledge, sitting alone at night and chuckling over each new fact or insight and sweeping them into the dark coffers of his mind at the approaching footstep for fear that someone else might know what he knows, he benefits not even himself. We admire the generous mind which delights in knowledge and even more in the sharing of that knowledge; the man typified by Chaucer's famous line, "Gladly would he learn, and gladly teach."

A man may achieve great political power, but if he uses that power only to line his pockets, or to increase his self-importance, we call him a tyrant and hold him up to public contempt. If, on the other hand, he uses that power to benefit the people, to put into effect great plans by which all are given better, more meaningful and productive lives, we hold him in high regard.

The lesson taught by the parable of the talents is that an obligation exists to use what we are given and increase its benefits; and the more we are given, the stronger is that obligation.

As Pike remarks:

"The most striking feature of the political state is not that governments, nor constitutions, nor laws, nor enactments, nor the judicial power, nor the police; but the universal will of the people to be governed by the common well. Take off that restraint, and no government on earth can stand for an hour."

Masonry is concerned with the public or civic life of man as it is concerned with the private life. No man is an island. We live in societies, and we decide, by our actions, how kind or cruel, sensitive or indifferent, compassionate or harsh, upright or corrupt that society is. We cannot separate ourselves from the world, nor should we wish to do so. It is a beautiful place. It is our duty, as Masons, to work in and with society. We have a responsibility to improve it in all the ways we can. That is Hiram's legacy to you. And it is intended to be your gift to mankind.

Finally, this degree reveals to us the chief attributes of Deity—Beauty, Wisdom, Mercy, Omniscience, Eternity, Perfection, Justice, Compassion, and Creation. These are the meanings of the four letters written around the circle within an equilateral triangle in the East of the lodge.

The search for divine Truth requires Charity and Benevolence among men. Indeed, good will and tolerance are necessary to accept the different approaches adopted by others in their search for truth. To be patient and even-minded makes this search easier when we are confronted with adversity in life. God is Love, and every impulse of charity that dwells in us is a participation in this divine nature. Love of God and love of one's neighbors, love of life and love of the world in which we live, whatever the ordeals we may come across. Benevolence and Love are the antidotes to inevitable wrongs, suffering, sorrow, poverty and need in the world. These virtues enable us to maintain our living temple as we cope with the vicissitudes of time.

LODGE OF PERFECTION

QUESTIONS TO CONTEMPLATE AS INTENDENTS OF THE BUILDING

1. How do we accept a Mason as a brother when we believe that he has done little to earn the qualities of Masonry, and deserve its benefits?

2. What is the lesson being conveyed by Hiram when he personally participated in selecting those who would take his place? What does this lesson have to do with Masons living in the 21st century?

3. What are the characteristics of knowledge and wisdom? How is each gained?

4. What is the difference between knowledge and wisdom?

5. What is the role of a teacher? How do we, as Scottish Rite men, instruct those around us?

6. How can we make Masonic education an important element of the lodge experience? What will be required to make practical and intellectual learning a part of the Masonic experience? Why is this important?

7. What characteristics represent an important balance between management and labor in all successful enterprises?

8. What does the concept of Masonic jurisprudence mean to you? To what areas of life does it apply?

9. What is required for political systems to be kept in equilibrium? What are some consequences to society when they are not?

THE JOURNEY OF THE ELU TO ENLIGHTENMENT

NINTH DEGREE.

9°
ELU OF THE NINE

"We must always be aware that ignorance is the principle enemy of human freedom"

The 9°, Elu the Nine (Master Elect of the Nine), carries great significance in the Scottish Rite. It is steeped in symbols and emblems which recur throughout the journey of the Rite. There are the black hangings strewn with silver tears, lamenting the prevalence of ignorance, error and oppression in the world. There is the cave, symbolizing the imprisonment of the soul and intellect. There is the lamp of spiritual despotism, the stream of water flowing from the past to the present, having its roots in ignorance, fraud, and falsehood. Our quest as a Master Elect is to help set right the things which are wrong in the world. The seeds of evil and kindness are in the conscience of men. And when the actions of men have unbalanced society, it is our duty as ethical men to try to make things right. Wrongness has no limits in its effects, and thus moral bravery as a weapon of the Rite is as important as physical bravery. Freedom is not possible in the context of ignorance.

We cannot but recognize the invasiveness of ignorance around us, but we remain resolved to overcome the sufferings of humanity and strengthen our determination to fight the evils of the world through the instruction we receive in our Masonic Degrees. This instruction derives from the virtues we have studied as we have progressed through the Symbolic lodge and the Lodge of Perfection. Virtues are principles of truth. Our task is to integrate those virtues into our daily lives, which enables us to take on a more courageous way of living that is affirmed in the Ninth Degree. The virtues stressed in this degree are represented by nine candles or lights; 8 placed in an octagonal form around the altar, and one between the altar and the east. These luminaries depict Disinterestedness, Courtesy, Devotedness, Firmness, Frankness, Generosity, Self-Denial, Heroism, and Patriotism; the virtues used to fight the evils in the world.

The principle causes brought out in this Degree, and the resulting commitments we are to make in addressing them are focused on four important ends—the commitment to the pursuit of knowledge, or education; the commitment to the pursuit of freedom, or the empowerment of men and women to do the utmost with their lives; the commitment to the pursuit of patriotism, that is, the love and devotion we practice toward our homeland to sustain its preservation and honor and protect the welfare of its citizens; and the commitment to the pursuit of individual and social enlightenment on behalf of all people.

These commitments seem obvious enough on the surface. Freedom is not possible without vigilance. We don't need to be reminded in our day that an ignorant populace is a powerful threat. The elevation of the people so that they are more and more fitted for freedom and knowledge is the greatest single task of the fraternity.

Education, including self-education and practical education, is the only path of overcoming ignorance. In a real sense, education is not itself so much an idea as it is a theme to which all great ideas become relevant. Education should aim, above all else, to make men good as men and as citizens. Plato writes, "If you ask what is the good of education, the answer is easy—that education makes good men, and good men act nobly, and conquer their enemies in battle, because they are good." Bacon adds, "men should enter upon learning to give a true account of their gift of reason, to the benefit and use of men." It is a common opinion in all ages that education should seek to develop the characteristic excellence of which men are capable and that its ultimate ends are human happiness and the welfare of society.

In this Degree, the emphasis of education is directed at the mitigation of ignorance. But, in a larger sense, Masonry teaches the importance of education as the single most significant preparation for good citizenship. Nothing can take the place of active participation in life. Men become citizens by living and acting as citizens, under the tutelage of good laws and in an atmosphere of civic virtue.

Tyranny and intolerance also seem an obvious enemy to freedom. Certainly, totalitarian systems tend to keep themselves in power by maintaining their people in ignorance and exciting them against those who show the truth. But not all tyranny is political. Tyranny takes place whenever any person or group says, "What I want is more important than what you want. My desires are more important than your desires. I matter more than you matter." We must never forget that a minority can tyrannize a majority; a single man can tyrannize a nation; a man or woman can tyrannize a family; a teacher can tyrannize a student; and employer can tyrannize an employee; a nation can tyrannize another state. Tyranny and intolerance are attitudes. And the essence of both is selfishness; selfishness in the world of material things and selfishness in the pursuit of power. Intolerance is selfishness in the world of ideas and beliefs. No man, no state, no church, no nation, has the right to insist that it knows the truth and that all others are wrong No one has the right to say, "I have the truth and the only truth. If you dare to disagree with me, I will have you oppressed until you admit that I am right."

The highest price to be paid for freedom is to allow others to be free. For this to happen, principles should always prevail over sentiment. As an Elu of the Scottish Rite, your task is to stop the bullying in the world.

Commitment to patriotism requires not only that we love our country enough to care about the welfare of its citizens, but that we also love it enough to carefully criticize its failings, and the weaknesses of our society, in order to protect and preserve it.

Commitment to individual and social enlightenment means that we liberate ourselves from our own lethargy, that is, going through life in the pursuit of pleasure and materialism through inactivity, rather than productivity. It is only through unceasing effort that we can attain any great purpose, affect any great cause, or fit ourselves for eminence in any profession.

Masonry makes very real demands upon those who

truly follow her teachings. It is not a matter of meeting for a few hours in a reunion, watching or acting in the degrees, having a good meal and some fellowship and then putting it back on the shelf like one's cap, until it is dusted off again for the next reunion.

Masonry has its being and does its work in the real world, in dealing with the problems of the real world. It requires of us that we strive to become a better man in our dealings with others on a day-by-day basis. It is imperative that moral and ethical men be concerned with the state of the people. The Mason knows that, especially in a democracy, an ignorant populace is indeed a real threat to freedom. Time and again, politicians have been elected by playing on the base fears and doubts of the population, rather than by calling forth the best that is within them. The Mason opposes this utterly.

Only the free choice is a meaningful choice. If I had a gun to your head and say "Your money or your life," I can hardly be said to be giving you a choice and you can hardly be said to be choosing freely. And yet, any choice based on fear, on ignorance, on prejudice is just as limited, just as unfree.

Because freedom and liberty are important, we obviously must strive to make them possible in the world. It is not enough to speak out against ignorance; we must strive to increase knowledge. Thus, it is, that we support scholarship programs, urge quality education, and insist upon good public schools which are supported by the community at large. Thus, also, it is that individual Masons volunteer for adult literacy programs, support public and educational television, give to colleges and universities, or find some other way to assure that information is freely available to the people. If we cannot found a university or endow a chair of learning, a lodge can at least contribute to the education of some boy or girl. From such small steps of charity and benevolence, great benefits have been given go the world. This truly is a means of protecting our nation, and a Mason's nation is important to him. Patriotism is a virtue, and not an old-fashioned sentiment of which one should be ashamed.

A Mason has an obligation to instruct and enlighten the people, and this responsibility must be carried out on the basis of sound principles, resolute knowledge, and unceasing commitment.

Our labor in the arena of life is to instruct, inform, and enlighten our fellow men. Hiram is the symbol of liberty or freedom--intellectual, physical, moral, political, and spiritual freedom.

The elevation of the people so they are more fitted for freedom and knowledge is the greatest aim of the Scottish Rite.

QUESTIONS TO CONTEMPLATE AS AN ELU OF THE NINE

1. How can we force a person to accept a law or practice deemed best by society when he holds beliefs which differ, even though his beliefs may cause personal harm, injury, or death only to himself?
2. Can democracy work in a country where most citizens are not knowledgeable enough to understand the complex issues confronting society?
3. What is the relation between moral knowledge and moral conduct?

4. Why does a man who knows what is good or right to do in a particular case, do the opposite?

5. With voter turnout so low in most elections, how can the government represent the will of the people? Is it important that it do so?

6. Do you believe there are absolute standards for good and evil? If so, what are they?

7. How is it that the ruffians represent the "chief foes of human liberty?"

8. What are some ways that human freedom and civil liberties are compromised in our own time as the result of ignorance?

9. Do principles shape and control our conduct, or are we more guided by sentiment? What price do we often pay for maintaining our principles against a popular sentiment?

10. How does defending the interests and honor of one's country help preserve freedom? How does it serve to restrict freedom?

THE JOURNEY OF THE ELU TO ENLIGHTENMENT

TENTH DEGREE.

172

10°
ELU OF THE FIFTEEN

"Seek the company of virtuous men"

The legend of the Ninth, Tenth, and Eleventh Degrees of the Scottish Rite go together as a group, and are often conferred as one. What is conveyed in one is reinforced in the other two. All three introduce the theme of the capture and punishment of the murderers of Hiram presented in the Third Degree of the English York and Emulation Rite. It also introduces the Gnostic concept of the Elus, the enlightened possessors of divine knowledge acquired through personal revelation.

In the 10°, Elu of the fifteen (Master Elect of the Fifteen), we are reminded that our quest for perfection must be made without fanaticism. This degree continues the lessons of the 9° and teaches us the consequences of selfishness. To know the principle enemies of human freedom and dignity in order to combat them. Tyranny and intolerance are again highlighted. Proclaiming what is right, what is important, what matters, in a way that holds one person or group above another is tyranny. Tyranny is always political because it is an attitude. The tyrant riding over the people, like the Kahns riding over the peasant, is a powerful image, and one can see the wrongness of it at once. But the problem is that most of our images of tyranny are historical. Tyranny was "back then." It couldn't happen now. But it can and it does, as was brought out in our discussion of the 9°. It is very important to remember that tyranny is not limited to the emperor who taxes his people unmercifully, or who demands to be worshipped as a god.

For tyranny does not equate with authority, but with attitude. We do not call the skilled and caring teacher who maintains order in his classroom a tyrant, nor the king who governs for the best interest and welfare of his people, nor the husband who discharges the offices of the household with love and concern.

The essence of tyranny is selfishness. The tyrant, being an individual, class, or nation, is willing to deny to others their own dignity, to reduce people to the status of things in order to gratify his own desires. As a Mason, we are obligated to fight against tyranny wherever and whenever it exists. It truly is our obligation to stop the bully and the brute.

The second great wrong against which this Degree warns us and against which we must fight is intolerance. As tyranny is selfishness in the world of material things and power, intolerance is selfishness in the world of ideas and beliefs.

The difference between fact and truth are especially important here. We have a right to insist on fact, at least until it can be replaced by a more fully developed fact. We have a right to say that the earth is roughly spherical and that those who claim it is flat, to the extent that they are describing a physical reality, are wrong. But no man, no state, no church, no nation, has the right to insist that it knows the truth and that all others are wrong. When truth is confused with fact, and when one then insists that others also treat that truth as fact, the essential selfishness of intolerance becomes apparent. "I am right, and you are wrong, and therefore you will change!"

In Masonry, the three ruffians represent ignorance or darkness, superstition or error, and egotism or ambition--the attributes of tyranny and oppression. Our challenge as men with passions, errors, judgments, faults, etc., is to find a cooperation between the Hiram (the forces of good and right) within us and the ruffians (wrong and evil) within us. This degree also focuses on the first and foremost goal of human life, which is the quest for spiritual enlightenment. Such spiritual growth is achieved through higher, more refined levels of consciousness; that is, concentrating one's mind on one's innermost self, his center of being. It is deep, pure, and non-descriptive, and wholly detached from ego. This state of being cannot be achieved as long as ignorance, tyranny and fanaticism linger in our minds.

Ignorance impairs intelligence by preventing the mind from being opened to the infinite richness of knowledge, and developing an understanding of the essential reality of the universe and mankind. Ignorance keeps man bound by the illusions of his shallow perceptions. This results in self-centeredness, selfishness, and overvaluing oneself to the point of overpowering others, which is tyranny. When it is applied to ideas and beliefs, this attitude leads to denying others their right to approach truth through their own means and from their own perspectives. When one human concept of truth is imposed on others as the only rightful, tolerable truth; such is fanaticism.

It is therefore a sacred obligation for a Mason to eradicate these three fundamental obstacles to wisdom. Again, this is achieved through education, the main focus of the Ninth Degree, and toleration and liberality, the two additional virtues emphasized in the Tenth Degree. Toleration is defined as every man's duty to respect the opinions and faiths of others, and accept their actions, as long as they do not infringe on his own freedom of action. Liberality is based on the principle that truth is one, but it is recognized through many different concepts. Therefore, no man or group of men has a natural right to impose his own concept as the one and only valid and acceptable truth.

This Degree is devoted, then, to the causes of people who struggle against any form of oppression; of those who defend the right of free thought against the tyranny of public opinion; to the employee asking for fair wages; to patriotism warring against the tyranny of party; to toleration against intolerance and fanaticism; to civilization, instruction, and enlightenment against savagery, error, and ignorance; to free thought, free speech, and free conscience.

The conclusion is that Masonry's natural religious concepts are only those on which all men can agree, and they are essentially centered on the brotherhood of man under the fatherhood of God; the notion of a universal supreme mind, a simple morality and courtesy, freedom of investigation on human essence and destiny, and, above all, selfless, unconditional love for one another. Our virtues are to be demonstrated in ordinary, day-to-day efforts to contribute to individual and collective harmony and happiness.

LODGE OF PERFECTION

Let the light of freedom illuminate the world,
The light of religious and political toleration
rise upon the world,
The light of education and intelligence
shine in all corners of the world.

QUESTIONS TO CONTEMPLATE AS AN ELU OF THE FIFTEEN

1. How can we show tolerance for the views of others with whom we do not agree, without seeming condescending, or appearing to accept their point of view just to please them?

2. What rights are so important that if the government tried to take them away from you, or others, would you be prepared to fight for them?

3. How do we distinguish between fanaticism and zeal?

4. How do we distinguish between ignorance and lack of information?

5. What does being tolerant mean?

6. How should we react to the destruction of, say, important icons of freedom, by being tolerant of the fanaticism and intolerance, which brought them down?

7. What are the consequences of being intolerant of actions of which we do not approve?

8. How can we contribute to the development of learning, and not just be critical of ignorance?

9. How would you go about applying the rules of Masonry to international peace initiatives?

THE JOURNEY OF THE ELU TO ENLIGHTENMENT

ELEVENTH DEGREE.

11°
ELU OF THE TWELVE

"There is no evil in death but that which life makes"

The 11°, Sublime Elect of the Twelve, continues the teachings of the Ninth and Tenth Degrees by admonishing the Elus to be leaders of mankind in its search for personal development, spiritual enlightenment, social justice and harmony. In the 10°, we explore the consequences of selfishness resulting in tyranny and intolerance. In the 11°, we go past merely saying that the Mason must oppose tyranny and intolerance and point out that he must be engaged in the positive act of actually trying to benefit other people as much as he likes to benefit himself. Life, for a Mason, can never be a matter of "looking out for Number One." We must be concerned with others because we realize that we are a part of that "other." We

THE JOURNEY OF THE ELU TO ENLIGHTENMENT

should not only avoid selfishness, but practice selflessness, or, as Pike called it, disinterestedness.

The story of this Degree involves the Elu of the Twelve who were elevated from the preceding Knights of the Fifteen to become Governors over the twelve tribes of Israel. It is important to note that the Elu of the Twelve were not elevated because of their birth, rank, or titles; instead, they were rewarded for their zeal and devotion toward the cause of justice. Each of us has an obligation to be concerned about the social welfare of the people as a whole. As an Elu of the Twelve, our duties are to be sincere in protecting people against illegal or unjust impositions; contend for their political rights, make sure they are not oppressed, and that they have access to legal means to redress their grievances. This is the mandate for good citizenship.

The problem is that most men are content with being passively involved in governance and civic affairs. We literally leave our individual freedom to the judgment of others whom we often don't even know. We also know from experience that, left to their own devices, men tend to find more differences than similarities between themselves and others. We may agree with the Biblical condemnation of those who say, "*Lord, I thank Thee that I am not like that man, a sinner,*" but rare indeed is the Mason who can truly claim not to have said the equivalent of, "*Lord, I thank Thee that am not like that man…a liberal…a Democrat…a Republican…an uneducated fool…an educated fool…a libertine…a prude…a liar…a nobody…a stuck up snob…a materialist…a spendthrift…a poor provider…a money grabber…a bleeding heart…an uncaring heel…an irreligious lout…a pious hypocrite…*" etc. etc. etc. Yet, this degree demands that we take an active role in ensuring that truth, liberty, justice, and proper governance are preserved and carried out for the benefit of everyone.

Standing up for what is right and just can be difficult, especially if a society, or those in power have become corrupt. But we must have sympathy with our kind because we recognize the human race is one big family. Unless we direct our zeal and devotion to the causes of truth, liberty, and justice, the ideals and cornerstones of our society can be eroded away. It has been said that, "the only thing necessary for the triumph of evil, is that good men do nothing." Therefore, it behooves us never to sit idly by.

Masonry also teaches us to take pride in our abilities, but not use that pride to denigrate others. We teach self-development so that we can be of aid to others, not so we can look down upon them from a loftier pinnacle. We seek for the things which unite us to mankind, for our common humanity, and not for artificial and meaningless discriminations so that we can feel superior to "the masses."

We also learn in this degree that the right of a people to representation is consecrated. One of the central issues addressed in this Degree is the question of "who shall guard the guardians?" True liberty cannot exist without an independent judicial body—which in our country is a jury of twelve whose verdict must be unanimous to convict of crime. A strong, impartial, accessible, and compassionate judicial system is essential to the happiness of the people and the welfare of the state. These are the Elect of the Twelve, the only true "guards of the guardians."

Trial by jury is important not because it releases the judge from his responsibility, but because it assures that the judgment of several persons is involved and thus has a better chance of being fair. The scales of justice should be adorned by the symbols of the affections; expressions of justice should be tempered with mercy so that laws are conceived in a spirit of love. The happiness of a people does not exclusively depend upon rigid expressions of wrong, but also upon a generous display of sentiment.

Further, no person is free, in whose courts do not sit upright justices whom power cannot terrify, nor wealth corrupt, nor ambition seduce. No person is free in whose court's power can convict the innocent or acquit the guilty; and the right of trial by jury is of more worth to a man than the right to vote; individual liberty and immunity from wrong and oppression being much more dependent on it.

These things are important to understand if we wish to stay a free people.

Finally, the 11° teaches that the most indispensable duty of a Mason is to devote himself to practice virtue. The inflamed heart adorning the apron is a symbol of our ardent devotion to the cause of Masonry and of zealous charity--for charity, more than all other virtues, is the principle virtue which satisfies humanity.

Thus, the characteristics of an Elu of the Twelve are that he be frank, sincere, reliable, just, of perfect honesty and integrity, and a lover of truth; that he be fair, faithful, and cognizant of God's will. This higher level of humanity is reached only by men who are wise, pious, temperate and just, frugal and abstinent, magnanimous and brave. We are the champions of human freedom. It is essential that we be earnest in doing what it is our duty to do, that no man should be disappointed because he has relied upon our word.

Life is a good school in this respect. It is indeed through the constant conflicts with life's difficulties, that we acquire relativity, or disinterestedness, with regard to ourselves. Virtue and morality are the only tenets which ensure peaceful living for ourselves and our society. And spiritual development is the only way to transcend natural drudgery and degradation, and open up to a future existence and an intimation of immortality.

Once this level of wisdom is reached, the better knowledge of one's own struggle and suffering leads to a better understanding of the suffering of others, which is the source of sympathy and compassion. This is what naturally impels us to labor for improving and protecting others as we do our selves.

QUESTIONS TO CONTEMPLATE AS AN ELU OF THE TWELVE

1. Who should be selected to "guard the guardians," that is, to provide an effective check and balance against negligence or apathy of those who rule?
2. What lesson in this Degree addresses a possible resolution to the problem of inequity in poverty?
3. What is the meaning of "a higher level of humanity" in the context of the quest of the Lodge of Perfection?
4. Why is it posited in this Degree that the right of a trial by jury is of more worth to a man than the right to vote?
5. What qualities are required to be a leader of mankind in the context of the requisites of freedom presented in this Degree?
6. What is the difference between Education and Enlightenment? How are they the same?

THE JOURNEY OF THE ELU TO ENLIGHTENMENT

TWELFTH DEGREE.

Reverse

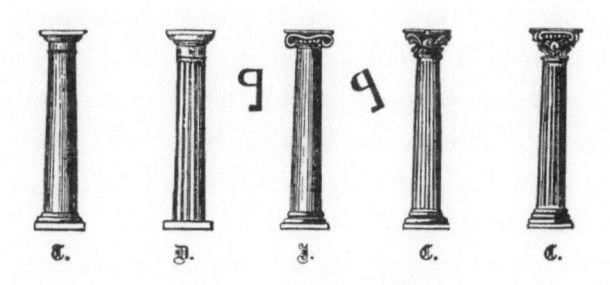

12°
Master Architect

Seek Wisdom

The ceremony of the 12°, Master Architect, is brief, but its significance is profound. The candidate is received in the Chamber of Designees, which had been assigned for use by the Master Hiram in the House of the Temple of Solomon. At this point in our journey, we have ceased to work with the instruments of the laborer-- the square, level, plumb and trowel—and we now assume the working tools of the Master Architect or Geometrician; the protractor, plain scale, slide rule and parallel ruler. Here we are taught the symbolic meanings of these tools, the most important of which instructs us to solve the great problems presented by the universe and be a part of its existence; to know and understand the lofty truths of philosophy and to communicate these freely with others; to live not only for ourselves, but for others; to be upright in all our actions. By their use, we advance beyond right angles and horizontals.

The mathematics of the heavens is before us. We advance from the realm of morality to that of true philosophy. From this point forward in our journey to the Royal Secret, we will deal with spiritual problems rather than material ones. The Master Architect approaches the symbolic sanctum sanctorum, or holy of holies, and begins to understand what Freemasonry really is.

There are two very profound insights to take from this Degree. The first is conveyed in the opening scene where the Junior Warden informs us "the Lord gives wisdom; and out of his mouth come knowledge and understanding." The second is given us by the Sage when he admonishes us "never to forget this truth: the eye makes that which it looks upon—the ear makes its own melodies and discords. The world without reflects the world within."

When it is said that the "Lord gives wisdom," what is meant is that wisdom is a divine aspect of human nature and is endowed within the soul, mind, and the will of every human being. There is a spark of divine light in all hearts, in the sanctuary of every man's soul. And within that divine enclosure is kept the essence of pure love, unlimited kindness, and the profound value and worth of all things in the world.

The problem is that we, and not God, determine what we encounter in our life. We choose to be ignorant. We settle for complacency and shallowness. We thrive on distrust and discontentment. We never seem to know what anything means until we have lost it. We may be proud of our mental and intellectual powers, yet perceive nothing of the worth of our soul. We are the possessor of great wealth, but we fail to take an accounting of our own treasure house.

There is no man, so vile, so base, so low, that he does not have some traits of that sacredness within him—some sanctuary in his soul, where no one may enter; some sacred spot where the memory of his childhood is, or when love was once felt, or the echo of some word of kindness once spoken to him—an echo that will never die away.

Thus, everyone has the power to make all situations, temptations, and trials as instruments to promote his virtue and happiness. Life is what we make it; the world is what we make it. Our task is to discover its allegorical meaning to us. Pike said, "The eyes of the cheerful and of the melancholy men are fixed upon the same world, but they do not see it the same way." The selfish man must not expect to find charity. The cold-hearted man will meet only coldness. The rude man will encounter violence. Those who ignore the rights of others must not be surprised if their own rights are forgotten.

Yet, the gentle man will be gentle, the kind man will be kind, the good man will find goodness all around him, an honest man will find there is honesty in the world. And the man of principles will find integrity in the minds of others.

The same is true of a community or society. The life of a community depends upon its moral condition. Intelligence, uprightness, kindness, a public spirit, will make it a happy community and give it permanence. Selfishness, dishonesty, corruption and crime will make it a miserable community, and will eventually bring about its ruin. All people live one life. We cannot be separate, no matter if we separate ourselves from all others.

Our quest, then, is for wisdom. This Degree teaches us what wisdom is and how knowledge and contemplation give access to it. We are all naturally endowed with all the necessary functions to learn and think. But it is only through the path of knowledge that we acquire wisdom. Wisdom is not possible without the acquisition of knowledge; and knowledge is only attained by great will. It is always the awakening of consciousness that awakens our will. And it is the faculty of the will that distinguishes us from the brute. It is the power of the mind that gives all situations and fortunes their character. The bottle is either half empty or half full, depending on the disposition of our mind. It is important to know that it is the very glory of a man that he can bend the circumstances of his own condition. The mind has the power to shape reality. And the mind will be happy or sad in proportion to its wisdom. We create our own future by our actions; thus, there is no such thing as an unimportant action.

The ultimate objective of Masonry is that we will use our precious mind to commune with God's spirit and, thereby, understand and even "feel" the essential reality of creation in our existence. The ultimate purpose of our life is to fuse into God's oneness. Creation is full of wonders and we all have a natural sense of these wonders. It is a great truth that the most significant attribute of God's will is to be found in the divine aspect of human nature. We are all endowed with a soul and mind; and the will necessary to discover these wonders. The result can be nothing less than the improvement of humankind.

One of the melancholy realities of our life is that there is yet to be discovered unity of mankind. Yet, God has ordained that life is a social state. Individual wisdom contributes to making social wisdom possible for the very reason that we interact with those around us in society and in our lives. We can change the way a person treats us by the way we think about that person; and even if we fail to change that individual, we can change our own perceptions of him.

Wisdom is indeed the true Masonic Light. Upon all conditions of men, there is one impartial law—to all situations, to all fortunes, the mind gives their character. Situations are not what they are in themselves, but what they are in the feelings of their possessors. Likewise, everything in Masonry is allegorical and symbolical. By means of its morality, we advance toward its philosophy—every degree is a step in that direction.

THE JOURNEY OF THE ELU TO ENLIGHTENMENT

QUESTIONS TO CONTEMPLATE AS A MASTER ARCHITECT

1. When faced with an opportunity to address a social ill requiring a considerable tax increase, how can we tell if our resistance is based on the guidance of our own soul or higher self, or from a selfish instinct to avoid higher taxes?

2. What are some of the consequences when we select other than the best as our public representatives?

3. What changes would you suggest be mandated to ensure that we select only the very best in our society to govern us?

4. The Sage in this Degree makes a note that we never seem to know what anything means or is of worth until we have lost it. What does this tell us of our own worth that we usually forget to consider?

5. What can we personally do to improve the lot of mankind?

6. How do we reconcile the ideas of individualism and freedom with community and morality?

7. What kind of virtues and qualities make a community a happy one?

8. How does the soul differ from the mind?

LODGE OF PERFECTION

THIRTEENTH DEGREE.

Reverse

191

13°
ROYAL ARCH OF SOLOMON

"We are a mystery encompassed with mysteries."

The 13°, Royal Arch of Solomon, together with the Fourteenth Degree, represents the capstone of the Lodge of Perfection. The legend of the Royal Arch Tradition as exemplified in the Scottish Rite can be summarized as follows: King Solomon had decided to build a temple or palace for the administration of justice on the outskirts of Jerusalem, thus covering and purifying a site which was believed to be an old pagan temple. Three of his architects were sent to survey the sight. Upon close examination, they discovered a ring, set in a heavy stone. Moving the stone, they found a chamber underground, with a similar stone in the floor. In all, nine chambers were discovered, each located under the preceding one. In the last chamber was a triangular pillar or pedestal of alabaster, in which mysteriously burned a flame, although no human hand had been there to feed the flame for centuries. Resting on the pedestal was a cube of agate, bearing a triangular plate of gold on which was inscribed the name of Deity—the whole being a great Masonic treasure.

The three took the cube back to Solomon, who recognized it for what it was—the promise made by God to Noah, Moses, and David to have His True Name revealed to mankind on a gold plate. Solomon rewarded the three brothers by advancing them to the Sublime Order of the Royal Arch.

What the brothers saw, without knowing it, was the Lost Word, the great symbol of Freemasonry. It is called ineffable because its true pronunciation has been lost to time. The degrees of the Lodge of Perfection are styled "ineffable" because they communicate truths and concepts which cannot always be expressed by words alone. The symbolic images in this Degree are profound, and represent some of the most important interpretations of symbolism in all of Masonry.

The descent into the nine arches can represent many things. It may be emblematic of the difficulties encountered by those who endeavor to discover the truth about God and the world around us. It may represent the self-exploration each of us must make in our quest for truth. Self-discovery was the purpose of all true ancient initiations; hence the Greeks adorned their temples with the words "Know Thyself." In this Degree, the descent itself has a secret meaning. *A Mason gains access to the knowledge of the divine truth only by seeking ever deeper within his inmost self, his soul.* This is what the candidate means when asked; "How did you receive this distinction?" and he answers, "By reaching the center of the most sacred place in the world."

Metaphors of ascending or descending occur in all three of the Craft Degrees of Freemasonry, and are encountered in a number of the Degrees of the Rite. The fundamental meanings for the individual contemplating them are self-awareness and transcendence. In this Degree, the descent into the nine vaults represent a movement downward into the personae of one's own mind and sub-conscious to discover his own true nature and his connection with nature, or the universe, or the divine. The ascent from the vault symbolizes changes in levels of consciousness, increasing awareness, and ultimately knowing Deity in a way that can only be experienced within oneself.

Adoniram, Yehu-Aber and Stolkin were the three architects who discovered the nine subterranean arches, all three being at the top of Solomon's selection among the Elus. Adoniram replaced Hiram Abif, as he was the only one who understood the Master's architectural knowledge. Yehu-Aber was selected for this psychological refinement and appointed as the King's Intimate Secretary, the only depository of the King's secrets. Stolkin was the first to discover Hiram Abif's corpse and realize most consciously how catastrophic the loss of the "True Word" was for mankind. These three symbolize the human potential for divine knowledge. They represent the three letters, YOD, HE, and VAV, that is to say, the most advanced stage in human understanding of God's nature and attributes.

On each of the nine arches preceding the nine compartments is written one of the 9 attributes of God; namely IOD, or principle; IAHO, or existence; IAH, or deity; EHEIAH, or essence; IAHEB, or concession; ADONAI, or potency; EL KHANAN, or mercy, and IOBEL, or bliss. In the French rituals, these are replaced with the 9 sephiroth of the Kabbalah.

The vault symbolizes the human search for the

essential reality and attributes of Deity. In Masonry, all circular symbols like the vaulted ceiling, the arches, the jewel, together with the number 3 refer to a divine level of consciousness which is represented in the phrase "passing from the square to the compasses." The torch carried in the hand of the candidates (architects) making the descent represents the Light of Masonry.

The ritual mentions the ninth compartment, where the divine treasure lies, is made of solid rock, and that Enoch's Temple was made of unhewn stones. This means that the ultimate objective of man's spiritual quest and his own soul, the vehicle to reach it, are of divine nature; "not made with human hands." This is what the prohibition against the "sound of hammer, or any tool of iron" meant in the construction of King Solomon's Temple.

The cubical stone is also presented for the first time in this Degree. This symbol is also found in the Hebrew and Christian scriptures. From here it was introduced into Alchemy, and from there, into Freemasonry. It represents created nature, that is, man's development potential. The luminous alabaster pedestal, which lights up from within, symbolizes "the perpetual flame," the soul of man; which is of identical nature with the God of the universe.

Thus, we travel successively through the Nine Arches named the First Cause or Principle, Existence, God, Immortality, Fortitude, Toleration, Power, Mercy, and Joy, meaning:

    God is the Principle
    God is Life
    God is Power
    God is Eternal
    God is Infinite

God is One
God is Love
God is Wisdom
God is Justice

As Freemasons, as enlightened men, we have a natural impulse to see God in the mystery of our own being. An understanding of the true nature of God and man's relationship with God is the most sacred treasure of Freemasonry. Yet, this principle is too often hidden in darkness, concealed from those who are not prepared to receive it.

We must never forget that it is easy for the name of God to get lost. It is easier to create God than to know him. This Degree informs us that the higher concept of God often gets lost in the course of time. It is frequently replaced with "substitute gods," that is to say, ideas about the Deity which result in angry, jealous, violent, whimsical, revengeful, man-mad entities capable of ordering any number of selfish and intolerant acts toward others which represent only the state of mind of those who create them.

Further, this Degree warns us that it is easy for a man, a nation, or a culture to "lose the name of God," which is to say, to lose a true awareness of His nature. Few things seem so easy as for a people to turn away from the truth. The Bible records many such instances, but our own personal experiences and observations also furnish abundant evidence. Just as the name of God may be "lost," so may the knowledge of God be lost in superstition and myth.

To mention only a few examples of our own experience, we know, as Masons, that God expects us to deal fairly and compassionately with others. Almost all of us would agree that is right, proper, and just. But we may pocket the extra change given to us by error in the supermarket.

We know that, as God is forgiving, He expects us to forgive. Yet we may hold a grudge against another for years.

We know that, as He freely gives us the gift of life, so He expects us to be generous and charitable in our dealings with others. Yet, when some charity or some other such organization contacts us, we may grudgingly give the minimum amount we think we can socially "get away with," or simply lie about having already given.

There is also a public, or civic, association with the arch or vault itself, and especially the keystone, that serves to remind us of the fact that the freedoms of a people are best assured when guaranteed by some instrument such as a Constitution, which sets forth the general rules and philosophy of a nation, and which is not easily changed. A nation is at risk when it must rely upon the good nature or kind intentions of a ruler or assembly, without some sort of check which supersedes that authority. A written constitution is like the keystone in the arch; it gives definition and stability to the political structure of a nation. Without such an instrument, it is far too easy for a nation to lose its sense of purpose and its guiding political ethic.

This is the same principle upon which the ancient landmarks, charges, and constitutions of Freemasonry are based. These are the compass that keep us centered on our organizational structure, and its foundational aims and purposes.

The final instruction of the 13° relates to the True Word. The meaning of the True Word in Masonry is that the true knowledge of God, of His nature and attributes, is revealed only to those who are endowed with the requisite amount of intellect and intelligence to perceive it. The search for the Master's Word is nothing less than the search for the true knowledge of God. It is the hero's quest. And the Royal Arch Degree very powerfully informs us that we can indeed gain access to the knowledge of the Divine truth only by seeking ever deeper within our inmost self, our soul.

The thing to be gained on this journey into oneself is insight, not just knowledge. That is why it is a personal quest. Knowledge can be gained from books or from a teacher, but insight must be the result of the individual's confrontation and exploration of his own thoughts, feelings, experiences and understandings. Real knowledge of yourself cannot be given you by someone else. You must go deep inside yourself to discover the meaning of your existence. Again, it is the internal and not the external qualifications that make a Mason. A man's soul is his spiritual dimension of the universe. It is the inmost part of his being where alone he may feel and realize the nature of God and find peace within himself. This state of mind is nothing less than the discovery and experience of one's own spirituality, "the alabaster pedestal lit from within."

As Masons, the process of discovering the luminous pedestal and the agate cube is an obvious allegory for the effect which the discovery of the nature of God is intended to have in our lives. The fact that the triangular plate bearing the name of God is sunk into the cube tells us that this awareness is intended to enter into us and change us. And if no such change occurs, then we still have not descended into the nine arches (looked deeply into our own souls and consciences) and found the mystic cube and plate. We are to seek the spiritual center deep within ourselves.

It is in the grave, in the rubbish of the temple, in the depths of the earth, in the experience and trials of our own life, that the "corruptible puts on incorruption, the mortal puts on immortality!" As Royal Arch Masons, we are to be constantly engaged in the noble labor of consciously rebuilding ourselves from the shattered temples of our own passions, intolerance, and ignorance; discovering beneath the rubbish the lost treasure of Light and Truth.

This is the personal transformation of which Masonry seeks for every man.

QUESTIONS TO CONTEMPLATE AS A MASON OF THE ROYAL ARCH

1. How do we know, in addressing a problem in our own life, that we are asking the right questions of ourselves to solve it?

2. Who do the three architects selected by Solomon represent in Blue Lodge Masonry and what do they symbolize?

3. Masonry is defined as a system of hieroglyphic instruction veiled in allegory and represented by symbols. What is revealed in this Degree that clarifies and explains the cryptic nature of this earlier definition?

4. This Degree suggests that most of life is a search, not for answers, but for the right questions. How do we go about deciding what to ask? Where do we look for answers? Can you think of what situations in your life may you be asking the wrong questions?

5. What does it mean when it is said that it is easy for the name of God to get lost?

6. How do we interpret the concept of an Elu in a society that insists everyone is created equal?

7. What is your interpretation of limiting the utterance of the Lost Word only to the High Priests of Israel?

8. What do the many different denominations of faith which are prevalent in the world today suggest to us in regard to the metaphor of the Lost Word?

9. This, and many other Degrees of the Scottish Rite, make reference to various attributes assigned to Deity. Why is it necessary to assign attributes to God? Why can one not simply know who God is?

10. Why are there so many different systems of faith in the world if there is only one Truth?

LODGE OF PERFECTION

14°
PERFECT ELU

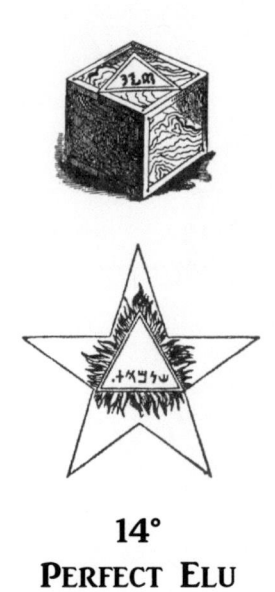

"The Glory of God is to conceal the Word"

The 14°, Perfect Elu, represents a secret underground vault or crypt in the shape of a perfect cube which is King Solomon's personal chamber for private conferences with the other two Grand Masters. When Enoch's Treasure was brought back to Solomon and he recognized the True Word, which had been lost since Hiram's murder, he decided to conceal it in a sacred vault under the holiest place of his own temple, the Sanctum Sanctorum, at the end of a secret underground passageway. He also decided in order to avoid another loss of the Word following his own death, to reveal this treasure to a select few whom he deemed most "perfect" of his master staff. These "Perfect Elus" formed an elite circle, based on their superior knowledge, wisdom, moral and spiritual qualities. Their ideal was to continue the Creator's work by improving mankind and leading it on its ascending path back to Deity's unity and perfection.

Unlike the vaults discovered in the 13°, this crypt was approached by a horizontal vaulted passageway with nine arches. While the passageway itself was dark, the Sanctum Sanctorum was brightly lit with 24 great lights, arranged by 3 in the South in the form of a triangle; 5 in the West forming a square with one in the center; 7 in the East in the form of a square enclosing a triangle; and 9 in the form of a triple triangle located in the East between the throne and two gilded columns. Amid these columns stood a triangular alabaster pedestal lit within. Upon it is set an agate cube on which a shining gold triangle is laid. The triangle bears the True Name of God in Phoenician and Sanskrit on its upper face, while 9 words written in different languages run around the three sides of the plate.

Like the Thirteenth Degree, the lessons in the 14° are conveyed largely through the symbols shown or introduced in the setting of the Degree itself. For example, the dimly lit passageway symbolizes the darkness of man's ignorance, a life through which he gropes for his ultimate aim, which is the discovery of truth, but which he is not yet able to attain because he is without possessing the tools necessary to help him in his quest.

In a sense, the passage toward enlightenment is a preparatory journey we all must take before we can receive the full light of knowledge. It has the same symbolism as the Chamber of Reflection prior to initiation in Craft Masonry, or that part of our circumambulation in the Entered Apprentice Degree which encompasses the north side of the lodge. It represents non-existence before birth; dark before light; ignorance before knowledge.

The crypt, or vault, is an inward symbol reminding us yet again that it is the internal qualities of a man that make him a Mason. Enoch's vertical vault in the 13° refers to the spiritual dimension of the universe and the soul of man, that fundamental part of himself where only he can feel and realize God within himself. Solomon's horizontal vault refers to the earth and society, to the King's wisdom and justice as an earthly ruler of men. The two together, uniting the vertical and the horizontal, create the symbol of the cross representing human perfection; and thus, the title of this Degree.

The distribution of the great lights (3, 5, 7, 9) also symbolizes the profound relationship intended between God and man. The number 3 refers to divinity, as it appears to man. The letters, YOD, HEH, and VAV characterize this stage of our human level of understanding, and correspond in Kabbalistic terms to Hochmah, or wisdom; Binah, or understanding; and Tiphereth, or beauty; which enables Kether, God's ineffable Being, to somewhat be felt by man. The number 5 refers to human perfection on our earthly plane of existence. Number 7 expresses God's Creative Power in the universe as well as the first step in man's spiritual ascent toward the Creator's truth and unity. Number 9 symbolizes the essential reality and attributes of Deity, Omnipotence, Omnipresence, and Omnificence—or God's Perfection.

Thus, we can see, in the 14° the most profound philosophical truths are presented as axioms, without being discussed, inciting us to pursue studies into their meaning on our own. We are put in possession of the Lost Word, and pointed in the direction toward the application of this newfound knowledge. We are consecrated to truth, and more deeply bound to our Brethren, the fraternity, and the ideas and truth Masonry hopes to promulgate. The Degree of Perfection is both a celebration of the revelation we received in the Thirteenth Degree, as well as an examination of our worthiness to possess it.

Knowledge, without its application is of little use or no value. With knowledge comes responsibility, and one must prove oneself worthy to possess it. The mere possession of knowledge is not a virtue. Yet knowledge, properly applied, results in wisdom, which the Biblical Proverbs say was coexistent with creation.

It is useful to be reminded that the ancient initiate could not have arrived at the hidden vault of Enoch had he not also mastered all the requisite lessons; mastered a practical application in his personal life with the lessons taught him. The rewards of the practice of virtue and upright living are what were discovered. What remains for us, as an inheritor of this ancient system, is to learn how to apply what we have discovered for ourselves. We are symbolically purified and consecrated to living virtuously, acting worthily, and deciding justly. And we obligate ourselves to strive hereafter to speak truthfully.

The Temple, the abode of the living presence of God represented by the sacred treasures placed in the Sanctum Sanctorum, has been built. Its most obscure recesses have been discovered, and that which was discovered has been secured. *"The Word, that which has been discovered, represents the limited utterance of the Grand Architect of the Universe. Here we arrive at the Perfection of the Master's Degree of the Symbolic Lodge with the discovery that knowledge of God is of His invisible nature, revealed to us in the Created World. Hence, we say, "The Glory of God is to conceal the Word."*

In the 13°, we saw that the True Word or True Name of God means the right concept of God's nature and attributes. But man's finite and imperfect nature limits his understanding of God's nature. We reduce the eternity of God to forms that come only within the grasp of our limited sense and intellect. God becomes an incarnate Divinity with man's attributes, which include love as well as hatred and violence. This is what Masonry calls the loss of the true Word.

However, despite our limitations, the true word of a Mason is the highest and noblest perception of what we call God that our limited mind is capable of forming. This word, whatever it is, is ineffable because one man cannot communicate his concept of Deity to another. Perfect truth is simply unattainable. We learn that it is up to each individual Mason to discover the secrets of Masonry by reflecting on its emblems and upon what is said and done in the work. The secrets are the insights which we can and must develop through the interpretation of our teachings. That happens when we think about the symbols, the lessons, the virtues, and consider their meanings in our own life.

We must prepare ourselves for knowledge. We can only learn when we are prepared to learn. We are each a part of a large Masonic family on the path to knowledge, using God's concept of His divinity in Man to create a universal union of morality and virtue.

It is also important that we remind ourselves that an understanding of the concept of God as a Trinity did not originate with Christianity. It is a far older concept, reaching back as far as we have any records of man's religious thought.

It was seen that God must necessarily consist of three aspects. First of all, there must be an intellect. The universe is not mindless, and its organization shows an intelligence of great scope. To conceive of the natural laws and foresee the consequences which would result from the establishment of those natural laws is a task of unimaginable complexity.

But the intellect is not enough, for it there were no Power or Will (force), then the idea conceived by the intellect would have remained formless. When the intellect interacts with the Power, a result comes forth. That result is known as the Word, the Logos, or any one of several terms in which man has attempted to express the concept.

Man, along with all the natural universe, results from that interaction. It is beside the point, for us, how man's body came into being. Whether it was directly created by an act of God, or whether it evolved according to a set of laws and processes set in motion by God is not a question appropriate to Masonry. But the soul, the spirit of man, is a different matter. This we can state, backed by the universal opinion of thoughtful men from every nation, every creed, and every time, is the creation of God. The method by which this took place is not known, and perhaps unknowable. Nor need the mechanics of the event concern us as Masons. The great truth with which we are concerned is that man is more than animal, more than accident, more than chance, more than chemistry, more than sociology—and that the essential nature of man is a question to be answered and explored by faith, reason, and philosophy; not by physics, biology or chemistry.

Our most glorious activity, the activity in which we most clearly demonstrate our connection with the Divine, is thought and study, and especially thought and study about man, God, and the nature of man's relationship with God.

But this is not an easy study. There are many markers on many trails, and the answer is not given to us directly. Nor can it be. To truly know is the result of insight and understanding, not merely of the accumulation of data. We may read all that the great writers have written—but unless we read with understanding; unless that knowledge brings about some fundamental change in our thinking, our perceptions, our understandings; the effort is wasted. Just as no one can become a mathematician by thumbing through a book of mathematics, so no one can become enlightened merely by casually reading the works of those who are enlightened. The process must enter the soul.

LODGE OF PERFECTION

QUESTIONS TO CONTEMPLATE AS A PERFECT ELU

1. How do we know when our life is what we want it to be?
2. Should any man be entitled to become a Mason?
3. Should all men be equally eligible to lead a country?
4. Do real leaders always represent the will of the majority?
5. What are some examples where society, culture, and whole civilizations have been harmed or even ruined because of a failure to adhere to the Elu Principle?
6. What is the real mission of the Elu in society?
7. How can you apply the Elu Principle in your own life?
8. The search for the Lost Word means many things. One of the most basic is each man's search to understand what he truly wants and who he truly is. Is your life what you want it to be? If not, how will you create what you want?
9. What will be required of you to become an Elu?
10. If perfection is not attainable, for what does the Perfect Elu strive?

THE JOURNEY OF THE ELU TO ENLIGHTENMENT

Chapter of Rose Croix

The quest of the Lodge of Perfection, then, is to come as close to Perfect Truth as we are able in this life. Masonry is above all a philosophical society. God has arranged his great purposes that each man has a work to do, a duty to perform, a part to play in the gradual enlightenment of the world. The completion of our first quest of the Scottish Rite—the quest for self-discovery and the awakening of our own spirituality—is made in an underground room, a cube, wherein we are instructed in the final mysteries of the Lodge. We have prepared ourselves to then purify and strengthen that spark, once awakened, and to make it the guiding force of our life. The first two degrees in this series deal with questions of ethics, and how ethics should aid us in our life decisions. In the Seventeenth Degree, we learn the power of our own spiritual force, and the Eighteenth degree informs us how our spirituality transforms us in a profound way. This is the quest of the Chapter of Rose Croix.

This guiding force which is within us is nothing less than our own empowerment as men. This newly discovered insight, this uniquely beautiful mystery within us enables the possibility that we may secure for others a balance of love, faith, and reason essential to universal harmony and a better world for all. Once armed with virtue, the quest of the Chapter of Rose Croix is to decide what we do with our own empowerment. This is a journey to light and knowledge, the inevitability of change, and the law of love.

THE SECOND TEMPLE OR NEW JERUSALEM

In a real sense, every brother is engaged in the process of building and rebuilding his life once he becomes consciously aware that the goal of human existence is to make the best we can of it. As we take on knowledge and wisdom we are naturally inclined to make progress. But the question is will we work hard enough at the process of growing spiritually to overcome the mundane setbacks that we encounter almost daily? The captivity in Babylon introduced in the legend of the 15° represents such periods of darkness in our life, where we are at sea in regard to the internal influences which enable us to strive for perfection. The reconstruction of the temple after the deportation to Babylon symbolizes the "restitution of primitive truth to men," that is, the highest concept of God in man's mind. Without a sincere belief and hope that we can throw away the rubbish of our life and literally recreate ourselves as enlightened men, more worthy of God's will; our mind would wander through the infinite desert of its old conceptions, without attraction, destiny, or end. Man's free will is God's instrument, like all other forces in nature, to bring the soul of man back to its own source, back to itself, back to its own natural virtue, rest and bliss, after wandering in the ignorant and violent profane world.

The goal of the Lodge of Perfection is to awaken us to the ruffians within ourselves and take control of their influence in our life so that we can become real Master Masons. Likewise, the Chapter of Rose Croix Degrees aim at raising our minds in such a way as to understand in the best way possible what it means to live in the consciousness of God.

It may seem obvious that the rebuilding of a material temple is purely symbolic, but the lesson of the New Jerusalem or the Second Temple building narrative is to help us understand the whole world, the big picture, the universe at large; and, above all, that every human heart is God's Temple. We can only do this by communing with our Self, our inner nature, so that we may feel and hear the voice of the spirit guide us in the significant moments of our life. In the context of the philosophy of the Rite, liberty, equality and fraternity in the soul of men and nations form the true Masonic temple, which must be built and rebuilt and defended against ignorance, intolerance, fanaticism, superstition, error, and selfishness.

The Great Work of Speculative Masonry is not the raising of grand buildings, but the raising of grand souls. We are each making a holy temple of ourselves, while also working together to make the world a temple of truth and liberty. This is what the Second Temple represents in Masonry.

THE JOURNEY OF THE ELU TO ENLIGHTENMENT

Fifteenth Degree
Plate 1st

CHAPTER OF ROSE CROIX

Fifteenth Degree
Plate 2nd

15°
KNIGHT OF THE EAST, OF THE SWORD, OR OF THE EAGLE

"It is to single men, and not the united efforts of many, that all the great works of man, struggling toward perfection, are owing"

The 15°, Knight of the East, is the first of two Chapter Degrees which serve as a transition between the Lodge of Perfection and the Rose Croix tradition, and deal with the Second Temple of Jerusalem, built by the Jews returning from the Babylonian captivity, and who brought with them a rich culture and oriental mysticism. The Fifteenth Degree informs us that our world has changed. The temple of Jerusalem has been destroyed and most of us have been carried away into

CHAPTER OF ROSE CROIX

Babylon. Since we are the captives, what does Babylon then represent in our journey to freedom? It was a world capital, a place of scientific learning and great wealth. It was a center of reforms in government, in health and commerce. Like all important cities, it was also seen as a great source of corruption and evil. To us, it symbolizes all the things of the temporal world—wealth, power, might, knowledge, even pleasure. It represents the opposite of the first city we encountered on our quest; the city of Jerusalem, the center of spiritual awareness, things of the spirit in opposition to things of the world.

In the character of Zerubbabel, whose name translates as "seed of Babylon," the candidate represents a great warrior in the armies of Cyrus and also a direct descendent of the King of Israel. He leaves behind a life of power, honor, wealth, and ease in Babylon and travels to Jerusalem to implore Cyrus, an initiate of the Mithraic mysteries, a Son of Light, to help him rebuild the temple. Cyrus recognizes Zerubbabel as an adept of the mysteries but tests his virtue by tempting him to reveal the secrets of the order and offering treasures from the temple. Zerubbabel refuses these temptations and is rewarded with the status of authority to return to Jerusalem to rebuild the temple. The lesson here is that it is only when our beliefs and principles are tested that we discover if they are strong enough to hold to our convictions of doing what is right. Then, as we grow in spiritual awareness, we must rebuild our lives to reflect our new understanding. We must leave the comforts and corruption of Babylon, which represents our old selves.

It is also essential that we understand the second temple to be only a pretext illustrating the mystical return of our own soul to its divine source within ourselves. This can only be achieved if freedom of thought and conscience is ensured. The path to liberty, equality and fraternity is a slow ascent (symbolized by the 70 years of captivity in Babylon), informing us that we must constantly pass through darkness to reach the light.

There is a great law of ebb and flow in nature. The full moon begins to wane the moment it reaches fullness. Nature teaches us, by example, that perfection is not a static state but an ongoing process—a process of gradual and cyclic progression towards greater perfection. This process requires work, effort, and vigilance on the part of every individual. Without an unceasing focus aimed at positive endeavor, it is easy to stray from truth and doing what is right. Confronted with the reality of polarity, or opposition in all things, we are forced to see a solution in apparent enigmas. We must ask, "Why are there so many opposites?" "Can they ever be reconciled?" and, "If so, how?"

Great swords are made by repeatedly plunging their blades into the extremes of hot and cold. Likewise, we here learn a lesson that foreshadows the reconciliation of opposites: we are taught to make advantage out of adversity. This reconciliation is one of the secrets of the Eighteenth Degree. However, in this Degree, we are taught that, above all things, we must remain faithful adherents to the truth and practice correct behavior. Integrity is extolled as the rule and bylaw of our personal code. By the words "Liberte' de Passage" we mean freedom of thought and conscience; political and religious liberty.

In this Degree, Zerubbabel struggles to choose between the temptations offered him by King Cyrus in exchange for secrets of the Mysteries of Solomon, or Freemasonry. Yet he remains true to the words he spoke in taking the obligations of Freemasonry. The obvious lesson here is the importance of maintaining one's integrity.

Resisting temptation is easy, as long as it isn't the right temptation. A man who does not like country western music will have little trouble resisting the person who tries to bribe him with tickets to a country western concert. Even a moderately good man may well be unwilling to barter his life for something against his principles.

The difficulty comes when we are tempted to do a "minor" wrong in order to achieve a great good.

Principles ethics is a specific area of philosophy which takes into account the particular context of an act when evaluating it according to absolute moral standards. Many examples can be given. Suppose you could, by condemning to death an innocent bum, eliminate poverty from the world (or establish universal peace, or accomplish some other great and universal good). Would you be justified in doing so? There is no question that to cause the death of an innocent person is wrong. There is also no question that the elimination of world poverty is a great and universal good. Does the life of an innocent man count against all that good? If so, how much? Should one do a "little" wrong in order to accomplish such good? Is it justified?

And there is the temptation.

If it is justified to take the life of an unknown man to remove poverty from the whole world, is it justified to take his life to remove poverty from half the world, from the United States, just from your own state, you own town, your own family, yourself? How do we find the way, or have some assurance that we are right?

We respond to situations by knowing what we believe, testing that belief as best we can by thought and insight, and then holding fast to our obligations; by being loyal to those principles we know to be true, even in the face of temptation to abandon them to do good. That does not mean that we do not change, develop, and raise our ethical sights. Indeed, as Masons, we have an obligation to try for even higher standards of honor and behavior. But we must always be sure that it is an advancement, and not a retrogression.

Zerubbabel realized he had the freedom to make an ethical choice. The great lesson to gain from this Degree is that we alone are the ruler of our own mind. A man who knows that his decisions cannot be blamed on circumstances or the will of other persons is a man who has truly embraced his freedom of thought in that moment. This is what liberty of thought, or Liberte de Penser, means.

The incident of the battle of the bridge is intended to be a lesson that change and development does not come quickly or easily. On the surface, this seems unreasonable. Surely any people would want to be free, would want to be in control of their own lives. But the experience of every great reformer teaches us just the opposite. Most people prefer the security of the cell they know to the great but insecure expanses of freedom. It is tempting for a people to sell their birthright. Even today, if we were to offer people a guaranteed income, guaranteed health benefits, guaranteed jobs if they would give up the right to work where they wished, give up the chance to earn more if they worked harder, give up the chance to participate directly in the political process, a distressing number would jump at the chance.

Our enemies represent the constant struggles we are faced with in life: ignorance, intolerance, selfishness, greed, jealousy, apathy, indifference of the world at large, the tendency to adjust to any evil to avoid difficulties in our little habitual way of life. The power of evil is far stronger than the power of good, and it demands a heroic strength and resistance not to yield to it in this world. Forces are always on the lookout to tear down what others have built, sometimes apparently or really with the best of intentions, that is, the roar and crush and hurry of life and business, the tumult and uproar of politics; the good intentions of folk who become intolerant of others just because they sincerely, and out of ignorance, believe they are right and others are wrong.

It is true that we make progress slowly, two steps forward and one back. But we do make progress. The yearning toward liberty and freedom is inherent in any people who are not utterly crushed. This drive can be very powerful, but the transition from slavery to freedom; from ignorance to knowledge is not and cannot be sudden. Rather, such a transition is progressive—a series of small steps, each taken as the last step is mastered.

Zerubbabel's character embodies that kind of individual, that kind of exceptional hero, a true Mason, who goes out in the world with staunch fidelity to duty and honor, constancy and resolve, and despite all odds, perseveres in reaching his goal, encouraging the disheartened, cheering the timid, inciting the indolent, forcing the apathetic and reluctant; constantly passing through the darkness to reach the light.

The Journey of the Elu to Enlightenment

Questions to Contemplate as a Knight of the East

1. What does the Babylon captivity symbolize in Masonry?
2. How can liberty for the individual and liberty of the society coexist?
3. Are liberty and freedom the same thing? How can we be sure we are motivated by high ideas and not by selfishness or stubbornness in disguise?
4. What sort of things cause the destruction of a Mason's "first temple?"
5. What is the meaning of the Second Temple? What is the symbolic goal of building it?
6. What is the difference between fact and truth? Does it offend you when you are misled by half-truths?
7. What do you see as the ethical distinction between lying and intentionally leading people astray by cleverly telling them only parts of the story?
8. What enemies of progress are highlighted in this Degree?

CHAPTER OF ROSE CROIX

Sixteenth Degree

223

16°
PRINCE OF JERUSALEM

"Everything acts upon and influences us"

The 16°, Prince of Jerusalem, continues the lessons of the Fifteenth Degree with a particular emphasis on the belief that God aids those who pursue good work, are faithful, and can practice the virtue of wisdom. This Degree teaches us that in our quest for self-development and creative living there are subtle temptations which can sidetrack us. We can live irresponsibly and without direction. We can be tempted by materialism and the pleasures of the flesh. We can surrender control over our life to some authority figure, such as a church, government, a parent, a peer group, or even a friend. Yet, only a sincere determination to follow Truth and Light will lead to a union with God's spirit. The Chapter of Rose Croix aims at raising the Mason's mind to a higher level of mystical consciousness. This Degree finalizes the necessary moral foundation that makes this mystical ascent possible.

The setting involves a halt in the progress of rebuilding the temple caused by objections of the enemies of Israel. The candidate sets out with Zerubbabel to request the new king Darius to honor his father's commitment to the rebuilding project. At Zerubbabel's request, Darius orders a search to be made to see if Cyrus did indeed decree the rebuilding of the house of the Temple. A unique provision of the laws of Persia was that a law or decree, once committed to writing, remained in force forever and could not be changed by a subsequent king or even by the king who first made the decree. The scroll is discovered and Darius orders that it be honored.

At a point during a feast, Zerubbabel (the candidate) is challenged with a riddle he must solve (as is often the case, whether progressing in the world or in a spiritual quest or ascent). Riddles are often encountered in symbolic quests. Their meaning is that as we progress in life, we are confronted with problems at all times which we must solve before we can proceed further. In this Degree, these tests examine three aspects of the human condition.

The first test is a life based on pleasure; the temptation to a life of ease and unconcern. It is the life of a person who "goes with the flow," happy and uncaring, his senses dulled to the sorrows and the potentials around him. Such a life produces nothing of value, either for the individual or for the world. There is no struggle for development, no attempt to make things better. It is, in essence, a life founded on the avoidance rather than the performance of duty.

The second temptation is to a life in which sensual pleasure predominates; not just in the indulgence in irresponsible sexuality, but in all the pleasures of the flesh.

It is the "eat, drink,' and be merry, for tomorrow you may die" philosophy. Masonry, on the other hand, says "work, care, labor, perform your duty, for tomorrow you may die; and if so, all the good that you might have done will remain undone for all eternity." The temptation is built on passion and desires rather than on self-control and responsibility.

The third, and most subtle temptation is to a life that avoids responsibility by obeying the orders of others without question. This is the temptation not to take control and responsibility for our own lives—to let others make the decisions and take the chances. It is the temptation to place both responsibility and blame on outside forces, to blame fate or circumstances for our own decisions not to act to improve ourselves and the world. In its most insidious form, it encourages us to let others do our thinking for us. It represents an unthinking yielding to authority, even if that authority is not appropriate.

Many centuries of darkness and near slavery clouded the earth because men took the pronouncements of others as authority without thinking for themselves, validating the experiences, and standing up as free and independent thinkers.

As we strive to build ourselves up, it indeed often seems that insurmountable obstacles block our progress. We are attacked by some who see us as vulnerable idealists, or by others who deny our right to try to change things or question our wisdom to change things. How do we persevere at such times? One very important response to such obstacles is to ally ourselves with those who share our commitments, and to both seek and provide support to each other in persevering. Yet, even our closest companions in this work, succumbing to their own frustrations and discouragement, can say and do things that sap our enthusiasm. Even within our own hearts and minds, we can discover different thoughts and feelings coercing us to stop fighting the temptations, to give up the work, and to distract ourselves and our companions with less noble pursuits.

The three vices exemplified in this Degree are often used as excuses for not holding to what we believe to be true and virtuous. In a very real way, we deny ourselves our liberty when we succumb to vices and temptations. We wrongly imagine that we can somehow avoid accountability for our own choices and actions. Yet, the truth is that we are still making our own choices and we are still responsible for their consequences.

The fourth answer given to the question, "Truth is stronger than all things," is the key to independent, creative, and productive living. A concern for truth—an attempt to see things as clearly as possible, to make decisions, to accept responsibility for the consequences of those decisions—is not the easy path. But it is the only one which the Mason can follow with honor. The truth abides. Even when we try to avoid it behind deceptions, distractions, and excuses we present to ourselves and others, truth always remains.

Thus, in this Degree, as in life, the quest of Truth wins out. The original order by Cyrus regarding the rebuilding of the temple is reaffirmed. On his return, Zerubbabel finds the city in ruin and appoints a set of judges to reinstate peace. The candidate is named a peacemaker, teaching us that before building our inner temple, we must first establish peace and love within ourselves.

This Degree is therefore an allegory of the trials that man faces when he decides to build a life of goodness and ethics based on love, truth, peace and toleration, intended to benefit others. Our obligations to others are stronger than the wars of nations or political conflicts. People are capable of atrocities when they forget that their obligations to other humans are superior to their allegiance to institutions. We must resist temptations to let others control our thinking, to live for pleasure, or just "go with the flow." The more we try to do good, the more some men will oppose us. This is why we must always carry the sword and the trowel, buoyed up by our hope for the eventual victory of good and the glory of humanity.

Questions to Contemplate as a Prince of Jerusalem

1. What does it mean to be in control of your own life? What does it mean to be an autonomous man? How can autonomy fit with social responsibility?
2. How does one go about measuring the effects of truth?
3. How can judges rule in righteousness when we cannot decide what it means to be righteous?
4. What does the sword and trowel symbolize?
5. We are to leave a noble heritage to those who will follow us in this world. What is a noble heritage?
6. Being dedicated to peace, under what circumstances are we justified in using violence?
7. Can a lie ever be used to further a truth?
8. What is your obligation to the future?

CHAPTER OF ROSE CROIX

Seventeenth Degree

Reverse

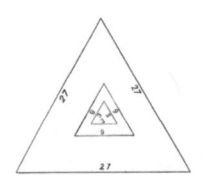

17°
KNIGHT OF THE EAST AND WEST

"Listen with your mind, your heart, and your spirit"

The 17°, Knight of the East and West, represents a turning point in Scottish Rite philosophy because it is here that we shift from temple-rich imagery to temple-free desperation. The two consistent motifs we encountered throughout the Blue Lodge and the Lodge of Perfection have been 1) adversity—battling with the shadow side of our personality, which serves as a catalyst to self-improvement so long as we stay active and keep moving toward our goal; and 2) the majestic Temple itself, which is analogous to a permanent, immovable jewel and the source of Masonic Light.

We encounter adversity again in the first two Degrees of the Chapter. It is noted that, in each, a test is made of those who are incorruptible. The central teaching has been that one who sincerely endeavors to acquire knowledge, and who is committed to the quest for higher truth, cannot be morally or ethically compromised. In the 15°, there is the temptation of wealth, and even the most sacred relic of history was offered our hero in a ruse to try and prove that honesty is a fallible human quality. In the 16°, we are reminded how easy it is for leadership to ignore the legal and societal commitments of the past. Our hero is confronted with a test so he can gain an audience with the king to redeem an older covenant which would change the world. When we are engaged in the work of building our lives and rebuilding the world into a more just and equitable place, there will always be adversity, temptations, and distractions to pull us away from our path.

Secondly, we note that, while adversity remains a constant throughout life, the temple motif is transitory and less permanent. Herein lies the major shift which occurs at this point in Scottish Rite instruction. All the historical events which were represented allegorically in the 1st through the 14th Degrees occurred exclusively during the idyllic four centuries of Solomon's Temple. Despite all the adversity we symbolically endured while advancing through these Degrees, we managed to do so because we had the reassuring presence of the Temple, along with all the mythical lessons associated with that grand edifice.

And then just when we had achieved our Masonic goal of discovering and pronouncing the Ineffable Name of Deity at the conclusion of the Lodge of Perfection, adversity struck again. Everything that we had gained seemed to evaporate. The Ineffable Word was again lost. There was no longer a *Sanctum Sanctorum*. This is the epitome of adversity, both temporal and spiritual.

The 17° alludes not only to the loss of the Temple but also explains the migration as an exodus out of the promised land that mirrored the intensity of Judaism's original exodus into the promised land. With the destruction of the Temple and the loss of the Ineffable Word, there is no longer any guaranteed sense of spiritual security or stability for either the devout believer or the sincere Mason. Not only is the Temple gone, but there no longer is either a royal figure like Solomon or a Messianic figure like Zerubbabel. As Knights of the East and West, we wander like the ancient survivors of that calamity, not knowing what the future will bring.

But still, we are not left without resources. Until such time as a physical temple is rebuilt to fulfill Danial's apocalyptic prophecies, we must find solace in the quiet sanctity that we strive to inculcate within our own being. The significance of the 17° is that its compelling lesson is essential to a complete understanding of how to live an authentic Masonic life.

We now must look inward, become more introspective and contemplative, and construct a spiritualized temple because we have no surrogate to rely on. All the other players have left the scene. The outward appearances no longer matter. Only the lessons we have learned in the preceding degrees can now come into play as we endeavor to create a brave new world that is very unpredictable, potentially unnerving, and hopefully thrilling.

The candidate represents a weary Prince of Jerusalem wandering along the shore of the Dead Sea, which symbolizes the stark and dry speculations of national philosophies that give no real hope for peace in the world. This journey requires reflection on the amount of time wasted in wrong or useless thoughts, words and actions. He comes to a community of the Essenes to request admittance and initiation. The series of trials he encounters demonstrate the purification and regeneration required for one to become a soldier of God, a knight prepared to give his life for his God, his friends, his country and mankind. After passing the trials and purification, he is received into the Order. John the Baptist, the most well-known member of the Essenes, delivers a prophecy and instruction from the Book of Revelations.

Among its many important lessons, this Degree teaches a principle recognized and deeply revered by all the great traditions of faith and philosophy. It is the principle of impermanence—observable in the fact that destruction, decay, and death are inescapable in this world.

In Masonry, rather than shy away from this truth, it faces it directly in its teachings, whether through the murder of a great and good man by envious ruffians; the sacking and ruin of a beautiful temple by conquering enemies; the execution of righteous people for speaking unvarnished truth to the proud and powerful; the disintegration of a soul into madness because of its vices; or the divine overthrow of a corrupt order to make way for a new dawn of enlightenment. Simply put, all things must pass, and we, as Masonic philosophers, are challenged to thoughtfully incorporate this truth into our spiritual and moral edifices.

Because Masonry teaches us to regard the internal before the external, we should ask ourselves how our mythic stories of death and destruction speak to our inner being. The answer is simple. Who and what you now think you are must fall in order to make way for the greater potential of who and what you are capable of becoming. In every human being, this profound change represents a psychological death. It is the release of the ego's attachment to a permanent self-concept, and the acceptance that we do not, and cannot, fully know ourselves. Every attempt to finally define who and what we are is really only an illusion.

Our personalities are never permanent, and we should strive not to think and act as if they are. Whether we realize it or not, our personality is always changing, always shifting and adjusting, always dying, and always being reborn into something new and different. The more rigidly we resist such change, the more difficult it is to blossom into our greatest potential. In our liberty of thought, we have the blessed opportunity to awaken to the breaking of the seals on the book of our own souls.

By studying the truths known and appreciated in the past, we give greater depth and scope to our own understanding. By learning of the errors of thought in the past, we help to avoid those errors ourselves. The more we study, the more we learn and appreciate that many of the differences in religion and philosophy are only surface interpretations, and that there are deep truths, known to be true by many different thinkers from many different backgrounds in many different time periods.

In the context of the historical setting of the Degree, we are reminded that, at some time, a resolution between the apparent forces of good and evil will take place. On an immediate and personal level, it teaches the importance of being on the side of the positive, rather than the negative. We should take every opportunity to make things better, for ourselves and others. By the same token, we should avoid at all costs the temptation to the negative. This isn't always easy, because the negative is very tempting.

It is not possible to make an exhaustive list of ways in which one can "join forces" with the negative—to fight on the side of the devils—but it is important that we recognize what this looks like. The following may give some idea.

We join the negative when we tell jokes which "put down" another person, sex, or race; when we pass rumors, or lie to those who trust us. We join the negative when we "get back" at others, trying to hurt them physically, emotionally, or financially; when we refuse to forgive others, or refuse to seek forgiveness; when we hate; seek revenge; ignore the suffering of others; sneer at another's religion; decide that, because we are right, we are justified in doing anything to make sure we win.

But there is an accounting! Whether one is a Christian, and a little uncomfortable about the day when He says to you, "Why did you do these things unto Me?" or a Jew, with an awareness that such things are outside the Covenant; or a follower of Islam, knowing that such things are forbidden to the Enlightened; or a Gnostic, knowing that such activity delays the Union with God; or a Deist, aware that the Overspirit requires positive rather than negative actions because they defile the spirit. Indeed, if you are a man of ethics at all, and your membership in Masonry proves that you are, then you must have an awareness that to hurt others is wrong, and to help them is right.

The quest path is never easy. Knowledge and insight are only won through suffering and pain. Neither has to be intense or overwhelming, but they must be real. It is never comfortable to move out of a rut, but it is essential to one's growth. Remember that growth implies change; and our own development must benefit not only ourselves but others in important ways. The purpose of the quest is never selfish; its benefits cannot be self-limiting.

The world moves in great, centuries-long patterns. We are participants in those patterns. The search for Light is a process, accomplished in small steps taken in humble determination.

Beware of ego. A self-centered man will never find Light. Truth prevails in people's words and deeds. There is a fundamental unity to all great systems of thought and philosophy which underlie any apparent differences. All human beings are related to each other in profound and primal ways.

It is the task of man to gather these scattered sparks of Light and to create, for himself, a true philosophy. This Truth, which will produce perfect harmony and insight when it is properly understood among nations, must be cherished, protected, and spread. The Knight of the East and West understands that peace, happiness, and welfare are possible through mutual respect, tolerance, and love. As a Knight, you now know that no matter whether you be from the East or the West, your journey is to spread the basic principles throughout mankind to enable people to live fraternally together by laying aside animosities and quarrels.

QUESTIONS TO CONTEMPLATE AS A KNIGHT OF THE EAST AND WEST

1. Are there many paths to God, or just one?
2. Does the acquisition of Truth require that you give up another Truth?
3. What does the desert represent in this Degree?
4. What are the major tenets as taught in Masonry of a "natural religion on which all good men can agree?"
5. What is knowledge designed to do for an individual? What price must we always pay for knowledge?
6. How do we go about giving up some long-held belief such as prejudice against another race or group that is different than we are? What would be our motivation?
7. Does increasing Masonic Light require that you give up a religious faith or a true philosophy?
8. Can a man change the world decisively for the better?

THE JOURNEY OF THE ELU TO ENLIGHTENMENT

CHAPTER OF ROSE CROIX

Eighteenth Degree
Plate 2nd

18°
KNIGHT ROSE CROIX

"The power of Knowledge is Transformative"

The 18°, Knight Rose Croix, completes the second quest in the Scottish Rite, the quest to strengthen, purify and direct the spark of the divine which we are progressively discovering in ourselves. It represents one of the most important Degrees in Freemasonry, and can be traced to the most ancient and highest initiation traditions in the West. It encourages earnest thought and introspection. It explores one of the great enigmas of the universe: the question of opposites, and the reconciliation of sin and wrong, pain and suffering, with the theory of the unbounded and unwavering beneficence of God. Pike suggests this reconciliation is the path to Light:

CHAPTER OF ROSE CROIX

"Light, as contradistinguished from darkness, is Good, as contradistinguished from Evil: and it is that Light, the true knowledge of Deity, the Eternal Good, for which Masons in all ages have sought."

The candidate is received in the dark chamber of a meeting room hung with black as a symbol of mourning for every great martyr who has given up his life in trying to better the world. The candidate agrees to help the brethren in the search to find the Lost Word, and thereby restore the working tools and broken column.

Perhaps the greatest and most perplexing question man must confront is the existence of evil in the world. How are we to understand the existence of evil in a world created by a God who is omnipotent and perfectly good? Since God is good and since everything which happens is within God's power, how can we account for the sin of Satan or the fall of man, with all the evils that occur as a result, without limiting God's power or absolving the erring creature from responsibility?

The problem is with our inadequate concepts of the nature of Deity. It is not that we need to prove that God exists, but rather that we need to find out what God is like. If we define God as that eternal order of things of which both the physical universe and man are but partial expressions, then we can focus on the nature of order in the universe. This has wisdom because it brings reason into the equation and enables science and religion to stand side by side. The nature of God is clearly revealed in the eyes of reason, which can then be balanced by any form of organized faith.

No man should be proud of ignorance. Given the total knowledge available in the world, ignorance is inevitable. But it should never be a source of self-satisfaction. And yet, a lot of men claim that "not knowing" is a virtue. This is especially true in the area of religion. Some act as if knowledge and faith were antagonistic; that the only way to bolster or secure one's faith is to remain as ignorant as possible of the faiths of others. This even applies to the history of one's belief. Indeed, much of the contemporary debate between Christianity and Islam is a contest fueled by ignorance.

For a Mason, this kind of attitude is problematic. One of the great lessons in Masonry is toleration of others, and especially of their beliefs.

There is simply no definition of what God is that is universally acceptable. There is only the conviction of the human heart; and we all know that the heart can be deceivingly expressive. Thus, we have many interpretations of the Grand Architect. There is God, the builder; God, the destroyer; God, the preserver. There is the One God; and the many Gods. There is the God of the Gentiles, the God of the Christian Trinity, and the God of Unity to Islam. Then there is the God of the Philosophers, the God of Mystics, the God of Reformers, the God of Enlightenment, and a whole host of Gods being proclaimed by contemporary spirituality gurus with all manners of thought.

All this should offer at least a hint that there is really only one enduring characteristic of God; and that is that God cannot be defined. God is a symbol, a mystery, a hieroglyph, a metaphor. Of God, there is understanding, reason, knowledge, touch, perception, imagination, name, and many other things. But God is not understood, nothing can be said of It. It cannot be named. It is not one of the things which is.

Regardless of one's faith system, or from what culture

one's understanding of God has evolved, reading the scriptures of faith alone is not the process for deriving the truth about God. God must be discovered or tapped into by ascending to God Itself. It has to be a kind of metaphysical reality, since there is nothing of this world which can be compared to It.

However, if we acknowledge that God is the source of all things, then we can suggest certain things about this Source. We can also believe that because goodness exists, God must be essential or necessary. We can say that because we know life, power, and knowledge exist, then God must be alive, powerful and intelligent in the most essential and complete way.

The outcome of all this is that we can gain an intuitive, imaginative knowledge of God which might well transcend reason; but, in the mortal scope of things, we can only know God by interpretation. This is why the instruction in Freemasonry urges us to see God as a symbol—because a symbol can mean what the symbol user interprets it to mean. The good result of this kind of teaching is that, since every one of us is confined to know only what we can see and feel about God's nature, this gives us the right to believe what we believe, and to hold firmly to that belief as the Truth. But it also admonishes us not to deny others the same right, even when we fundamentally disagree with their belief.

When issues of religion are raised to a level of national debate, it would be nice for once to have a dialogue which is focused, not on differences of faith, but on the great balance of faith, hope, charity, reason, and the natural order of the universe. The man who has hope and faith and benevolence in his heart, might well say, "Perhaps this evil and chaos is only apparent. Perhaps there is order in the world, even though I can't see it. I shall believe that, and act as if it were true."

In Masonry, light over darkness manifests itself in many dualistic forms—liberty over tyranny, peace over war, compassion over cruelty, and learning over ignorance. But there is always a "resolution of contraries," implying that some guiding principle, harmonizing power, divine attribute, or cosmic law is so ever-present, all-encompassing, and transcendent that all forces eventually bow to it and serve it in some way, even despite themselves. This is why we can find balance in our own life, even when the turmoil of the moment may seem to be overcoming us.

A Knight Rose Croix should know that the greatest law of all trinities, or balance, is the Law of Love. Love, in its grandest sense, has no opposite, no contrary. In its fullness, it is not merely the sentiment of affection that can be opposed by hate. It is not the feeling of attraction contrasted by fear or disgust. It is not a generosity offset by selfishness. It is not a sense of care and concern challenged by apathy. Love, in its mysterious wholeness, is a light that is present even within the darkest shadows. It is the alchemical secret to the resolution of contraries.

It is infinite and eternal, and therefore just as impossible for us to completely comprehend as the Godhead. Thus, it is no wonder that John the Evangelist declared that God is Love. Yet, as invisible as that divine ideal of Love is, we are always connected to it. It is like a ray of light that leads directly back to its Divine Source. This is why the great exemplar and messianic figure in this degree added his powerful and far-reaching voice to the timeless chorus, declaring the Law of Love as the Great Commandment served by all other teachings and laws.

It is the transformative force and principle of life in all-conscious beings. It is the force that has the power to overcome hatred, evil, violence, selfishness, negativity and confusion. And it is not limited to any particular religion. It is the gift of God to Man.

It requires that we put others' interest ahead of our own, and to do so willingly and not grudgingly. It takes a profound faith to treat others with love rather than suspicion. And it requires the most profound act of faith of all to love our enemies. Yet, there is no other profitable way to live, no other answer. For hatred and anger always poison the soul. God has written the answers to the great mysteries throughout nature, but we must be sensitive and in tune to read them.

In this quest, then, you have strengthened the spark until it is a flame of power. You have also learned to express that power, that spirituality, in terms of the Law of Love, which assures you that you will bring benefit rather than harm to people.

As a Knight of the Rose and Cross, ever strive to be mindful that your faith and hope in service to Love, and thus the fruits of your care and affection, your compassion and generosity, as limited as these may be, are always in conformity with the highest of all laws.

Question to Contemplate as a Knight Rose Croix

1. What, if anything, do you do to increase the general good rather than that of only yourself and family?
2. What responsibilities do you feel toward other people in our society?
3. What is the essential nature of transformation? How does it apply to the basic purposes of Masonry?
4. What do the Rose and Cross symbolize to you?
5. What is the True Word in Masonry? What does it mean?
6. It is said that the great majority of mankind makes little or no use of its divine gifts. What are some divine gifts that all human possess?
7. What is the "silent inner word of the spirit? How can you access it?

XI

COUNCIL OF KADOSH

With the 19°, we enter the philosophical journey of the Rite, comprising the Nineteenth through the Thirtieth Degrees. The word "Kadosh" is Hebrew and means "consecrated or dedicated." Its members are dedicated to the discovery of philosophical truths and chivalric virtues. The Degrees present various concepts of Deity and man's search to discover the meaning of God. The lessons are provided as instruction, not doctrine. They examine various philosophical, religious, and knighthood traditions.

We leave the mystical field of pure knowledge and love, to engage in the world of action. We are again reminded that we are on a journey to become transformed in the consciousness of God. And that transformation, being a metaphorical process, involves a journey where powerful forces are encountered. In the Council of Kadosh, the quest is to express our strengthened spirituality in the matters and affairs of the world. In the classic representation of the hero's journey, the great mythologist Joseph Campbell explains:

> "A hero ventures forth from the world of common day into a region of supernatural wonder; fabulous forces are there encountered and a decisive victory is won; the hero comes back from this mysterious adventure with the power to bestow boons on his fellow man."
>
> *–Hero of a Thousand Faces*

THE JOURNEY OF THE ELU TO ENLIGHTENMENT

We are entering a new phase of our journey. Masonry is philosophy teaching by symbols; as history is philosophy teaching by examples. It is a sad comment on the human condition that philosophy is no longer seen as a worthy partner with scientific development and economic progress. It is often characterized as useless, or at best ornamental in the practical affairs of society. Yet, this is a very recent attitude that has arisen only in the last half century. All visions of the ideal state, of virtues in human thought and the accomplishments of science, are steeped in philosophy. After all, the crown of knowledge is wisdom; and wisdom is attained only as one rises in the hierarchy of knowledge; either to the highest science, or the ultimate attainment of philosophical inquiry. Nearly every noted philosopher has agreed with Hobbes, who presented his classification of the types of knowledge under the heading "science, that is, Knowledge of Consequences, which is also called Philosophy." It is no insignificant thing that the authors of the books which are today regarded as among the foundations of modern science—Galileo, Newton, Huygens, Lavoisier, and Faraday—refer to themselves as philosophers; and to the science in which they were engaged as aspects of natural philosophy.

Philosophy is as much the love of the attainment of wisdom, as it is the love of wisdom itself. And, from a Masonic perspective, this is an important distinction. A man would not be called a scientist in a particular field like, say, mathematics, unless he actually had some mathematical knowledge; but a man who is not actually wise can be called a philosopher by virtue of his effort to become wise. In Masonry, we are to practice out in the world the wisdom we have acquired in the study of our art; which is wholly philosophical. And the practice of it is as important as its content.

How do speculations concerning the nature of things affect the theory of human life and society? Or the practical principles by which man tries to lead a good life and organize a good society? What relation do the truths of physics and metaphysics bear to the truths and issues in psychology, ethics and politics? Upon the answers to these questions depends the varying esteem in which philosophy has been held in the great periods of western culture. Unlike supernatural religion and empirical science, it does not promise eternal salvation or earthly prosperity. Its uses must somehow be assessed in terms of the love of wisdom, and the search for wisdom, which is, at once, speculative and practical Masonry.

THE JOURNEY OF THE ELU TO ENLIGHTENMENT

NINETEENTH DEGREE.

Reverse of Jewel ----- †

250

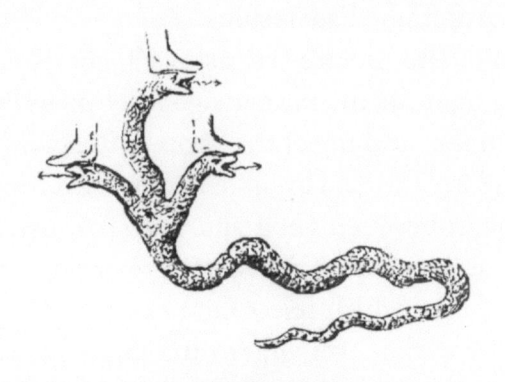

19°
Grand Pontiff

"It is our business to plant the seed"

The 19°, Grand Pontiff, gives us a hint of its lesson in its name. The expression "Sovereign Pontiff" was created in the distant past in honor of Horatius Cocles who saved Rome. "Summus Pontifex" was the title bestowed on Julius Caesar and thereafter to the Roman Emperors until the 3rd Century when the head of the Catholic Church, the Pope, took it for himself. "Pontifex Maximus," or Grand Pontiff, literally means "Great Bridge Builder." Since it is not possible for any man to know at what point in time truth, honesty, honor and loving kindness will forever eradicate error, falsehood and intolerance, the duty of the Grand Pontiff is to hope with confidence in the final victory of good over evil, and act as a bridge builder for future generations by laboring in the present for the improvement of human society without any false expectations of immediate results.

The candidate is received as a Knight Rose Croix, prepared to fight for the ultimate good of mankind. He is instructed in the meaning of the Sages of Religion. He then hears a prophecy foretold by all religions when a final battle shall be fought between good and evil. The instruction is interrupted as an evil spirit appears and tempts the candidate with philosophies which reject God as either powerless or uncaring. The spirit is overcome by the appearance of a good spirit, the spirit of Masonry, which urges the candidate and others in the room to reject such philosophy, and work for enlightenment in the hope and belief that the will of God will bless such efforts by establishing the "New Jerusalem", that is, by restoring mankind to its original divine nature after the final defeat over evil.

The principle teaching of this degree is that we are to labor diligently for the future not only to make the future better for mankind, but also in making man's existence a bridge to eternal life. However, the fight for the ultimate good of mankind requires the eradication of evil. Since this must wait for God's appointed time, we learn that our best weapons are faith, hope and charity; and we fight for truth, light, love, tolerance, the rule of law and peace. Our quest is to destroy evil that exists in the form of error, falsehood and intolerance. The victory for good takes the form of truth, honesty, honor and charity.

The esoteric meaning of the Degree reveals that the

twelve tribes of Israel and the twelve Apostles symbolize all those who have labored to reform, instruct and elevate mankind. Thus, to a large extent, the past controls the present and the present controls the future.

In a very real sense, today is governed by yesterday. We know that the influences of the childhood years have a profound effect on the adult life of a man or woman. It has become popular to mildly sneer at the idea of "truths learned at the mother's knee," but such truths (or errors) are learned and have a lasting effect.

Suppose one child grows up in a home in which the mother and father are always fighting and arguing, and violence is a frequent event. Suppose that another child grows up in a home in which the mother and father respect each other as individuals, and resolve conflicts quietly and in a spirit of love and friendship. Will anyone be surprised if the first child, as an adult, believes that contention is the way to resolve a conflict, and that violence is an acceptable tool; or that the second child, as an adult, believes that people can almost always resolve conflict peacefully, if each is only willing to listen and work with the other?

In the life of every culture, nation or civilization, today is the result of yesterday. The young often wish to rebel against the past, without being aware that the very rebellion is made possible by the past.

Our actions, for good or bad, will reverberate down through the centuries, in ways we can't imagine. There is no such thing as an unimportant moment. Let us take a semi-hypothetical example.

A young man, at the turn of the 19th century, is deciding whether to go in business or farming. He tries business for a while, decides against it because a recession nearly wipes him out and so goes into farming. He has been engaged to a young woman, who decides to marry someone else. He finally marries another young woman who, as it happens, has been brought up in a family which values education, although she herself has gone only as far as the fifth grade. They have a son. The son, growing up on the farm, becomes interested in living things and the ways in which they grow. The father tolerates this interest as long as it does not get in the way of the farm chores, but the mother encourages it. Together they find and read books on biology and botany. The son develops a stronger interest, and decides that, as an adult, he wants to teach biology.

He becomes a teacher and, because he loves the subject, he is a good teacher. One of his students is a bright young man, with no interest at all in biology, taking the class because it was a required subject. But he becomes infected with the enthusiasm and excitement of his teacher and decides to make biology his profession.

Some years later, he develops a vaccine which protects all mankind against a great killing and crippling disease, saving untold thousands agonizing pain and death.

All because one man made an "inconsequential" decision to take up farming.

Each of us has, as we said, a profound effect on posterity, and we cannot know in advance which actions will have those effects. It behooves us, then, never to think of ourselves or our actions as unimportant. The great good or evil we do will manifest fully long after we are gone. The best we can and must do, is to act at all times in the best way we know, and never assume that something we do "won't matter."

The present is the result of the past. Good and wise

men in the past, powerful because they were in touch with their spirituality, have done things which have shaped the world. That is our task as well. Our quest should be to strive to leave a legacy of positive actions, deeds and influences behind us.

> "To sow, that others may reap; to work and plant for those who are to occupy the earth when we are dead; to project our influences far into the future, and live beyond our time; to rule as the Kings of Thought, over men who are yet unborn; to bless with the glorious gifts of truth and light and liberty those who will neither know the name of the giver, nor care in what grave his unregarded ashes repose, is the true office of a Mason and the proudest destiny of man."

Questions to Contemplate as a Grand Pontiff

1. How do you become a different person?
2. What is the battle in which we are personally engaged? Why is a battle necessary?
3. What are some potential consequences of not learning of the past, or paying attention to the "great flow of time?"
4. Can you remember moments in your life when something said or casually done by another person made a strong positive or negative influence on you?
5. What can you do to improve the lives of those yet to come?
6. Why is a man seldom able to reap what he sows during his lifetime?
7. What must we learn from the past?

THE JOURNEY OF THE ELU TO ENLIGHTENMENT

TWENTIETH DEGREE.

20°
GRAND MASTER OF ALL SYMBOLIC LODGES

"Do that which thou ought to do; let the result be what it will"

The 20°, Master of the Symbolic Lodge, illustrates the quintessential task of every Mason—to prepare himself, by thought, study and reflection, to be a leader of his Brethren. The Degree goes back to the themes presented in the 15° and the 16°, namely the reconstruction of the Temple. However, this Degree also refers to a legend alluded to in the Seventeenth Degree, that of erecting a personal inner temple that can never be destroyed. The Venerable Grand Master represents King Cyrus and the candidate represents Zerubbabel. The whole Degree aims at making the future "Grand Master of the Symbolic Lodge."

The symbolism and structure of a Masonic Lodge is so well known that it is often easy to dismiss its allegorical importance. This is particularly true with those of us who regularly sit in its tyled recesses month after month and contemplate its beautiful ritual language and ceremonial forms. We wholly take for granted that its design and workings are not a matter of mere coincidence. The charge of Masonry is to instruct and guide its members along the path of life. The lodge represents the world, and, on a larger scale, the universe. But it also symbolizes the life of the individual Mason. All that exists in life is contained in the mystic teachings of our royal art. This is one reason Freemasonry is as relevant today, as in any past century.

The arrangement of the officers and the layout of the lodge furniture and jewels are such that, if we learn the symbols and allegories represented by this structure, we can acquire a real understanding of ourselves, our nature, the mystery of life, the purpose of initiation, and a love of God and his plan for our lives.

Inasmuch as the lodge symbolically represents the life of the individual brother; then the Worshipful Master of the lodge represents mankind in its ideal. He, too, represents each individual brother, just as the universe is reflected in each person. The first lesson we learn as Entered Apprentices is that each person is a model of the universe. This means that each of us indeed has control over our own destiny. Life is not a throw of the dice. We are not intended to be victims, but masters, over ourselves. But we must pay attention. One of the great purposes of Masonry is to teach us how we go about controlling our life in a way that can affect the noblest of ends.

The idea of attaining mastery over ourselves is not only to aid us in perfecting our own journey; but that we can also lead and teach our fellow men by our own example. To do so requires a lot of work; but the principle work in which we are engaged is to become virtuous men.

The question is: Why do we care? Why, after all, should we live a moral and ethical life when we all live in such a "dog eat dog" kind of world where everyone seems to be looking out only for themselves? To do the right thing often seems to place us at a disadvantage. Why should we strive for virtue and morality?

Admittedly, these are not easy questions to answer. To make it worse, there really are no half-way compromise answers. It doesn't work to strive to be "sort of moral" or "more or less honest." Living a moral life is rather like shooting at a target which is some distance away. We have to aim higher because gravity (or our own animal nature) is always pulling us down. Thus, the man who tries to be only somewhat honest will find that he constantly falls short of that goal; just as the man who strives to be completely honest falls short of his goal. So one is primarily dishonest, and the second can hope, at best, to be honest most of the time.

But again, why should we strive for virtue and morality? The reason is that society will not work if no one strives for some sort of virtue. We must often remind ourselves that the media through which we receive much of our information will tend always to bring us the worst examples of the human condition. But our own life experience informs us that, in fact, most people are honest and will do what they say they will do. Pure legality just isn't enough. If every sale or contract had to be enforced through the courts, if every income tax return had to be audited, if people restrained their impulses to violence only in the presence of policemen, the hospitals would be filled in half a morning (and who would restrain the violence of the policeman). So, if we wish to live other than as hermits, a certain level of morality is necessary.

But more than that, our actions shape and determine our "selves" just as surely as those selves determine our actions. A student may think of himself as an honest person, until he decides to cheat on an exam for which he is not prepared. It may not be a very important test; he may not even need the course to graduate. But if he cheats on that test, he will find it a lot easier to cheat on the next.

Dishonesty is like an addictive drug—there is no such thing as an amount so small that it's safe to play with. We shape ourselves by how we think, believe and act. Virtue strengthens us as men, helping us develop into the kind of individual we want to be; while a lack of virtue sets us ever further back from true self-realization and fulfillment. The truth is that the honest man is happier, has fewer fears, and lives a better life than the man who must always look over his shoulder, fleeing even when no man pursues him.

Virtue and morality are also an expression of gratitude. God has given us much, and asked little in return. And what He asks, He asks for our benefit, not for His. We live in gratitude to God to try to live as best we can. It is what the highest nature within us compels us to do. Whenever we intuitively come in touch with our higher self, we are feeling a spark of virtue within us whispering divine counsel. It is nothing less than God's instruction to us. And since it is God's way of pointing us in the right direction, to live on the square of virtue and morality is the least we can do.

These are the reasons that it is important to live a moral and virtuous life, and that is the reason that the Scottish Rite teaches the importance of virtue and morality.

The plan and layout of the lodge informs us in all we

need to know to become better men; to live in the presence of God's will for us. Knowing that our lodge is a symbol of the construction of our own temple to God, we need only to work out the path which leads us to build as well as we can. We are each the architect, the building material, and the builder of our temple to God.

Our principle work is to strive to bring into balance the opposite lines of force which are constantly at play within ourselves. Each degree we attain, each office we hold, each ritual element we learn symbolizes some virtue to be attained, some divine quality to be manifested, some labor to be worked out, some ruffian or pitfall to be overcome, some teaching that advances our state of mind and being, some awakening of consciousness to an assimilation of our higher, spiritual nature.

We must work with patience and persistence to achieve what is possible in perfecting ourselves as men so that we can make a positive difference in our own life, and the lives of others. Never forget that the structure of Masonry is such that we have to do the work ourselves, with the help of our brothers. As we study, contemplate, and apply the lessons of each degree to the plan of our own life, the secrets of life itself are revealed to us. That is the key. We are each the solution and the enigma of our own self- improvement. The 20° is styled the Master of the Symbolic Lodge. It informs us that holding a Masonic office is of extreme importance and is not to be taken lightly. It is not about the titles and the jewels. The Master of the Lodge should be chosen with the greatest of care because his personality and knowledge of Masonry greatly effects the progress of the lodge. In many lodges, the energy and knowledge of the Master is reflected in the lodge itself. An energetic, knowledgeable, passionate Master will be reflected by the energy, instruction, and passion of the lodge. When a Master chooses to do nothing but while away his time in the chair, the lodge often relaxes with him. But when the Master strives toward the ideals of Masonry, his brethren benefit greatly by his interest and wisdom.

No other way is better in reaching the goal of this degree than meditating on and practicing the 20 Masonic virtues so eloquently illustrated in its ritual instruction—including the virtues of Prudence, Temperance, Chastity, Sobriety, Heroism, Firmness, Equanimity, Patience, Purity, Honor, Fidelity, Punctuality, Charity, Kindness, Generosity, Liberality, Disinterestedness, Mercy, Forgiveness and Forbearance.

In addition, the nine great lights or virtues represented by the geometric points of the tracing board are Gratitude to God, Love of Mankind, Confidence in Human Nature, Veneration for the Deity, Devotedness to Family and Friends, Patriotism, Truth, Justice and Toleration.

The whole ceremony of the Degree aims at making the future Master of a Symbolic Lodge deeply conscious of his duties and the qualities required to discharge them. His task is to prepare men to govern themselves so that they will be law abiding citizens worthy of a free society.

Yet there is one other hidden lesson conveyed in the Degree which is perhaps the most important: We are all Masters of the Symbolic Lodge! As Master Masons, we are charged to:

> Love Your Neighbor as Yourself
> Forgive your enemy and be reconciled with him
> Do not do to others what you would not like them to do to you

Be good, kind, humane and charitable, and console the afflicted
Be faithful to your country
Be tolerant of all political and religious opinions, and do not seek to make converts
Fraternize with all men
Think well, speak well and act well
Do that which you ought to do and let the result be what it will
Take the wise and good as models, and place the sage above the soldier, the noble, and the prince.

The bottom line is when we can attain mastery over our own conduct, we will be better prepared to lead, and others can learn by our good example. Indeed, inspiring others to shape their conduct by our good example is the surest way we can hope to expect to live respected and die regretted. That is our duty and aim as Masters of our life, which is our true symbolic lodge. Individually, our quest is to become master of our own temple of consciousness.

QUESTIONS TO CONTEMPLATE AS A MASTER OF THE SYMBOLIC LODGE

1. How can you prepare yourself to be one of the few who accomplishes real purpose in life?
2. What are some of the costs of real progress to humanity?
3. Why are not all men fitted for such labor?
4. What does this say about whom we choose to be a Master of a Symbolic Lodge?
5. What is the fundamental obligation of a Lodge Master?
6. What is the balance between strength and loving kindness?
7. What is the relationship between the square and the triangle in Masonry?
8. What does the octagon shown on the trestle board of this Degree represent?

COUNCIL OF KADOSH

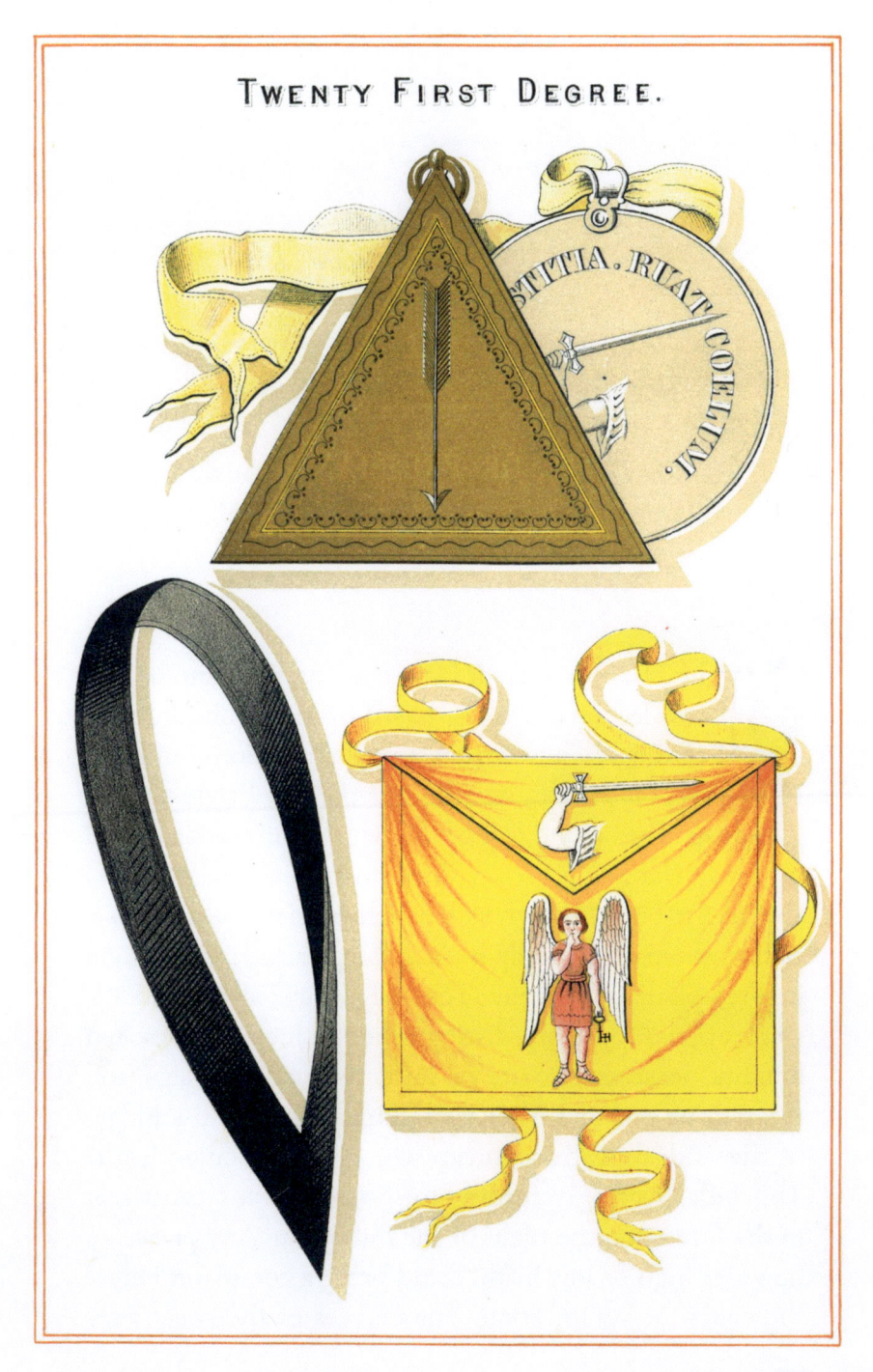

TWENTY FIRST DEGREE.

21°
NOACHITE, OR PRUSSIAN KNIGHT

"It is the basest office man can fall into, to make his tongue the defamer of the worthy man"

The 21°, Noachite, or Prussian Knight, is founded on two legends; the first based on the Biblical Tower of Babel (a word meaning confusion) built by Phaleg, as grand architect, who was the Noah's great, great grandson. The second legend, on which our modern ritual is based, relates to a 12th century closed secret all powerful German tribunal known as the Vehmgericht, which was a court system of the Holy Roman Empire, having its origin in Westphalia, Germany. The judges, called Freishoffen, were originally highly distinguished princes, nobles and knights possessing a rite of initiation, a secret sign and recognition greeting. They were similar to the Frank Judges of the 12th to 15th centuries which are presented in the Thirtieth Degree. According to the legend, the court met in the forests on the night of the full moon. Any prince, of however high or low birth, could bring a complaint before the court for adjudication. The decrees of the court were final and absolute, and the court had the power to enforce its own sentences. The candidate represents Adolph the Saxon, a Knight of the Holy Cross who has just returned from a crusade to find that his lands have been taken and divided between the church and Count Reinfred, a high placed member of the Vehmgericht. After a trial by ordeal goes against Reinfred, Adolph is offered and accepts the seat on the tribunal which had been held by Reinfred.

The instruction of this Degree focuses on the virtues of modesty and humility. A self-examination and awareness of one's own weaknesses are the best tools to eradicate vanity, conceit and pride from our consciousness. The humble search for divine wisdom, rather than the destructive arrogance of trivial pursuits, should be the ultimate goal of human beings.

We must also refrain from judging what we cannot fully understand. Ignorance leads to arrogance, unfair judgments, and criticizing others. One of the greatest failings of men is when they think their own intelligence is wiser than God's wisdom and providence. We must never forget that, however certain we are that we are right, we may be wrong.

Much of the sorrow and pain in the world has been caused by persons convinced that they alone knew the truth. Advances in medicine and physics have been delayed because the director of a laboratory "knew" that the approach suggested by some young subordinate had to be wrong. Men have been tortured because those in religious authority "knew" that other opinions and beliefs were false. Mobs have risen up and murdered innocent men and women whom they "knew" to be guilty of some crime.

Brother Benjamin Franklin, in moving that the

Constitutional Convention adopt the draft of the Constitution, urged those who still had disagreement to "doubt a little of their own infallibility on this occasion" and join him in voting for adoption.

It's good advice for all Masons on all occasions.

The problem is not so much in being sure that we are right; the problem comes when we extend our concept of rightness to the point of saying; "I am right. Therefore, you are wrong." That is a statement which Masons should make only with the greatest care and precaution. It is, perhaps, most easy for us to be wrong when certain that we are right. The thinking Mason must always entertain the idea that he may be wrong, no matter how strongly his belief and the evidence of the moment may suggest he is right. We should never become so wedded to our view of reality that we ignore or discount information which contradicts that view. This Degree admonishes us to guard against the arrogance of our own perceptions—the certainty that we know the truth and others who disagree must be wrong.

It is a grave error to insist that only that which we can see, touch, taste, or otherwise experience through the senses exists. Science has taught us that reality is only a perception. We cannot see or measure reality. Thus, it is essential that we stay focused on the spiritual rather than the external or material perceptions of things. There is a power and force in Truth, and it is the central quest in this Degree.

The second great lesson is equity in dealing with others. We may remark that we do not look down on those who are "lower" than we, nor fawn upon those "higher." Indeed, we may insist that, in a democracy, there are none lower or higher. And yet we are tempted to treat the receptionist briskly and the president of the corporation with great respect. We may speak of someone as being "only a secretary," or "only a janitor." When we do that, we are not treating all people alike, assuming that all are equal worth in the eyes of God.

The same inequity can exist in the respect we show others based purely on what they have chosen to do in their life. We give high regard to the medical doctor who can cure the common cold, yet place little value on the teacher who will determine if our child will succeed in life. This degree teaches above all else that we must respect all men and women for themselves, not for the positions they hold, the good we hope they may do us, or the harm we fear they might cause us.

The just and honest man is just and honest to all, regardless of the status and power or humility of the person with whom he is dealing. It is just as wrong to be arrogant toward those you perceive as "lower" than you as it is to be envious to those you see as having power and position.

The Tower of Babel serves as an important allegorical reference of this point. The story also instructs us that we should be humble and modest men, rather than act conceited or belittling to others. This lesson applies not only to our approach toward the Grand Architect of the Universe, but also to our relationships with our fellow man and even to our own inward attempts at improving ourselves.

Freemasonry bestows many titles upon men. However, we cannot use the titles we may receive in this organization or any other as a shield for arrogance, conceit, or impartiality. Nor should we rely on these titles, or nobility or wealth, as a basis for our conduct in our relationships with God and our fellow man.

As Masons, we are engaged in a work to make ourselves better men.

THE JOURNEY OF THE ELU TO ENLIGHTENMENT

Indeed, there is great virtue in humility and modesty. We exude the virtues of charity and generosity when we hold our tongue rather than speaking of the faults of others. We exude the virtues of fair-mindedness and respect when we recognize that we are no better than our peers, regardless of rank, nobility, or wealth. That is the mandate of the Prussian Knight, to represent before yourself, your God and your fellows, a degree of humility and modesty.

Honesty is honesty. Justice is Justice. Be true to yourself—and everyone else.

There is also a significant esoteric consideration woven within the fabric of this Degree. Phaleg is an important figure in the Noachidic tradition of Freemasonry, and the Noachite or Prussian Knight of the 21° of the Scottish Rite. He is also the Standard Bearer or head of the tent of the Elus of the Nine, Twelve and Fifteen in the Masonic Camp in the 32° ritual. Yet, no story is created about him in our liturgy. So, what makes him important to the Scottish Rite?

The 21° is based on two legends. As mentioned above, the legend we follow is based on a secret German tribunal of the Middle Ages. The Degree appears about 1758 at a time when high Scottish Rite degrees were mushrooming within the Council of Emperors of the East and West in France. It abandoned the legend of Hiram in favor of Noah's tradition, the origin of which is older than Solomon's tradition by several centuries. The original exemplification was about the esoteric Bible legend of the Tower of Babel, built by Phaleg, its grand architect. Phaleg, a descendent of Noah; who, by that time, had forgotten all about God's covenant with Noah that he would not again destroy the earth. The tower was built with the idea of reaching heaven to make Man equal to God. In order to punish such self-conceited effrontery, God confounded mankind's languages and dispersed them all over the world; the first human diaspora.

Phaleg withdrew to what became Prussia in Northern Germany, and repented his Promethean ambition. It was reported in 553, while excavating salt mines there, a triangular temple was discovered. On the base of a white marble column inside the building, the entire story of the Tower of Babel was written in Syriac language. A tomb was found close by, with a stone of agate (the symbol of purity) indicating that this was Phaleg's grave and that he implored God to have pity on him since he had regained his humility and had thus purified himself. This is the reason that Germans traditionally consider themselves as the descendants of Noah's grandson.

The ancient order of Noachites became the Order of Prussian Knights, as Prussians came to see themselves as descendants of Phaleg. The Grand Master of Prussian Knights was Frederick of Brunswick, or Frederick II, King of Prussia. As we know, the 1786 Constitutions make him the Founder of the Scottish Rite. His ancestors protected the Prussian Knights for three centuries. According to the Francken Manuscript, their annual festival of the Knights was held on the full moon in March. As these knights became members of the Vehmgericht, the tribunal came to adopt that night for its secret trials. This is what inspired Pike when he developed our modern degree. He wanted to return to medieval Christian knighthood. During the Crusades, all European knights were initiated into the Catholic tradition, and the Prussian knights, who were highly respected by all, accepted that the Knight Masons of the Hiram tradition might be initiated within their order. Now, what does this mean? Phaleg is the password of the 21° Degree and Shem, Ham and Japheth are the sacred words. So, we are dealing with the older legend here. As you may recall, elements of the Noah tradition appear in several other degrees of the Rite.

Phaleg's tent in the 32° corresponds to the letter X in the motto of the degree "SALIX NONIS TENUS", which expresses the Royal Secret. It is an anagram for *Let the Light which is within us guide us*. The letter 'X' in Masonry always stands for change. This gives us an insight as to the esoteric meaning of Phaleg. As Phaleg is also the head of the 9th and the 12th degree, we can note that this change is the change from the ignorance represented by the ruffians to the wisdom of the seers; and the change represented by the arrogance of Count Rienford and the modesty of Adolph the Saxon; or the change represented by arrogance toward God, as represented by the Tower of Babel, arrogance toward our fellows, as represented by the Vehmgericht; as compared with the refraining from judging those things we cannot fully understand.

Questions to Contemplate as a Prussian Knight

1. Does any human being have the right to condemn another to die? Upon what basis is such judgment justified?
2. Is it possible for individuals in today's society to be protected from lies, slander, gossip, partisanship, etc.?
3. What are the requirements of individual protection and civil liberty?
4. What does a free, independent and impartial judiciary teach us about human freedom?
5. Why is the judiciary one of the three principles in the trinity of democracy?
6. What is essential for justice to be rendered impartially?
7. What are some examples of unfair judgments we encounter every day? How do they affect our lives?
8. What are some ways we can refrain from judging others?
9. Do you think of yourself as a man of integrity? Would you lie to save a friend? Should you? Would you lie to save yourself? Does it make any difference whether we violate our own ethics to benefit another? It if does, would the most ethical position be to violate our ethics for someone we have never met?

THE JOURNEY OF THE ELU TO ENLIGHTENMENT

TWENTY SECOND DEGREE.

22°
KNIGHT ROYAL AXE, OR PRINCE OF LIBANUS

"There is no nobility in idleness"

The 22°, Knight Royal Axe or Prince of Libanus, is a degree whose legend is centered on the Cedars of Lebanon. It is said that when Adam was expelled from Eden, he took a sapling of the Tree of Life and planted it in Lebanon. The wood from these cedars was used in the construction of Noah's Ark; the coffin holding the murdered body of Osiris; the Ark of the Covenant; Solomon's Temple; Zerubbabel's Second Temple; the cross on which Jesus is said to have died. Cedars are still to be found in the structures of Christian basilicas, Moslem mosques and Jewish synagogues.

Upon the same mountain from which the cedars of Lebanon were cut to be used in the building of the temple, the King of Tyre established a corporation of craftsmen to handle these noble trees. Within this body, mathematics and astronomy were studied, as well as architecture, masonry, and the crafts of metal work and stone carving. These craftsmen were recruited from the Druzes, and were part of the Mystery tradition. The Druzes were a secretive mystical community of Islam tribesmen descending from Abraham through Ishmael, which had settled from time immemorial in the mountains of Lebanon. They were grouped into colleges of artificers, the leaders of which were recruited through initiation. The reason we call Tubalcain an artificer is that he, too, was a member of the Mysteries. A large portion of the period of initiation was spent in hard physical labor in the practical aspects of craft work. Their Mysteries were said to have been transmitted to the Crusades who took them to Scotland where the Order of the Royal Axe is believed to have been established.

The candidate represents a Prussian Knight who has come to the college in order to further his study of Masonry.

The forests of Lebanon have two meanings. First, they represent the primeval forests of the world. Primeval means ancient, primitive, unhewn, uncivilized. It refers to the condition of the world before knowledge. When the Degree was written, the forest was a symbol of barbarism, that is, an ignorant society which is ruled and consumed by animal passion—selfish, unloving, uncaring. We are told that the axe cuts or fells the trees of Lebanon. This axe is mightier than the sword because it represents the forward progress of civilization. It cuts away the prejudices of ignorance, the absurdities of superstition. The trees which are felled are intolerance, bigotry, superstition, uncharitableness, idleness—anything that impairs improvement and the progress of civilization.

The key association we can make with the axe is that an axe splits things. Thus, like the square and compasses, it is an emblem of duality—the opposition of good and evil in the world. The poisonous trees in the dark, primitive forest of intolerance, ignorance, and such, represent the evil which must be cut down so that divine light, the sunshine of truth, reason and love might be let into the human heart and mind.

The other association has to do with the work of the axe itself. When a forest is felled, what do we see? Light—In Masonry the hewing of the trees of Lebanon lets in the light of truth and reason upon the individual's mind so that he can no longer be duped by the darkness of vice.

It is also interesting for us to catch the fact that the ceremony of the Degree opens as the cedars wait to be felled, and it closes when they have been felled. The second meaning of the forest relates to its clearing, and the deep significance the tree has in history. The Tree of Life, the Tree of the Kabbalah, the Cross—all evoke regenerative processes, growth, proliferation, immortality—especially evergreens like cedar. Thus, we have this dichotomy of darkness and light associated with the forest and it's clearing and regeneration. They allude to the central quest of the candidate in this Degree: his noble search for his original divine essence at the innermost core of his individuality. He learns that such a goal is only possible through hard spiritual work.

And therein is the challenge. It is common enough for us to complain about having to work. We complain when the alarm rings in the morning; we look forward to the weekend; and we dread the approach of Monday morning and the beginning of the work week. We dream of having enough money that we never have to work again.

But, for most of us, that is social ritual and playing.

THE JOURNEY OF THE ELU TO ENLIGHTENMENT

Take away our ability to work and most men become very unhappy indeed. It is often seen in a forced retirement—if the man has nothing of interest to do, nothing with which to fill the time, death often comes quickly. Only the truly perverse man enjoys the feeling of being useless. We may enjoy the temporary cessation of work, but we also enjoy starting it again. We have a deep, inner need to be doing something useful.

This need to build, to be constructive, to create, to employ our time in something worthwhile, is one of the strongest indicators of our relationship with God. For the essence of God is creation. It is in the results of His great creative act that we see and become aware of Him.

Whether that act was a series of individual acts of creation, or whether it was one great act that established the natural laws which resulted in the "big bang" and a series of evolutions, predicated by and necessitated by whose natural laws, is not a question or concern of Masonry. But as Masons, we do believe that, however it may have been done, God was the architect and author of the Universe. His was the idea, and the act was creation. It is perhaps His greatest gift to us that we are allowed to participate, in however limited a degree, in His creative nature. We, too, can build. We can conceive an idea and bring it to being.

Work also fulfills another important role for a Mason. As Masons, we are forbidden to be parasites upon society or the world. The great rule may be stated thus:

"Let no one be poorer because you are richer; Let no one go hungry because you eat."

If we earn our wealth, if we earn our food, then we have created value at least equal to that which we have taken. Thus no one suffers because of us, and such comfort and ease as we may enjoy are untainted by the knowledge that they have are acquired at the price of the well-being of others.

We may create that value by physical or intellectual labor; we may create it by the product we make or the service we perform; we may create it by the lending of our resources or the utility of our advice. But so long as we have created something of value, we need not feel that we have injured another.

There is also an important civic or public duty taught by this Degree. We are to strive to make the life of the working man better. This is not the rather condescending duty it may at first sound. It does not mean that we, from our position of greater insight and luxury should tell the working man how to live. After all, the vast majority of us are working men. But it means that we have a responsibility to make sure that certain benefits are available to man regardless of is ability to pay for them. Education is a good example. The Mason supports the public schools—if for no other reason—because they make education available free of individual charge to the children of those who live in poverty. And it has been proven time and again that education is almost the only way out of poverty.

We must look for ways to make the lives of even those who work for the lowest wages better—not through programs of governmental "give-away" but through programs and practices which benefit him while still preserving his God-given dignity.

Above all, we are required to work upon ourselves. Never forget that your life is an unfinished building, on which you must constantly labor so that it may be better and more beautiful. The task of building the Temple, in all its symbolic meanings, is work. Our quest is to build a beautiful and meaningful life.

Finally, in the lecture of this Degree, we are blessed to receive one of the most poignant phrases that Pike ever wrote. As I reiterate it here, think about the thousands of years of effort of the Princes of Libanus, employed from morn to dusk with the working tools of the craftsman; the saw to clear and prepare, the axe to split and refine, the plane to smooth the inequalities of the wood; the thousands of men who toiled in the Cedars of Lebanon—cutting away the darkness of ignorance with skill and learning, designing by geometry the right proportions and forms to be used in building; hewing the great planks of wood generation after generation which ultimately framed and adorned the great edifices which would be erected to God's name. Imagine such a college of architects and craftsmen—carrying the spirit of Noah with them, building and refining the structures of civilization in every age and every era. Doing the good work, the true work, the square work with the medium of wood.

Then, with this mental image we have formed together, contemplate what Pike has taught us in this Degree:

> "It is in the hands of brave, forgotten men that have made this great, populous, cultivated world a world for us. It is all work, and forgotten work. The real conquerors, creators, and eternal proprietors of every great and civilized land are all the heroic souls that ever were in it, each in his own degree: all the men that ever felled a forest tree or drained a marsh, or contrived a wise scheme, or did or said a true or valiant thing therein. Genuine work alone, done faithfully, is eternal... Whatever of morality and intelligence,

of method, insight, ingenuity, energy; in a word, whatsoever of strength a man has in him, will lie in the work he does."

Questions to Contemplate as a Prince of Libanus

1. What are the things you would like to accomplish during your lifetime?
2. How can you be involved in such accomplishments?
3. What are some of the virtues which you feel are directly tied to work?
4. What must we watch out for in a life of ease and luxury?
5. What has history shown mankind in regard to the accumulation of wealth?
6. What are some vices you feel represent the wrong use of work?
7. What duty do men, and particularly Masons, have toward the welfare of others?
8. What constitutes fulfillment in life?
9. What do you plan to do in your retirement years?
10. Should a person's appearance, life-style, gender or ethnic background influence you in hiring or promoting someone? In not hiring them? On what basis, if any, do you believe such criteria is justified, and why?
11. In the age of artificial intelligence and robotics, where many traditional jobs will be lost to humans, do you believe the teachings of this Degree will no longer be important?

THE JOURNEY OF THE ELU TO ENLIGHTENMENT

TWENTY THIRD DEGREE.

23°
Chief of the Tabernacle

"The world is not God, but the work of God"

The 23°, Chief of the Tabernacle, is the first of the Degrees based on the ancient Mystery Religions. The ancient Mysteries were a series of increasing purifications of the body and mind, and increasing awareness of one's spiritual identity. It was a journey--a process of self-discovery. The candidate in this Degree represents a member of the tribe of Levi, who has come to acquire the lowest degree of initiation into the mysteries of the Hebrew priesthood.

The sole purpose of the Mysteries was to explore the nature of God, Man and the Universe and their interrelationships. They came to be because they were the best tool devised by man in his perennial quest for a higher knowledge of the Truth hidden behind appearances in the universe and in him. They filled the gap created by the insufficiency of the popular public religion and worship to satisfy the deeper thoughts and aspirations of Mans' mind.

The basis of Hermetic Philosophy is that there has

always been this secret of secrets. That which is below is a reflection of that which is above. Each man is a microcosm, that is, a miniature model of the universe. The world is not God but proceeds from Him. This was one of the great insights of ancient wisdom.

It is a daunting thought that we are each a reflection of the Divine. Yet, almost all of the world's religions each teach the same thing. The task of Freemasonry is to inform you of that truth and encourage you to explore its implications. The Tabernacle, the setting of this Degree, was the earthly house of God. It represented the solitary place where the scientific knowledge of the ancient world was deposited. It was later replaced by the Temple built by Solomon, which has the same symbolism. The Lodge room always symbolizes the individual Mason and the universe in which he lives. Progress in esoteric knowledge cannot happen unless one is initiated in a place set aside for such purpose and discovery.

And the approach to such a place is by purification and contemplation. We were told in the first Degree of Masonry that we use the common gavel for "divesting our minds and consciences of all the vices and superfluities of life." Purification is the process of setting aside the errors and passions of the past so that we can start fresh. Contemplation is thought. It is a matter of sitting quietly and asking yourself what the symbols you have heard or seen or read really mean. Contemplation is the path to enlightenment. Our progress in Masonry is marked by our own self-improvement as a purer and better individual.

The Mysteries were meant to be the beginning of a new life of reason and virtue. They treated subjects mystically by illustrating through symbols what could not be explained, by exciting feelings and insight when one could not develop an adequate idea. Instead of a prescribed routine or creed, they invited men to seek, feel, compare and judge on their own. They impelled the initiate to study, interpret and develop the symbols for himself. Their purpose was to awaken the mind and develop its creativity, rather than fill it with ready-made opinions and dogma.

It seems the mind of man is drawn in two directions in his relationship with God. On the first, and highest level, we seem to know, intuitively, that there is a higher power, and that power is essentially incomprehensible. It is simply too large and too great for our minds to conceive. On the lower level, we seem constantly to create gods in our own image. We invest them with the worst, and not the best that is in us. As a few examples, consider these situations and statements in response which you may have heard others make, or even made yourself.

You see someone cheating and getting away with it and you respond, "That's all right, he'll pay for it on the Day of Judgment!" Someone makes you angry. You respond, "Damn him to hell!" Or you see a chance to make some money, perhaps in a way that is not completely ethical. You respond, "God helps those who help themselves." Your favorite football team has an important game coming up. You say, "Please, God, let them win!" Or you see a problem coming, you take no steps to help counter it, and disaster strikes. Your response is, "Oh well, it is God's will." There are many such examples.

But we have just described a god who is vengeful, craftily awaiting a chance to trip others, greedy, a partisan football fan, and who delights in pain and suffering.

Of course, that is not the God whom you truly believe. But

the process is the same which leads to the creation of an image demanding human sacrifice.

It is of great importance that we keep our ideas of God as pure and elevated as possible. Gods constructed in our own worst images tend to condone our own worst actions. It is then even easier to make a god of money, of social status, of power, or of ego. Divesting our minds is not only a matter of ridding ourselves of vice and superfluity. It is also a matter of ridding ourselves of prejudices and preconceptions.

As a Mason, our concept of God should constantly evolve to higher and nobler planes. As a part of that process, we must learn more; think more deeply; study more intently. That was the central lesson of the Mysteries. And Masonry still follows this ancient manner of teaching. Pike wrote;

> "Her symbols are the instruction she gives; and the lectures are but only partial and insufficient one-sided endeavors to interpret those symbols. He who would become an accomplished Mason, must not be content merely to hear or even to understand the lectures, but must, aided by them, and they having as it were marked out of the way for him, study, interpret, and develop the symbols for himself."

It is important to beware of literalism. It is impossible for a limited human being to truly conceive the unlimited. We must, of necessity, make do with concepts of God which fall far short of Him. Still, we can and must conceive of the best; our standard must be higher than ourselves. In the process of living out our quest by actions in the real world, we are to follow duty; not desire.

Questions to Contemplate as a Chief of the Tabernacle

1. What is the utilization of symbols and symbol interpretation designed to do? What is it meant to prevent?

2. What is required of you in making progress in esoteric knowledge?

3. How might you think differently about your own faith had you made as much possible in the study of the history, teachings, doctrine and philosophy of your faith as would have been required of the ancients?

4. What is the value of studying the major faith systems in the world in addition to your own?

5. What does this Degree teach us about the relationship between faith and reason?

6. A society's concept of God and the universe changes over time along with its scientific development and progress. What does this warn us about the nature of man and his practices of faith?

7. How has Masonry helped you affirm the validity of your chosen faith?

8. Why do you think this Degree was set in a tabernacle instead of a temple?

THE JOURNEY OF THE ELU TO ENLIGHTENMENT

TWENTY FOURTH DEGREE.

24°
PRINCE OF THE TABERNACLE

"Initiation tends to man's perfection"

The 24°, Prince of the Tabernacle, illustrates the common features of some of the world's major religions. The candidate is received in the court of the Princes of the Tabernacle and is consecrated by earth, air, fire, and water. He participates in the retelling of the mythic story of Osiris, murdered by Typhon, and reborn to life. The candidate is instructed in the theme of the hero who dies and is reborn. He is first purified by the elements of nature to remind him of the gifts these provide. He is then led into a tabernacle of darkness and silence which symbolizes death. The attempts to bring back to life Osiris, the god of the sun, of light, life and good using symbols representing science, reason and logic; all fail.

It often seems as if the world was composed of opposites, We speak of light and dark, good and evil, love and hate. Within ourselves, it often seems as if we are torn in two directions, between self and others, between honesty and expediency, between charity and greed. This apparent duality is profoundly revealed in this Degree with the confrontation between Osiris, and his brother, Typhon. It is this dual nature of mankind that led many early religions to postulate that there were two gods, one "good" and one "evil" which contested control of the world. But the initiates into those religions—those who were allowed access to the inner and higher mysteries—understood that the duality was only an appearance, and that there was, in truth, only one God.

The great Law of God, which underlies all religions, is the law of balance and harmony—of two opposing forces held in equilibrium and so resulting in a third force. Life and death combined result in the new life, eternal and perfect. There is no such thing as death. These truths are not provable by science or logic. They are established by faith and reason always in balance.

The Mason understands that neither faith nor reason alone is sufficient for full comprehension. Faith without reason becomes a destructive force, leading to intolerance, hatred, and horrible distortions. Faith without reason has created gods who delighted in sacrificing infants, in self-mutilation of their worshipers, and in actions which can only be described as mob insanity. Likewise, reason without faith doubts everything, and limits man's awareness of God to man's only limited intellectual processes—making a God a sort of celestial computer, if it does not deny His existence altogether.

But faith and reason, balanced, provide the best path we have to an understanding of God. Faith and reason, together, make clear the need for a Redemptive Figure.

In your personal path, that Redemptive Figure may have already come, or it may be yet to appear. But all the great ancient religions either announced His arrival or foretold of His coming.

That fact is not a cause for a weakening of faith, but for its strengthening. Either we are forced to believe that all civilized peoples, at different times, in different cultural conditions, have engaged in the same self-delusion or we must believe that some great truth communicates itself to man, and has done so for centuries.

We live in an age of mass-communications, in which we are accustomed to receiving information directly and clearly. Newspapers test the level of their stories with "readability scores" to make certain that someone with a ninth-grade education can read them. "Say what you mean, clearly and simply," has become almost a religious tenet among communicators.

And yet, all such tests, all such efforts, merely measure the technical difficulty of the material. A book may be very easy to read, and very difficult to understand.

The ancient religions were under no such compulsion. They taught not directly, but by symbols. One thing was said, another meant. One thing was pictured, another implied. For them, as for Masonry, the difficulty was intentional. Only by the process of thinking about a symbol or a truth, considering it from every possible angle, rethinking it again and again can we begin to apprehend the truth. Truth which is merely communicated is useless; to be of worth it must become part of the person himself, part of his thinking and his awareness of the world. This insight cannot be given to us. It must be earned by study and effort. This is the quest of a Prince of the Tabernacle.

THE JOURNEY OF THE ELU TO ENLIGHTENMENT

A powerful illustration of this idea is shown when the candidate is told the initiate is he who possesses the lamp of the Sages, the cloak of the wise, and the staff of the Patriarchs. The lamp is reason, by whose light the initiate traverses the fields of science; the cloak is liberty, or self-control, that is, the full possession of one's self, which defends him against the blind forces of instinct; and the staff of faith, the profound conviction that God is real.

It is a great truth that reason is not withheld from any man, but its possessors too often do not know how to make use of it. The use of reason is a science which must be learned. Likewise, liberty is offered unto all, but few have the power to be free. Freedom is a right which one must defend. In the same manner, faith is a free gift of God unto all men, but few dare to lean upon it. Faith is a power which one must take into himself. These three—reason, true liberty, and faith are the three great lights illuminated in this Degree. We are admonished to find the courage to accept these gifts of God and carry them with us in life.

The important thing to take from this Degree is a basic understanding of the objectives of the ancient Mysteries and how to make them work in your life. Initiation into the Mysteries was not only to learn the great truths, but also a process to awaken and develop the Divine nature within oneself. The object was to dignify man in his own eyes and teach him his right place in the universe. If his intellect could be improved and his soul prevented from being impeded by an overload of base physical needs, his life could be made more agreeable.

It is a hard lesson to learn but a man's happiness is increased when his soul is purified from the passions that disturb him. The issue is how to bring about the mental change which enables one to truly live a happy life. This requires purity of heart. There is both a material and a spiritual commitment involved in Masonic initiation.

And we must understand that one cannot assume holy responsibilities for which one is not fit. Remember always that the same fire which give the light by which the scholar reads and the physician attends at the bedside in the small hours, also, in the hands of the incompetent, consumes and destroys entire cities. Knowledge is always a danger to the fool, for with it he may destroy both himself and others. Moral instruction must be accompanied with a purity of heart. Take care, then, to learn well and study with an honest heart.

If the soul is to be re-established to the perfection it has lost, then exalting the intellectual and spiritual levels of the human mind and consciousness is necessary. Masonry imitates the methods of the Mysteries by also utilizing initiation as a way of elevating the soul from the sensual human life to a communion with God. The Mysteries explored the nature of mankind, and focused on the spiritual nature of humanity and its relationship with Deity. The great motto of the ancient Mysteries was to "Know Thyself."

To attain the science and power and understanding of the Wise Men, four things are indispensable: an Intellect, enlightened by study; a Daring which nothing checks; a Will that nothing can conquer; and a Discretion that nothing can corrupt. Thus, the four essential qualities necessary to become knowledgeable in the Mysteries are *to Know, to Will, to Dare, and to be Silent.*

"To Know" means to know yourself. "To Will" means to actively desire to know more, to grow and develop in knowledge. "To Dare" means to seek and question with courage, and not to accept ideas blindly. "To be Silent" means to understand that this is your personal and internal quest. It is not to be discussed with others except on your own terms. Real secrets are exactly that, secrets not to be discussed with those who are outside your circle of trusted friends.

As an initiate, you must be in the world, but not of it. The initiates are set apart. They interact with the world with care, love, compassion, and toleration, but they do not let the doubts, the skepticism, and the ignorance of the world touch them or influence them. As a Mason, you have taken obligations to yourself, and your brothers, to distinguish yourself from the rest of the community. You have chosen not to be a common man, and that choice is not reversible.

Questions to Contemplate as a Prince of the Tabernacle

1. Why is it better to be thinking men, when to choose to be so requires so much sacrifice and labor?
2. Do you think you are knowledgeable enough to make wise choices among alternative approaches to complex issues such improving education, combating drug addition, improving health care, controlling pollution, and strengthening the economy? What does this Degree teach us about the essential requisites for knowledge?
3. Can democracy work in a country where most citizens are not knowledgeable enough to understand the complex issues confronting society? What about a country where only a fraction of the people participates in elections?

4. Would you rather live in a democracy run by inept, corrupt leaders, or in a dictatorship run by capable honest leaders?
5. In what areas of life are we tempted to do what's "good enough," rather than what is best?
6. In this Degree, we are compelled to secrecy because of an important fear. What is that fear?
7. Why is secrecy both a sacrifice and a virtue?
8. What if anything do you think is the ethical distinction between fraudulently taking money from the government and fraudulently evading taxes so as not to give it to them?
9. Is it important for you to have freedoms you are unable to exercise? What freedoms do you value most?
10. Do you believe that everyone should have the same freedom of choice as you do?
11. If you were determining who could immigrate here, would you let in those you thought would contribute the most to your country, or those most in need of refuge?
12. Would you rather live in a country where your religion was the State religion, or in one where Church and State were separate and all religions were treated equally?
13. What modern conclusions can we draw from our study of the Mysteries?

THE JOURNEY OF THE ELU TO ENLIGHTENMENT

TWENTY FIFTH DEGREE.
PLATE 1ST.

TWENTY FIFTH DEGREE.
Plate 2ND.

25°
KNIGHT OF THE BRAZEN SERPENT, OR SUFI MASTER

The 25°, Knight of the Brazen Serpent, was renamed Sufi Master in 2006. The original ritual represents the camp of the Israelites in the middle of the Sinai Desert in the fortieth year of their wandering. The Lodge represents four apartments; the House of the Earth, House of the Planets, House of the Sun and Moon, and the House of Light. In the opening of the first three Houses, there is no teacher; only books which the candidate has to read. He is left silently to himself for nearly half of the Degree. The symbolic meaning here is that life is essentially self-instruction.

In the newer version, the Degree introduces us to Sufi teachings and traditions, and gives us clues on how this esoteric branch of Islam might help overcome the difficulties encountered in our attempts to advance in the Mysteries.

The candidate represents an initiate in the Islamic mysteries who has taken all the necessary vows and is devoted to the search for truth. The Degree makes a serious inquiry into our understanding of the basic tenets of Freemasonry, and the faithfulness in which we have personally followed its instruction. What are our vows? Who, after taking them, remembers them? Have we performed our duties better than before? Are we more forgiving? Are we more generous to the poor? Are we less selfish, less envious, less ungrateful? Do we make greater sacrifices for others? Do we accept wages for that which we have not honestly earned? Do we risk the guilt of perjury to the poor performance of our duties? In summary, this Degree asks us if we have truly performed all we have promised. It is the first question we should frequently ask ourselves.

In Masonry, we have assumed obligations to the performance of many duties. Our obligations are real. And we have agreed to live by them. If we do not do so, we are hypocrites and bring dishonor to the fraternity.

"Good resolutions are for the most part like words written on the sands of the seashore, over which the tide rises. Perhaps it is not well to require anyone to vow to perform any duty or avoid any vice. The vow rarely insures performance, and too commonly entails perjury. There are duties that you do not perform, or which you perform only occasionally, or reluctantly, or inadequately, or with only half your heart."

And so it is with every man. The reality of life is that the perfection idealized in the 14° is elusive, and the path to it requires constant attention.

One of the great lessons of this Degree is that knowledge and instruction is to be found everywhere—in nature, in our relations with others, in history, and in the everyday things of life. We only have to look for it with openness and understanding. Truth, knowledge, and opportunity for advancement often come to us in forms which are at first unrecognizable, and can even seem, at first sight, unacceptable, and even foolish. But if we withhold premature judgments, and apply mature reflection, we learn to recognize truth. In so doing, we broaden our horizons of understanding which leads to greater wisdom. Thoughts are our most basic and important tools. To think well and clearly is essential to human progress. The search for knowledge is indeed important. And insight and understanding are even more so.

It is easy to confuse the symbol with reality. One may set up a statue of a great man after his death, because one wishes to be reminded of his life, his values, and his teachings. But given a few decades of time it has not been uncommon to find that statue worshiped as a god. It is this tendency to turn symbols into reality which has given rise to popular superstition, to such pseudo-sciences as astrology, and to cults. It would be comforting to think that this was an error common to ancient peoples, but unlikely to happen today; but observation suggests otherwise. There are still, today, snake-worshipping cults, people who make decisions on the basis of the position of stars, and those who react to a picture of a rock music star as if they were in his actual presence.

It would be a close approximation of the truth to say that, historically, the masses have worshiped the symbols while the Initiates have worshiped the reality behind the symbol. Understand that the purpose of initiation is to produce change, change in yourself. Initiation, properly understood, is transformation. Once transformed, a man cannot view the world as he previously had, any more than the world of the butterfly is the world of the caterpillar.

It is important to understand that status, wealth, and educational degrees are all symbols. Status is a symbol of the power and ability to make changes in the world and in people's thinking. Wealth is a symbol of work done or of planning and investment—or the creation of something of worth. Academic degrees are given for study and effort, which creates a deeper ability to understand, comprehend, and contribute to the knowledge of the world. All three can be put to good and noble use. All three, so used, are honorable and legitimate goals.

Yet the Mason is as likely as any man to desire status as a thing in itself—not for the good he can do; to covet wealth, not as an evidence and consequence of the creation of worth, but as if it could by itself give him comfort; to be more interested in a piece of paper to hang on his wall or get a better salary than in knowledge for its own sake and for the betterment of both mankind and his own intellectual life.

A Sufi Master in this Degree states;

"The destiny of man is to make or create himself. He is and must always be the child of his own works, for time and for eternity. The necessity of competition is imposed on all men; but the number of the elect, that is to say, of those who succeed, is always small. In other words, men desirous of being important are numerous, but men who excel are always rare. Life is a warfare, in which one must prove his soldiership if he would rise in rank."

We must always be cautious not to be too hasty in

interpreting matters of truth. We have, at the click of a mouse, access to any point of view on any subject of public concern; often without the slightest documentation of its underlying fact, truth or reality. Some things are too valuable to be entrusted to those who are not worthy. It is a good lesson to be reminded that our ancient brethren, desirous of being admitted into our order, served a probationary period of a year, during which time his behavior and actions were carefully watched. It was only after affirming his sincerity and honesty that he was admitted to our mysteries.

Above all, the 25th Degree warns us against several mental attitudes which can cause trouble for us. One is intellectual laziness. How many times have we heard a brother complain that he was against education programs in Lodge? He had had all the education he wanted or needed in high school. This Degree suggests differently You should not be content with what you have already learned, thinking you may not improve your store of wisdom. It is easy for the mind of man to fall into the rut of not thinking. The average man cannot and does not choose to think deeply, and has, in all times, been content to let the fake practitioner enslave him in some way. As Masons, we simply cannot fall into a state of indifference and inactivity. If, having attained the degrees of the Rite, we convince ourselves there is no further need for study, no further requirement to learn anything more, no compelling reason to regularly and actively participate in the learning experiences offered at our reunion gatherings; we will, in that case be, like the knight who lets the sword of his father's rust in its scabbard, and the glories of his race die out. This only paves the way for losing what you already possess. You will have been given a great treasure, yet choose to live in poverty.

In the earlier version of this Degree, the candidate visited the four apartments of the Lodge. In the House of the Earth, he was taught the basis of philosophy and the development of his own spirit. In the House of the Planets, he was reminded how the knowledge of the world enters the mind and soul through the five senses, but there is a sixth sense which represents that knowledge which only arises from thought and introspection, in which the soul itself examines. In the House of the Sun and Moon, he learns of the great cycle of life, and is reminded that, as the Sun holds dominion over the planets, so should the Scottish Rite Mason hold dominion over himself, his passions and his weaknesses. This is the only way one can reach his fullest potential as a man and spiritual being.

As men, we are called upon to think, to study, and to consider. We are to seek after wisdom, which is the ability to apply knowledge and insight to the problems and questions of the world. Never judge any group, organization, culture, or civilization by its symbols. Judge, rather, by the knowledge those symbols represent.

The quest is that we continue our development to express our moral and ethical self in the world. But we must ever be cautious that we do not fall into the error of confusing symbols with the thing symbolized. The distinguishing characteristic of a Mason is that he is not philosophically blind enough to confuse the symbol with the reality behind it.

The Journey of the Elu to Enlightenment

Questions to Contemplate as a Sufi Knight

1. Do you value wealth as a symbol of success, and not because of the good you can do with wealth? What does this say about your understanding of the difference between perception and reality?

2. It is said the enlightened man has no need of ordinary light. He is not dependent on the light or knowledge of other men. Why is this so?

3. One of the Sufi Masters tells us: "A wise man can find knowledge, even in the act of fools." Can you give an example from your own life which might confirm this observation?

4. What are some modern-day examples and consequences of turning a symbol into reality? Of focusing on a symbol, rather than the thing symbolized?

5. All Mysteries have taught the common core of wisdom and love in all men, hidden under different uniforms which history and politics have woven around them. What does this teach us?

6. What must we free ourselves from to escape violence and spiritual death?

7. Pike states that all religion is symbolism since we can describe only what we see and feel. The real objects of religion are unseen. What does this say about literal interpretations of the Volume of Sacred Law? Is there a way to reconcile liberal vs. symbolic interpretations of matters of religion?

8. What do religion and philosophy have in common? How do they differ?

9. Is it possible to find your way to heaven alone?

COUNCIL OF KADOSH

TWENTY SIXTH DEGREE.

26°
PRINCE OF MERCY

Let us seek the things that are above

The 26°, Prince of Mercy, is the last of the four Degrees which have focused on the Ancient Mysteries. As you have seen, they present to us a series of increasing purifications of the body and mind, and an increasing awareness of our spiritual identity. It is intended to be a journey of self-discovery in which we learn that, by studying all faiths, and searching for universal archetypes that are common to all men; we can draw a common core of wisdom, love and compassion that can be found in all religions and moral philosophies.

The Twenty-Sixth Degree focuses on the Christian Mysteries and confirms that early Christians taught their creed through initiation and their ceremonies were performed in secrecy. It is important to understand why this is the case. It was for the same reason that Masonry has always used allegories and symbols to convey its lessons.

The fact is there is always danger attached to acquired knowledge. If ill-used, it is like "a sword in the hands of a child," as Clemens, Bishop of Alexandria, put it in 191 A.D. Truths which are taught through symbols and parables, as in the Gospels, are seldom understood by those whose spiritual and intellectual development has restrained them to believe in ideas only on their face value. It is a natural impulse for us to want to stick to the letter of the law, a story, a news report, or even a moral code without seeing the spirit hidden underneath, or applying it to a broader perspective or meaning.

The same tendency is prevalent in Freemasonry, where the value of its rituals is restrained when the goal is only to focus on the language of our art, and not its deeper meanings. The richness and fullness of its allegories and symbols is too often not explored, and therefore, sadly, never discovered by men in lodge. It is a sobering reality that truths are normally comprehended only by those who are duly and truly prepared to receive them.

St. Basil, the Bishop of Alexandria in 412 A.D., speaking of the symbolism hidden under the doctrines of the church, was even more caustic when he said, *"These mysteries are so profound and so exalted that they can be comprehended by those only who are enlightened. The ignorant person, not being aware of his own weakness of mind, often condemns what he should venerate and ridicules what he does not understand."* He even referred to the example given by Jesus Christ in this respect, saying; *"The Lord spake in parables to His hearers in general; but to His disciples He explained in private the parables and allegories which He spoke in public."*

THE JOURNEY OF THE ELU TO ENLIGHTENMENT

No man has ever seen God; we can only know of His attributes:

- Our soul is an integral part of God's own soul. A moral sense has a Divine source.
- Moral truths are a part of God's perfect nature and are as real as physics and geometry.
- The distinction between good and evil is essential and is the unique quality of man.
- God is the principle of morality.
- It is an absolute and universal obligation to conform to morality, to what is true, just, and good. It is neither variable nor contingent. No excuse can justify man's failure to exercise moral imperatives. We naturally recognize the distinction between the merit and demerit of our actions, and inherently know that vice and virtue are respectively punished and rewarded by some inflexible law of cause and effect.
- Charity is God's immutable law since God is Love. It is an obligation of mankind. It demands to be generous, to rejoice at the good fortune of others, sympathize with them in their sorrows and misfortunes, live peacefully with all men, and repay injuries with kindness.
- The laws which control and regulate the universe are those of motion and harmony.
- The balance of God's infinite and perfect justice and mercy expresses His wisdom. While infinite justice alone would call for man's utter destruction, and infinite mercy would allow the

most offensive hedonism, together they bring man both retribution and forgiveness, the conditions of his freedom of choice, the attribute of his divine superiority in the scale of creation.

The problem is that we know the attributes, but not the substance of these forces. We cannot realize infinity and eternity in space and time. The absolute existence of a Supreme Principle or Being is not within the reach of our senses or mind. It is nearly impossible for us to grasp the idea of an existence without a beginning or an effect without a cause. We are mysteries to ourselves. And this makes God an even greater mystery.

In this Degree, the relationship of the Christian Mysteries to the Craft Degrees in Masonry are particularly explored. The candidate represents a "Catechumen" (Fellowcraft) who seeks to become a "faithful," (as in Master Mason, or the third level of membership in the Mysteries). The three great attributes of God's essence are configured on three sides of an equilateral triangle with a flaming heart in the center. On the heart are the letters I.H.S, and on the three respective sides, are the letters W (Wisdom, or force to create), F (Force, or strength to build) and H (Harmony, the power to preserve, to uphold equilibrium and order, which is beauty). I.H.S are the traditional Christian Latin initials for "Iesus Hominum Salvator" (Jesus, the Savior of Mankind). It is also the initials of "Imperium, Harmonia, Sapientia" (the Masonic trinity of Power, Harmony and Wisdom, and the initials of the motto on the Christian Emperor Constantine's banner, "In Hoc Signo," meaning "Under this sign," which was followed by "vinces" meaning "you will conquer." The eventual victory of Light, Truth and Perfection is certain because Man has a natural instinct toward immortality. If this were not so, the world would be a theater of wrong and injustice perpetuated by greed and ignorance.

Thus, in our review of the Ancient Mysteries, we have learned it is important that we not neglect our faith while developing our spirituality. Faith is strengthened by questioning. To doubt and question does not weaken faith, but helps it to grow. When properly understood, there is no conflict between faith and science. Man has an inherent need to relate to God. As we become more aware of the Divine, we will find that all systems of faith have more in common than is often noticed. The quest is to overcome the obstacles that divide mankind so we can see the unity of the Creating Power within its own offspring. The perennial human attempts at understanding the ineffable mysteries of God, Man and Nature lead to the conclusion that toleration is one of mankind's most important duties.

Questions to Contemplate as a Prince of Mercy

1. Have you granted to all other people the same right to their own religious convictions that you rightly demand for yourself?

2. Why do you think that people fear asking questions openly about their own religion?

3. Have you ever confused the roles of science and religion, either rejecting some scientific fact because it appears to conflict with a religious truth, or discarding a religious truth because it seems to conflict with scientific fact? Are there circumstances where you feel you may have too hastily made a judgment in favor of one over the other?

THE JOURNEY OF THE ELU TO ENLIGHTENMENT

Twenty Seventh Degree.

27°
KNIGHT OF THE SUN, OR PRINCE ADEPT

"We can see only a small part of all that is."

The 27°, Knight of the Sun, Prince Adept, is the last and supreme philosophical Degree of the Scottish Rite. It is the most complex of the philosophical Degrees, but a Degree of great richness, and can, alone, provide food for years of thought. It is the complete recapitulation and synthesis of the scientific, philosophical and religious teachings of the Rite. It represents the true quest of the Spiritual Alchemist, which is the fusion of Man's mind with God's spirit. This search for the Absolute in Man and the purification of his soul is the Great Work.

The candidate is received in a council representing the ancient Adepts. He is instructed in moral philosophy, in the thoughts of the ancients concerning Nature and God, and in the symbols of alchemy. Much of the material with this Degree concerns the use and interpretations of symbols.

It is important for us to understand that all our religious concepts of God were developed by men who lived long before modern science; and the understanding science has given us as to how the world was created and formulated. Faith systems have historically feared addressing the idea of an evolving universe because they fear that thoughtful peoples will give up their belief in God altogether. When in actuality, the reverse seems to be occurring in our time; what people disbelieve in is hanging onto old and inadequate concepts of God.

We see this in young adults today. They find that the early concepts of God which they accepted at home or in Sunday school does not fit the new world of modern science which they now know. There is no place any longer for a benevolent and venerable old gentleman with white hair sitting on a throne somewhere up in the sky. Yet, unless a new concept of God which is adequate to our new knowledge replaces the old inadequate one, disillusioned youth may discard their belief in God completely.

The lessons of the Prince Adept again inform us that the real problem is not to prove that God exists; but rather to find out what God is like. Because reason exists in all things, it is clearly impossible for God to act on a whim. God cannot do anything that is not in accord with His own nature; that is, he cannot bring about things which are contrary to His nature any more than a triangle's three angles can equal anything other than two right angles. God's freedom must be understood in the only sense that freedom is possible in the universe. God alone is the free cause.

If we believe that there is a pattern to the universe that shapes nature, and there is a direction to the universe as a whole, then everything in that universe is a part of that Grand Design. This design, of course, is what we mean by God. The image of God, then, is the non-physical part of us—our soul. Where do we get our drive for morality and meaning? Where do we derive our urge to make a positive difference with our life? How do we acquire our tendency to love? That drive is from the soul which is the "image of God."

Living in the image of God means that we have the ability to choose how we want to be. It is this ability that makes us special. Life only becomes meaningful because of our ability to choose its outcome for us. The difference between being programmed to love and choosing to love is precisely what makes love significant. Similarly, if I don't have the choice to do good but am programmed to do good, then there's nothing meaningful about it. It is only because I have both the ability and choice to do good or evil that good becomes significant.

But it goes deeper still. For choice to be authentic, there have to be consequences. If every time I get in trouble, someone comes and bails me out, that is not really choice. Choice means consequences. When we think about it, all of history is based on decisions that human beings have made—and the consequences that flow from that. So, the image of God means that God created beings who have the ability to make decisions, and those decisions create consequences that make us all co-partners in the development of the world.

This brings up another complex idea revealed in the 27°. The universe is balanced between two forces, which maintain it in equilibrium; that which attracts and that which resists. The force which draws a planet toward the sun, and the force which repels it from the center, are antagonistic, but not hostile—their result is the harmonious and perpetual movement of the planet in its orbit. Thus, two conflicting forces, in reality, work together for resolution. Opposition develops talent, and criticism arouses genius. Statements of error provoke utterances of truth; imperfect creeds cause truer ones to arise.

In the world of morality, there are also two forces; one which desires and attempts, and one which restrains or atones for. These two forces are symbolized by Cain and Abel, by the good and evil principles taught by Zarathustra. These forces are represented in Masonry in the black and white tessellated pavement.

Thus, within us all, are passions, tendencies to anger, to lust, to selfishness, to greed. These arise from the animal within us. If we are to be balanced, if we are to advance, these passions must be opposed and overcome by the tendencies to compassion, to love, to generosity, to charity. And these arise from God within us. We have, within us, a soul which is eternal, immortal, and powerful. It is also active. It can perceive the world about it, both the world of matter and the world of spirit. Such perceptions come to us as insights, awareness's, intuitions. It can communicate directly with the souls of others. Thus it is that we can know, without knowing how we know, that one man is honest and trustworthy and another not to be trusted. Thus it is that we can be aware of the love another has for us, even if no words are spoken. Thus it is that we can share with others a sense of beauty, or wonder, or awe, or joy, or sorrow.

In our life, either the animal or the divine will predominate. Take care that it be the divine which triumphs. The spirituality of the soul is the foundation of immortality. We have an innate tendency to reject the idea of our death being the final end of ourselves. We have an innate thirst for the infinite, to become reunited with God. As we grow in knowledge and virtue, we intuitively come to accept that our individual personality is only an actor in the short drama we call our present life. There is a greater meaning to existence than merely to "eat, drink and be merry."

Our urging for immortality leads us to understand that God exists both within and without us at the same time. He exists within us, and is a part of us, not by our doing, but by His will. This intimacy, this God-in-us, can be a frightening thought for it means that there is no hiding, no such thing as hoping we won't get caught in our little acts of humanness.

So much, for example, for telling a joke to our buddies in a bar that we wouldn't tell in our church or synagogue. If we are there, God is there. If a word, a joke, a song, a story is out of place in a church, it is out of place anywhere, for the same God who is in the church is in us, and we cannot escape Him. That makes us uncomfortable.

Man is both animal and divine. Each day of our life, we make choices which celebrate the animal or the divine. We seldom get in difficulty by following our true higher impulses. We create few problems by being forgiving, kind, compassionate, tolerant, understanding, loving and truthful—we create many problems by being spiteful, greedy, uncaring, bigoted, hateful and dishonest. It is the animal side of us that gets us in trouble.

We tend to excuse our negative behavior by claiming it is "natural." I'm only human," we cry, as if that were some justification for giving way to our animal nature. But we don't do it very well. Animals are better at being animals than are we. Animals are not generally perverse. They do as their nature or genetic programs tell them to do, moderating it somewhat by learned behavior. But a man who gives way to the animal in his nature is perverse. He uses his reason, his intelligence, his ability not to further and develop his higher emotions, not to strengthen the Divine in himself, but to become more cunning and crafty—to out-beast the beasts.

We cannot forever ignore God-in-us. To celebrate the Divine is to come closer, even by a little, to our true nature; to celebrate the animal is to move further away from it. Masonry insists that Man's normal condition is progress from ignorance to higher and higher knowledge. For this reason, moral truth cannot be a mere abstraction. Seeking it is the ultimate justification of human life.

Finally, to know how to die is the ultimate secret that sets us above pain, above sensual appetites, above the fear of death. The last victory man can gain over death is to overcome the love of life, not through despair, but through a loftier hope, contained in faith. To learn to overcome oneself is to learn to live. What we are doing as Masons is working out our own process of refinement so that we can overcome ourselves, know the nature of good, and find true happiness in our life. The object of the ancient initiations was to find or form such men. And such is the object of Freemasonry.

If you are, or can become such a man, you will be worthy to be called Adept, and a Knight of the Sun.

For the true, final purpose of Alchemy is for man to understand himself and his relationship to God. As God is made visible in the natural world, so by studying the natural world we hope to better understand God. And by studying the relationship of man to the world around him, we hope to better understand the relationship of man to his Creator.

What, then does this mean to you?

As the alchemist strives to create the Philosopher's Stone, whose purpose is the preparation of life-giving medicines, so you must strive to convert your life into one that touches others with healing, and peace, and comfort.

As the alchemist refines metal in the fire, so you must refine yourself; burning away the base materials of fear, greed, envy, lust, anger, and those other elements which debase your soul and spirit.

As the alchemist distills liquids to arrive at the very essence of a substance, so you must distill your thoughts and actions, leaving behind what is of this world, and arriving at an understanding of your true nature as a spiritual being, connected forever with God.

This is what, in Alchemy, has always been called "the work." It is from Alchemy that Masonry adopted that term.

QUESTIONS TO CONTEMPLATE AS A KNIGHT OF THE SUN

1. If a spark of God exists in all men, what does that tell us about the way we should treat others?
2. Does it matter if others have different faiths, live in different cultures, or live thousands of miles apart from us?
3. Unity evolving out of duality is a central theme of the Degree. What are some practical applications of this them in daily life?
4. What kind of cooperation does it take for us to have within us "the immortality of the Sages?"
5. What must we do to refine our own base metal into Gold?

THE JOURNEY OF THE ELU TO ENLIGHTENMENT

TWENTY EIGHTH DEGREE.

320

28°
KNIGHT COMMANDER OF THE TEMPLE

"Times change, and circumstances; but Virtue and Duty remain the same"

The 28°, Knight Commander of the Temple, is the first of the Chivalric Degrees that emphasize the Knighthood Tradition of the Medieval period. It announces new and higher battles that Masons must wage within themselves and with society in the journey to enlightenment and mature masculinity. Having made yourself familiar with some of the great truths common to the world's great religions, and firm in what you have learned in all the Degrees up until now, you assume the vows of Knighthood and take up arms against injustice, falsehood and oppression.

THE JOURNEY OF THE ELU TO ENLIGHTENMENT

This Degree relates to the Order of the Teutonic Knights and that of the Knights of the Temple of Jerusalem, later called the Knights Templar. Knighthood was a Christian institution and it was conferred during a ceremony with sacraments similar to those of Christianity. Knighthood originated from cavalry warriors, hence the arming of the spurs, urging the knights to deeds of honor and virtue; a coat of mail, cuirass and gauntlets, symbolizing protection from vice; a belt and a two-edged sword symbolizing chivalric courage and justice. Knights were expected to be the most gallant and virtuous men. They dedicated their life to the protection of right and defense of the needy.

You represent the candidate, Constans, a young squire and Knight of the Sun, who wants to demonstrate his zeal for Masonry. Before being admitted into the Court, you would have had to prepare yourself in silence and solitude in a chamber of reflection lit by a single candle. The floor and walls are lined with black, and there is but a table upon which rest three skulls. You would have been left alone to contemplate, deeply, the meaning of the three skulls; to consider your own mortality, and the fact that, when you are gone, only your deeds done for others will be left. Nothing of selfishness will survive you, nor will men in future years care whether you were happy or sorrowful, at ease, or in pain. You would have found paper on the table, and a notice that, if there was anyone with whom you had an argument unresolved, or anyone with whom you were not at peace, you were to write to that person and make amends before you could proceed in the degree.

Argument and strife damage both parties. You cannot be angry with another without poisoning your own soul.

Do not let pride stand in the way of peace. The man who says that he will never forgive another or who takes pride in the fact that he will never apologize is taking pride in his own damnation.

You would have then had to commit yourself to stand vigil over your arms until dawn.

In this Degree, the candidate is confronted with three temptations. The first represents a life of sensual pleasure, but without faith or spiritual grounding. The second is a life based on spiritual values, but without any true human experience. The third temptation represents a life based on moral principles used as a pretext not to act for the sake of others at one's own expense. Thus, tempted by sensuality, by materialism, and by misguided spirituality to abandon his vigil and his honor, he resists; but ultimately leaves his vigil to help the battle when his city is attacked. To save the lives and liberty of his people, he decides to sacrifice his own career and rushes to battle. Because he is an excellent fighter, he turns the tide of the battle and the city and humanity is saved. Since he left his vigil unselfishly for the cause of justice and humanity, he is knighted a Commander of the Temple.

One of the questions we must ask as contemporary men, few of whom have ever put on a pair of spurs, is why should we preserve an obviously archaic tradition of another time? Do we retain the chivalric degrees in Masonry just so we can call ourselves Knights?

The answer is obvious. It is not the activities but the qualities of the medieval knight which we seek to emulate. And those qualities are as important today as they were a thousand years ago. Is a damsel any less in distress because she is suffering from a crippling disease rather than locked in a high tower by a cruel baron? Is the innocent child less deserving of help because he cannot read, hear, or speak rather than being the legitimate heir to the throne, kidnapped by an usurper? Are the poor more comfortable because they live on the streets of an American city rather than as serfs in medieval Europe? Is it less worthy to assist the sick by research done in Masonic hospitals today than to found a hospital in 1100 AD? Is it less contemptible to betray a friend, to cheat in order to gain financially, to use religion for political advantage, to make promises lightly and break them without thought, to fight in a court of law for something you believe to be wrong? It is less contemptible to do these things today than it was a thousand years ago?

While it is true that knighthood was conferred only on virtuous men, it is important to realize it was the qualities exhibited by the man through his actions that mattered. It was his virtues that were symbolized. And the knight's virtues were even symbolized by the equipment he used. For instance, nothing was more symbolic than a knight's spurs, which represented courage. When a young man was knighted, it was often said he had "won his spurs."

In truth, there was no such thing as a uniform code of knightly behavior in the Middle Ages. All of the characteristics of a knight were written sometime long after the Age of Chivalry by contemplative philosophers who compiled lists of virtuous qualities which they felt best defined chivalry. In this Degree, we raise up five of those assets and talents—humility, temperance, chastity, generosity, and honor. To be humble is not to think badly of yourself, but to think well of others. To be temperate means to live soberly, righteously, and godly, to walk honestly in life, to be moderate in thoughts, words, and deeds.

Self-control is essential to a virtuous man. To be chaste means to flee from youthful lusts. It is human nature to be both animal and spirit, but the animal must be subdued if the spiritual is to grow and flourish. To be generous means to be generous in spirit, not to return evil when evil is done to you, but with a generous spirit to return good. Sharing what is valuable in life means not just giving away material goods, but also your time, attention, wisdom and energy with others. This is what creates a strong, rich, and diverse community. Bitterness and revenge will destroy you, but mercy and generosity strengthen you and those around you. To be a man of honor means to uphold your convictions at all times, especially when no one is watching. Honor is nobility.

Each of these are important and admirable qualities; and when all of them blend together in one person, we discover the value and power of chivalry today as much as ever. As a modern knight, you should strive to keep these virtues alive in your own heart, and work to bring these qualities out in the people you see every day—at home, in the office, at school or on the street corner. A great power is wielded by the man who dwells in unity and love for his fellow man, who assists those in need and distress without any concern for self-interest or recognition, and who finds truth within his own heart through a deep and abiding trust in God.

The important lesson conveyed in this Degree is that the world is not black and white. Right and wrong are rarely absolute. What is right in one situation may be wrong in another. There is no "pre-programmed" path to right action. We must always evaluate our choices. Likewise, we cannot push the responsibility for our actions or decisions onto others. We ultimately must be responsible and accountable for our own life. We are not to judge too hastily the motives of others.

A Mason is a moralist, a philosopher, a symbolist and a spiritualist. He is also a soldier of honor, loyalty, duty and truth. But truth is always his first duty. It does indeed require knightly heroism to stick to fixed and pure spiritual values in a world of political, economic, and practical realities in which everything tends to become debatable and relative.

The world is in great need of men who say, "I will do the right thing because it is right. I will not do that which I believe to be wrong, even though it is convenient, advantageous, or popular. I will not convince myself that it doesn't matter, or that it's 'only a little wrong', or that since everyone does it, then it must be right." A person who lives by the code of chivalry in today's world allows everyone to see their best qualities reflected in his shining armor. As a Knight Commander of the Temple, you are obligated to be such a man.

Questions to Contemplate as a Knight Commander of the Temple

1. What brings us to truth in spiritual values?
2. How do we know when moral principles are not compromised by ethics?
3. What kinds of human enemies are Masons fighting today?
4. If you knew that you were going to die tomorrow, what are some of the things you would want to do? People you would want to see? Love you would want to express? Forgiveness from others you have wanted to ask?
5. Are there not times when the right thing to do is determined by the situation in which you find yourself? If it always wrong to lie? Is it acceptable to lie if only be doing so can you prevent harm from coming to another person? Is it wrong to kill? If a madman is attacking a school with an automatic rifle, and the only way you can stop him is by shooting him, thus taking a chance on killing him, are you justified in doing so? What do the questions of situational ethics teach us about who we are?
6. How can you be sure your actions are properly motivated?

THE JOURNEY OF THE ELU TO ENLIGHTENMENT

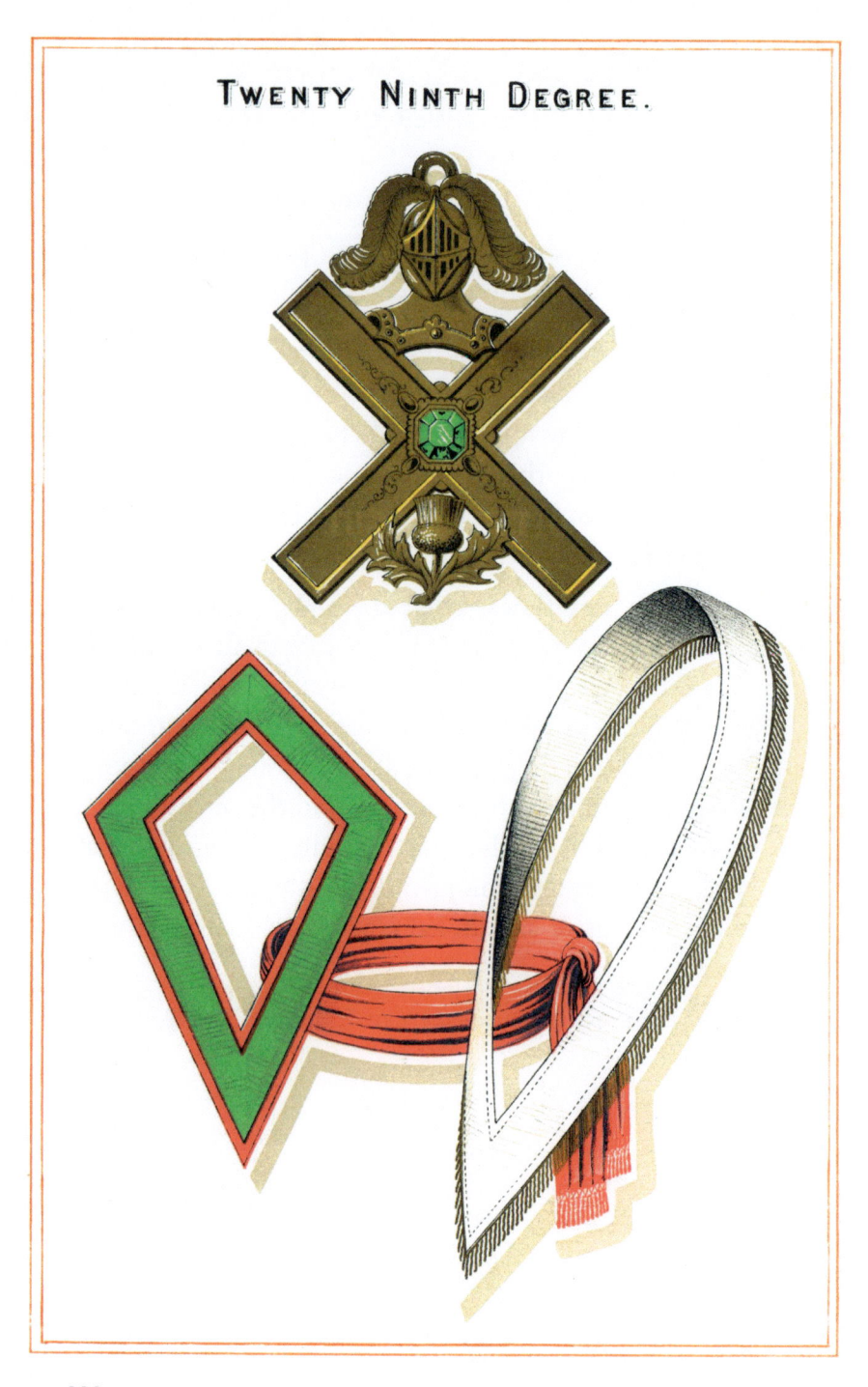

TWENTY NINTH DEGREE.

328

29°
GRAND SCOTTISH KNIGHT OF SAINT ANDREW

"Virtue and Wisdom, only, perfect and defend man"

The 29°, Scottish Knight of Saint Andrew, is one of the three Scottish Rite Degrees organized around the Knights Templar tradition. The 28° describes the foundation and development of the Order of the Temple; the 29° refers to the secret revival of the Order in Scotland; and the 30° presents the Order's revenge and eventual triumph. This middle of the three degrees representing the knighthood tradition of the Council of Kadosh once again illustrates there will always be a constant fight for virtue against ignorance, tyranny and fanaticism in order to improve men and society.

The candidate represents a Knight Commander of the Temple who seeks admission into the Knights of Saint Andrew. He falls into the hands of the Inquisition, and is threatened to be tortured if he does not renounce the Order and betray his friends to the Inquisition. He refuses, and then discovers that the supposed Inquisitors are themselves members of the Order who performed the tests because the lives and safety of the knights were, in reality, in constant peril of the Inquisition. By holding true to his honor, the candidate instructs us that truth and courage are essential to the quest for an ideal character. It is the character of a man that makes courage a virtue, and it is among the most universally admired of all the virtues. Courage is the capacity to overcome fear and cowardness and faintheartedness. And it is more than just bravery. It is having the daring of the heart necessary to undertake tasks which are difficult, often tedious and unglamorous, and to accept the sacrifices that are involved. Courage is the virtue of heroes, and who doesn't like heroes?

Advanced societies seem always torn apart by the struggle for wealth and power; the imbalance between the fortunes of a few and the poverty of the multitudes. Ends seem always to justify the means and office seeking is too often a manipulation of politics for place. The media seldom knows the truth and often distorts it for viewership and ratings. We live in a world that has no real belief in virtue and honor; and willingly accepts licentiousness and dishonesty as the way of the times. But that doesn't mean virtue is passé and no longer of any practical value. The chivalric degrees focus on the constant battle that must be fought for virtue against ignorance, selfishness, and fanaticism.

The world still needs heroic souls, even if it does not recognize that need. We are deeply moved when men brave space, flinging themselves toward the planets in craft smaller than some of the vehicles which travel our roads. We admire the doctors and nurses who risk treating patients with rare and contagious diseases, as we do the thinker who takes a leap into knowledge ridiculed by his colleagues and is proven right. We admire the soldier who is willing to put his life on the line to preserve the ideals of his country. We admire the man who refuses to compromise what he knows to be right. Folly it may be, but it is a glorious folly.

It may be that we cannot all be heroic souls, and we almost certainly cannot be heroic all the time. But we can, at least, avoid anti-heroism. We can constantly be about the business of being better fathers, husbands, brothers, friends, and members of our communities. We can endeavor to improve ourselves and the world in which we live. We can strive always to become better men. As Masons, we know that a single act of love and kindness is worth more than countless volumes of well-intended theory, speculation, or pontification.

The very essence of knighthood is action. Unless we act on the ideals we learn in Masonry, we can no more claim to understand virtue, honor, and truth than a man can claim to understand military service because he has read books about the subject of warfare. The horrors and abuses of human history teach us that the great ideals of virtue and honor must not be allowed to wither as only quaint notions and romantic theories which are no longer practical in a modern and weary world. As Masons, we plant the seeds of the great virtues through our actions, and the results bear fruit that sustains the victory of truth for humanity, even in its darkest hours.

In every degree of Freemasonry, the candidate seeks to attain light. In the philosophical degrees, the search is for intellectual light. In the chivalric degrees, the search is to be *illuminated by the knightly and heroic virtues which are the light of the soul.*

THE JOURNEY OF THE ELU TO ENLIGHTENMENT

As we make our quest to take virtue out into the world, we must always be aware that we will be opposed by weapons of fear, lies, and distortion. Our motives will be questioned. We will be held up to ridicule. The negative forces of the world will oppose us.

But virtue cannot be beaten, and a few battles do not a war make. In the end, it is truth, and not error, that is immortal. Pike has so aptly informed us so many times in our journey to perfection that *"men are great or small as it pleases God. But their nature is great or small as it pleases themselves. Men are not born, some with great souls and some with little souls. By an act of will he can make himself a moral giant, or dwarf himself to a pigmy. There are two natures in man, the higher and the lower, the great and the mean, the noble and the ignoble; and he can and must, by his own voluntary act, identify himself with one or the other."*

We are Knights for the very good reason that we are engaged in the battle to become all that we can become; to be all that we can be. Our own willpower is indeed the necessary condition of our freedom. But it also makes us fully responsible for ourselves. If we use the virtues taught in this Degree as active forces in life, and not just as abstract words, we can change ourselves and the world for the better. But we have to sincerely believe that good will win out over evil, and expand its influence, as we carry out the purpose of this quest—the development of actions in service to virtue into more and more areas of life.

We are bound to be the Almoners of God's bounty. As a father stands in the midst of his household, and says, "What is best for my children?" So we are to stand in the world and say, "What is best for my Brotherhood?"

Questions to Contemplate as a Grand Knight of Saint Andrew

1. What do the principles, heroism, thoughts and deeds of great men who have passed this life tell us about history that is worthwhile for us to know?
2. What has the most value to us when studying the past?
3. What does this tell us about our own lives?
4. We are told in this Degree that nothing of divine truth which comes into the world is ever lost. How do we know this to be true?
5. With what can one really conquer fear?
6. What kind of man and exemplar do you most honor, and want to emulate? What is required of you to attain the ideal of being a true brother of the mystic tie?
7. What must a man possess as a necessary condition of freedom?
8. What is it that makes a man fully responsible for himself?
9. What are some of the virtues indispensable in your efforts to exalt your nobler nature?
10. When many years from now you look back on your life, do you think you will be more disturbed by the times you tried and failed, or by the times you found excuses and didn't try? What have been the defining moments in your life that changed you for the better? What held you back from achieving your best potential?

THE JOURNEY OF THE ELU TO ENLIGHTENMENT

THIRTIETH DEGREE.

30°
KNIGHT KADOSH, OR KNIGHT OF THE TEMPLE

"A people will have such institutions as it's fitted to have"

The 30°, Knight Kadosh, is the last of the three Templary Degrees of the Scottish Rite, and was inspired by the murder of Jacques de Molay, the last Grand Commander of the Knights Templar. The word "Kadosh" means "separate," or "Holy," or "Sacred," that is, separate from the profane world.

At this stage of his journey, the Knight Kadosh is supposed to have reached a spiritual level beyond all material, moral and intellectual knowledge he has gained in the previous degrees. He is now armed inwardly with the most mystical concept of Deity, a love for his fellow men and knowledge of Truth. He has recovered his innermost unity and freedom and feels responsible to his purified conscience alone.

But he is still a warrior. Fighting not only with his own human imperfections, but against his external enemies, the fanatics, haters and intolerant of all types. He wants to restore the original powers and dignity in men which have been taken away by tyranny, in whatever form. The quest of a true knight is to express in the world the duties, obligations, insights and knowledge gathered in his spiritual journey; his awakened consciousness. And this quest never truly ends. It continues throughout his life. It is what makes him a warrior.

The importance of being a force in the world, in spite of the fact that it will expose you to danger and hatred, is the mark of every hero. Masonic heroism requires extraordinary strength, will and patience. Truth and justice must be defended in small things as well as large. It requires a lot of warrior energy.

Yet, we live in a time when people are generally uncomfortable with the warrior form of masculine energy. On the surface, this is easy to understand. Women, especially, have been victimized by it in every age. Warfare in our own time has reached such monstrous and pervasive proportions that aggressive energy is looked on with much suspicion and fear. Male abusers, exploiters, and oppressors have often made masculinity an ogre to be dreaded rather than a character to be admired. The problem is not that all warrior energy is bad; the problem is that men must be taught how to control it for positive and beneficial purposes. Warrior energy is an archetype of manhood. We can't just take a vote and vote the warrior out. Like all archetypes, it lives on in spite of our conscious attitudes toward it. And, like it or not, we have to face it. Warrior myths and traditions persist because being a warrior is a basic building block of masculine psychology. It is rooted in our genes. Being a warrior means being engaged with life rather than withdrawing from it.

In Masonry, it means being loyal to something—a cause,

a people, a country, a task—something larger than the individual. In the theme of knighthood, it can mean being loyal to the virtues of chivalry, and the God, or principle, that lies behind such things as noble quests. The warrior is often a destroyer. But the positive warrior energy destroys only what needs to be destroyed in order for something new and fresh, more alive and more virtuous to appear. Many things in our world need destroying—corruption, tyranny, oppression, injustice, greed, dishonesty, envy, hatred—and, in the very act of destroying, a warrior can build a new celestial Jerusalem.

Of course, it would be comforting to believe that all the major battles had been fought and won—that the freedom and liberty of mankind, at least in our country, were accomplished facts. But it would be an error. The most subtle temptation in this area is to preserve our own rights, while stepping on those of others. This is not an easy temptation to overcome—and it requires deep thought, not "knee-jerk" reactions.

For example, we believe, almost without qualification, in religious freedom. We believe that every man and woman have a right to practice their religion, even if we disagree with it or think it to be foolish. We believe that parents have not only the right, but a responsibility to bring their child up in a religion, and to provide religious instruction and environment for the child. But what if a person's religion forbids the use of medical attention, believing that God alone can heal and that reliance on medicine is wrong. Their child falls ill, the parents refuse medical help for the child, and the child dies. The State decides to pass a law which says that a child can be taken from the parents by force, and medicine provided. What is right?

We believe in absolute freedom of opinion and speech. A highly persuasive person appears, and is advocating hatred and fear, convincing people that they should treat some group with violence because they are responsible for all the evil in the world. A law is proposed to keep the person from speaking. What is right?

There are many prices to be paid for freedom, but perhaps the highest price is this: if freedom of speech exists, people will say things we do not like: if freedom of action exists, people will do things of which we do not approve: if freedom of religion exists, people will hold and practice beliefs we think wrong. It is easier to fight for what we believe to be right than to allow a person to express what we believe to be wrong, but we must be willing to do both if we are to have true freedom.

There is, unfortunately, a strong tendency in man to "sell out" for the short-term gain or for convenience. Governments in the world today, no less than yesterday, have been all too willing to accommodate that tendency.

> "We will take care of you from the cradle to the grave; we will see to it that you have a job, an adequate income, health care, a place to live. We only ask in return a few sacrifices which are logically necessary in order to accomplish those goals. If we are to guarantee you a job, we must plan for the economy so that there are enough jobs to go around. To do that, you will have to choose a job from two or three options we give you. If we are to guarantee you an adequate income, we must plan and control that income, so that someone else does not make too much. We must therefore set the salary, and it must be independent of your own efforts, else not everyone will receive the

same. If we are to provide health care, you will need to see the doctor we choose on the schedule we choose. If you are to have a place to live, you must let us select the place so that everyone can be served."

"And, of course, since we cannot plan effectively in the face of constant criticism and complaint, we must insist that you not meet without permission to dissent from the official positions, since that would introduce disorder into the system and hurt yourselves and others."

The 30° provides that Masonry is opposed at all times and under all circumstances to any arbitrary power that seeks to keep people in ignorance, or tell them what they should believe or think, or limit the knowledge available to them. If man is to be free, then he must be free; not partially free, or free with exceptions.

The Knight Kadosh fights against tyranny in all its forms; tyranny over thought, tyranny over speech, tyranny over belief, tyranny over opinion. And he must also be constantly vigilant in his own life to make sure he does not attempt to practice tyranny over the thought, speech, belief, or opinion of another.

This Degree teaches many lessons which have application in public and civic life, but its primary and profound revolutionary lesson, the great political truth of Masonry is this: *individuals are supreme over institutions*. It is difficult for us to realize, today, the world-shattering force of that idea when it first developed. The assumption was that institutions were superior over men. The Church had the power to torture and kill persons who disagreed with some small point of doctrine. The organization of the Church was superior to the mere men and women who

THE JOURNEY OF THE ELU TO ENLIGHTENMENT

attended church (an idea, by the way, as alive among the Puritans in New England as among the members of the Inquisition). Likewise, the king had the right to imprison, execute, or impoverish anyone he chose. Government was superior to the people governed.

But Masonry taught, and the world finally adopted, the idea that man was superior to any institution (not superior to God, but superior to the organizational institution of the Church; not superior to law, but superior to the organizational institutions of government).

This idea, that man is not mere fodder of the machine, but that the institutional machine exists to serve him and is legitimate only as far as it serves him was given its first formal expression outside of Masonry in the Declaration of Independence. It has now become the common-sense reality of a people, as it was first a sacred truth of Masonry. It is an essential ingredient of freedom.

Pike summarizes the battles waged by a Knight Kadosh, as follows:

- <u>Fight against ignorance:</u> Knowledge is power. Education is a necessary step towards understanding truth. Only the well-informed man is free. Ignorance leads to the slavery of emotions, and the rule of clever orators' corrupt logic. Ignorance is the cause of fanaticism. It nourishes tyranny. Knowledge frees men from prejudice and error and makes men more useful and beneficial to the community. The task of acquiring knowledge is a noble privilege of human nature.

- <u>Fight against Spiritual Tyranny</u>: Intolerance demands absolute surrender of the reason as well as the will. It primarily seeks the preservation of the institution, however wrong it may have turned, rather than the preservation of its original teachings, which may themselves be sublime.

- Fight against Despotism: Despots seek to control men's thoughts and actions. Mind-conditioning replaces education and freedom of expression. Patriotism and idealism can be used to mobilize popular sentiment, with a view to distracting the people's attentions from their corruption. Fake enemies are created to be feared and fought, instead of the despot's abusive authority. A well regulated and safely balanced republic expressing the will and assent of the people are the only forms of government an enlightened human being should submit.

- Fight against Vice: Vice will always thrive wherever ignorance, weakness, laziness and hunger exist and are exploited by greed. Ambition, fanaticism and superstition are at the same time the cause and effect of vice.

Reason and knowledge are the best weapons we have to ensure moral victory over vice. Together with virtue, love and charity, these are our divine weapons against ignorance; religious and political tyranny; and their effects. Constitutional governments, by their checks and balances, protect the individual against the natural despotic tendency to compromise any form of government. The separation of Church and State, in particular, ensures the independence of political institutions and frees political life from the fictitious promise of spiritual rewards, the hope for spiritual salvation, and the threat of punishments here or hereafter, used by clerical or other totalitarian establishments to enslave the people. The power vested in leaders democratically elected by the people at large should always prevail over self-appointed spiritual or temporal totalitarian individuals or entities of whatever strain. The heart of man craves only for justice and love. Men, created in God's image, are essentially good. Evil institutions alone have made them bad.

It is the duty of Masonry and every Knight to aid in leading them back to truth.

Questions to Contemplate as a Knight Kadosh

1. What can make politics and religion tyrannical?
2. What are the consequences of forcing something upon others when they are not prepared to receive it?
3. What was the Protestant Reformation and what did it have to do with the lessons taught in this Degree?
4. What do the lives of great men teach us? Do examples from the past have to be real?
5. What are some ways that freeing men from their ignorance might be accomplished today?
6. Who does DeMolay represent in Masonry?
7. Why is warrior energy as necessary today as in the past? How can warrior energy be used as a means for positive ends?

THE JOURNEY OF THE ELU TO ENLIGHTENMENT

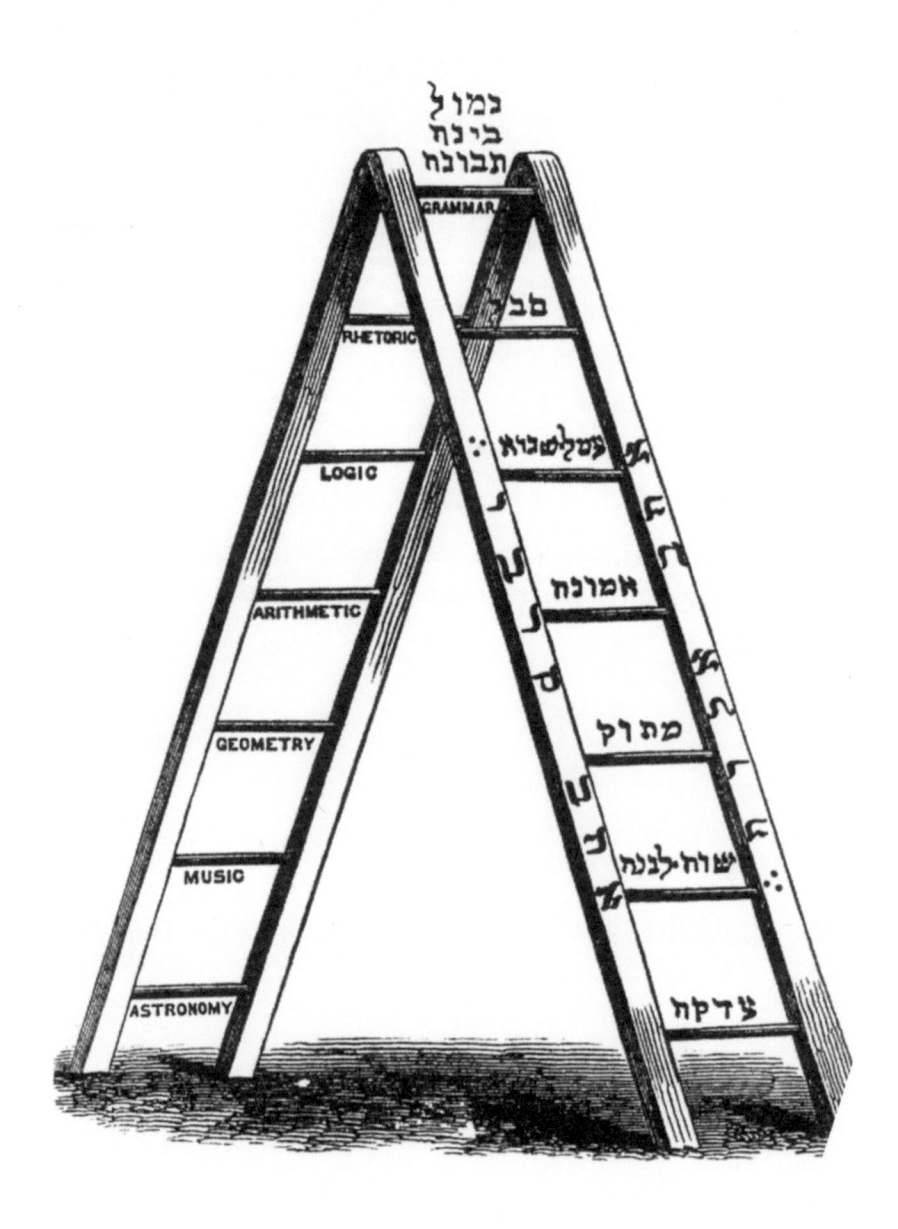

XII

THE CONSISTORY

The Consistory is the fourth body of the Rite and comprises the final two degrees that may be applied for in the Scottish Rite. It completes the quest theme begun by the candidate in the Entered Apprentice Degree of the Blue Lodge. In the Thirty-first Degree, the Knight Kadosh must finally encounter himself without armor to protect him. He is in the raw nakedness of his own being; examining who he really is in his own skin. He makes the deepest probe of himself that he has likely ever made, knowing that he can never be Master over himself, or Master of the Royal Secret, until he can assure to himself he is not acting in self-deception. He has to know that he has indeed moved from one state of his being to a higher principle in life. He has left the pettiness of mundane thinking, of assigning importance to the basest of his instincts. He has moved beyond the soul-destroying influence of his own ambition, his unfairness in judgments, his selfishness and self-centered ego, his jealousy and deceitfulness of others, his unearned privileges, and his failure to live up to his duties and obligations in life. He knows that it is not enough to have simply done no harm in life; he alone is responsible for actively doing good. He must pass the final trials of the Thirty-first Degree to prove oneself fit for the great duties assumed, and the profound lesson taught, in the Thirty-second Degree.

He cannot achieve his final goal in life, or realize the true empowerment of his soul, until he has made peace with himself; that is, affirmed himself in the nature of his entire being. He must be, and know himself to be, a good man.

The quest of the Degrees of the Consistory then, is the quest for self-examination and empowerment. Empowerment is within you. All answers in life are within you. Whether this realization and enablement comes as a powerful understanding which enables you to accomplish great things, or whether it comes and passes almost unnoticed depends upon you, and the preparation you have made with your life. If you are wise and heed the lessons which have been given you in the Rite, you will indeed become a Master among men, ruler of yourself and over circumstances and fortune.

What we know matters. What we know about ourselves matters. What we build matters. There is no such thing as an unimportant action. We build ourselves, and the selection of the materials we use for our own intellectual and spiritual life are the most important decisions we will ever make.

The Scottish Rite gives us the tools to have whatever life we want. We need only to select well, examine carefully, decide fairly, live spiritually, and love mightily.

CONSISTORY

THIRTY FIRST DEGREE.

31°
GRAND INSPECTOR INQUISITOR COMMANDER

*"You are to inquire into your own heart and conduct,
and keep careful watch over yourself,
that you go not astray"*

The 31°, Inspector Inquisitor, is the first of the two Degrees of the Consistory. The Sovereign Tribunals of Inspector Inquisitors used to be the Masonic equivalent of the Supreme Court of the Scottish Rite, with the right of judicial powers in enforcing and maintaining the Statutes and Regulations of the Order, as well as individual Masonic duties and codes of behavior.

It could administer justice and take disciplinary action to redress any breach of Masonic laws, regulations, and edicts. When an Inspector Inquisitor visited a lodge, the gavel of authority was automatically given to him upon his entrance.

This Degree therefore focuses on justice and elaborates upon the relationship between human law, as the guardian of social justice, and the law of God, or ideal divine justice. It teaches us to judge ourselves and others according to the wisdom taught in the preceding degrees, keeping in mind the difference between human and divine justice. Immortality demands that we convert our knowledge and faith into actual self-improvement, and not to confine them to mere external attitudes of morality and piety. Our spiritual improvement will reflect on society.

The candidate represents the soul of an Egyptian architect named Cheres, and is taken by Horus, son of Osiris, the god and judge of the dead, to a hall of justice representing the Egyptian Court of the Dead, to determine if he will be admitted among the gods. He is represented by an advocate, a defender, and a counselor, who presents conclusions of law. He is questioned about his life and actions.

The degree is not so much concerned with profane justice, but addresses the internal justice associated with man's spirituality; that is, on reaching a state of mind where he is one in himself. He has dealt with the apparent contradictions inherent in humanity, and has striven to reach a point where the duality or oppositions of his nature have merged together into a unity of the whole, of order and harmony. This represents the culmination of the human quest, wherein the candidate, like all other heroes of the great mythic cycles, must go through a deep purification

THE JOURNEY OF THE ELU TO ENLIGHTENMENT

process symbolized by the most searching questions asked by the gods during the ceremony.

The degree is not aimed at actually selecting saints, but at making the Mason realize what he is essentially, how much latitude he has given himself, and the degree of self-deception he practices. Thus, the Degree forces us to make an inquiry into our own truthfulness. We cannot be a moral man in attitude only. We have to walk the walk as well as talk the talk.

The degree is aimed at destroying all unconscious arrogance, reminding us to hold our obligations in our hearts; practice Masonry in our lives and not only with our mouths. This "change in heart" can be achieved by equitably redressing, correcting, adjusting or protecting the conflicting situations we encounter within ourselves and thus come as close as we can to absolute justice and equity of judgment on ourselves and our fellowmen.

The questions we must answer at this time powerfully reminds us that the better we live our life the less we will have for which to be embarrassed if/when we must face a divine tribunal of it. In the heroic journey into ourselves we have made in the Scottish Rite, we have been presented the virtues and wisdom that every Mason should strive to acquire. If we have truly been in touch with our own psychology of being, we will have reached a point where we are at one with ourselves. That is the place where real wisdom and justice reside.

It is not enough that we simply avoid wrong and evil. We must also do good. This means that we, as Masons, are required to be positive men; not merely to avoid being negative men. It is not enough to be able to say that we have not passed on rumor and slander about others. Rather, that we have tried to stop rumor and slander; that we have not done injustice to another; rather we have sought to treat men and women with justice and fairness. It is not enough for us to claim that we have never hurt anyone; we must also be able to claim that we have helped someone. It is not enough for us to claim that we have not taken advantage of those weaker than us; rather, that we have aided and assisted those weaker than us. It is not enough to claim that we have not taken advantage of political corruption; rather, that we have fought against political corruption. It is not enough for us to claim that we have not neglected the services of our religion; rather, that we have done our best to live as our faith directs. It is not enough to claim that we have not come between man and wife or parent and child; rather, that we have helped to heal the breach between man and wife, or parent and child.

This Degree teaches us in a very profound way that we have an obligation to inspect our own life, and make an honest inquiry into our own actions, motives, attitudes, and behaviors.

Impartiality in law is necessary, and most of us believe in it with a minor qualification: by "impartial" we mean that the court should not be prejudiced in favor of our opponent. For some reason, prejudice in our favor is seen not as partiality, but as "sensitive awareness of the special facts and the nature of the case." Yet true impartiality is impartial in the same sense that a traffic light is impartial. It cares not whether a President or a prostitute is driving a car—when its internal clock tells it to, it changes from green to red.

Your internal clock is ticking. Don't forget to be truthful to yourself. Make amends sooner than later.

The Journey of the Elu to Enlightenment

Questions to Contemplate as an Inspector Inquisitor

1. What does this Degree teach us about the human condition?
2. What does it teach us about contradictions?
3. In what way does the Degree parallel the mythic journey of the hero?
4. What is a change of heart? How does one have a change in heart?
5. What is required of us to balance the scale of justice? What have we achieved when we do?
6. What is the difference between appearance and reality?
7. What is the meaning of the Hall of Two Truths?
8. As inspectors, what are we inspecting?
9. What should be our motives when judging others? What should the focus of judgment be?
10. How do we know that crime and injustice do not pay when inhumanity, wickedness, partiality and vice seem so prevalent in the world?
11. Is a man a thief who steals a loaf of bread for his hungry children?

CONSISTORY

THIRTY SECOND DEGREE.
PLATE 1ST.

THE JOURNEY OF THE ELU TO ENLIGHTENMENT

THIRTY SECOND DEGREE.
PLATE 2ND.

354

CONSISTORY

32°
Sublime Prince of the Royal Secret

"Go, and serve by action as a light among men"

The 32°, Master of the Royal Secret, is the second of the Consistory Degrees. It summarizes all of the preceding degrees into a single coherent "holy doctrine" for the whole of the Rite.

The candidate is received in the camp of the 32°. By means of the camp, the teachings of the preceding Degrees are briefly reviewed. The candidate is reminded of the teachings of antiquity and is then permitted to take the vows which create him a Soldier of Light, a Soldier of Freedom, a Soldier of True Religion, a Soldier of the People, and a Soldier of the Scottish Rite of Freemasonry.

The basis of the fundamental truths and symbols common to all cultures and all ages has been that "dualism" exists in all of nature—one being the constructive force of light, or truth; the other, the destructive force of dark, or antagonism. These opposite forces are necessary for man to be endowed with free will and responsibility. In human terms, we think of these opposites as forces of good and evil which result from the condition of one's state of mind and character; that is, of man's virtues and vices. In Masonry, we often refer to this as the dual nature of man, the spiritual and material side of his being, which is symbolized by the square and compasses.

But this dual nature does not contain any principle of evil; rather, it is perceived like a coin that is a single thing with two sides of light and darkness, depending on the position of the observer. Light is a symbolic construct associated with existence and knowledge since, through light, man "sees" and understands the surrounding universe and his own inner being.

In this way, he also perceives that one of the fundamental principles in nature is that it ceaselessly moves in a cyclical fashion; things are born, exist, die, and are reborn. Just as the death of a seed is necessary for a new plant to grow, the death of man is necessary for a new life. This makes the general force of life permanent and eternal, and inspires man to strive for an ever greater spiritual awareness and understanding of the essential reality of himself, the universe, and its divine origin.

The ancient philosophers taught that truth and intelligence are thus eternal attributes of God. This idea has been handed down through the long succession of ages in the lessons of Freemasonry, wherein we read that "Truth is a Divine Attribute, and the foundation of every virtue."

The greatest glory in life is knowing that we are immortal. Pike suggests in the lecture of this Degree that;

"It is enough for us to know what Masonry teaches, that we are not all mortal; that the Soul or Spirit, the intellectual and reasoning portion of our self, is our Very Self, is not subject to decay and dissolution, but is simple and immaterial, survives the death of the body, and is capable of immortality; that it is also capable of improvement and advancement, of increase in knowledge of the things that are divine, of becoming wiser and better, and more and more worthy of immortality; and that to become so, and to help to improve and benefit others and all our race, is the noblest ambition and highest glory that we can entertain and attain unto, in this momentary and imperfect life. In every human being the Divine and the Human are intermingled."

The final instruction of the Rite is also given in Pike's words:

"You have heard more than one definition of Freemasonry. The truest and most significant you have yet to hear. It is taught to the entered Apprentice, the Fellow-Craft and the Master, and is taught in every Degree through which you have advanced to this. It is a definition of what Freemasonry is, of what its purposes and its very essence and spirit are; and it has for everyone of us the force and sanctity of a divine law, and imposes on everyone of us a solemn obligation."

"FREEMASONRY is the subjugation of the Human that is in man by the Divine; the Conquest of the Appetites and Passions by the Moral Sense and the Reason; a continual effort, struggle, and warfare of the Spiritual against the Material and Sensual. That victory, when it has been achieved and secured, and the conqueror may rest upon his shield and wear the well-earned laurels, is the true Holy Empire."

"You have been taught in those Degrees conferred in the Lodge of Perfection... to be true, under whatever temptation to be false; to be honest in all your dealings, even if great losses should be the consequence; to be charitable, when selfishness would prompt you to close your hand; to judge justly and impartially, even in your own case, when baser impulses prompt you to do an injustice that you might be benefited or justified; to be tolerant, when passion prompts to intolerance and persecution; to do what is right, when the wrong seems to promise greater profit; ...in all these things and others which you promised in those Degrees, your spiritual nature is taught and encouraged to assert its rightful dominion over your appetites and passions."

"The Philosophical Degrees have taught you the value of knowledge, the excellence of truth, the superiority of intellectual labor, the dignity and value of your soul, the worth of great and noble thoughts; and thus endeavored to assist you to rise above the level of the animal appetites and passions...and to find purer pleasure and nobler prizes and rewards in the acquisition of knowledge, the enlargement of the intellect, interpretation of the sacred writing of God upon the great pages of the Book of Nature."

"And the Chivalric Degrees have led you on the same path, by showing you the excellence of generosity, clemency, forgiveness of injustice, magnanimity, contempt of danger, and the paramount obligations of Duty and Honor. They have taught you to overcome the fear of Death, to devote yourself to the great cause of civil and religious Liberty, to be the Soldier of all that is just, right, and true.

"The Royal Secret, of which you are (Master), if you are a true Adept, if knowledge seems to you advisable, and Philosophy is, for you, radiant with a divine beauty ...is the Mystery of Balance. It is the Secret of the UNIVERSAL EQUILIBRIUM."

Thus, the Royal Secret, the ultimate objective of the Scottish Rite, is that we have the perception there is universal equilibrium in the universe, and it has application to our personal lives:

Equilibrium in the Universe—in physics there are four basic forces which affect the stability of the atomic nucleus. If any quantity was added to, or taken away from these forces, nothing would exist. This razor's edge, or equilibrium, upon which everything stands, is the major law of the universe. Scientists know the attributes of all the forces in nature, and they know there is a unified force which could synthesize and consolidate the four basic forces. But they do not know its essence. The search for this unified force is the Philosopher's Stone of the Alchemists, the Universal Knowledge of the Rose-Croix.

The secret of occult sciences is the secret of nature itself, the Creator's secret hidden in His Creation.

Equilibrium in our Personal Lives—finding balance and harmony between the opposite forces within and without us.

Individual equilibrium—what we try every day to establish in our ordinary life, whether we like it or not, to battle our own duality, find a balance and harmony between the constant opposing forces within us. Finding balance in all this is the secret for right living.

<u>Spiritual equilibrium</u>—realizing that evil is the shadow of good, darkness of light, sorrow of joy, suffering of happiness—all are complementary aspects of reality. We have free will to abide by, or break it. We utilize both reason and faith to come closer to truth. Whenever rational scientific knowledge is exhausted, we call upon intuitive faith in an eventual solution to lead us forward. Reason helps faith find a new path when it stumbles over dogma. Without a balance between faith and reason, we are confronted with either prophets without philosophy or common sense; or blind believers without truth; or philosophers without faith; or skeptics wallowing in the chaos of unproductive doubt.

<u>Moral equilibrium</u>—equity resulting in the balance between justice and mercy. Love is better than hate and forgiveness is wiser than revenge. If absolute justice prevailed, imperfect humanity would be annihilated. If absolute mercy alone were applied, the result would be universal chaos of corruption, vice and crime. Free will and responsibility must be in balance. Harmony and beauty result from a wise balance between love, intellect, reason and morality, on the one hand; and the appetites and passions on the other. We are to live "within the bounds of the compasses."

<u>Political equilibrium</u>—the essence of a harmonious society is to be found in the balance between obedience to law and liberty; subjection to authority and individual rights and equality; subordination to the wisest and best, and fraternity. Otherwise we will get insane anarchical

despotism or, in reverse, the endless despotic anarchy of revolt. A peaceful, naturally evolving society is based on a balance between the will and common sense of the past, expressed in universal moral rules and political constitutions; and necessary active institutional changes expressing the will of the present, in keeping with philosophical and scientific progress.

"And as in each Triangle of Perfection, one is three and three are one, so man is one, though of a double nature; and he attains the purposes of his being only when the two natures that are in him are in just equilibrium; and his life is a success only when it too is a harmony, and beautiful, like the great Harmonies of God and the Universe."

"Such, my Brother, is the True Word of a Master Mason; such the true Royal Secret, which makes possible, and shall at length make real, the Holy Empire of true Masonic Brotherhood."

My Brothers, you have been on one of the great journeys you will ever make in your life. You have probed the depths of your consciousness, reviewed the profound breadth of the human condition, explored the wisdom of the ages, and started the process of looking at yourself as you truly are. You have learned that you are a reflection of the universe, connected to every living thing and to every other person who lives or has ever lived. You now know what the true definition of Freemasonry is, of what its purposes and its very essence and spirit are; that it has for every one of us the force and sanctity of a divine law, and imposes on every one of us a solemn obligation that we conquer our passions, struggles, and shortcomings with reason and hope and wisdom.

We repeat again that there is no real secret in Masonry.

It is a state of mind. It is a virtual secret in the same way that reality is but our perception of what is real. The secrets are the mysteries of our own life which have not yet been revealed to us. They are the reality which has not yet been fully understood. And without a change in consciousness, they will always remain hidden from us. The major goal of our lives, as Masters of the Royal Secret, is therefore a search for those secrets. The Royal Secret, the ultimate objective of the Scottish Rite Mason, is to have the perception that there is an essential equilibrium in the universe, and it applies to our personal lives.

We must strive each day to establish a balance between work and leisure; joy and sorrow, contemplation and action; sympathy and antipathy; enjoying life and preparing for death; respecting others while realizing ourselves; dedicating our time to family and society; cultivating our own solitude and intimacy.

Life is a battle and to fight that battle heroically and well is the great purposes of Man's existence.

The mystery of the 32° is this: It inculcates the ideal that you can liberate yourself from the internal and external factors that have conditioned you; of discovering the Divine Light in yourself, and of believing this is possible. It is the only way you may attain freedom of thought, freedom of conscience and freedom of culture. And you can recreate others as you have recreated yourself. This is the ultimate goal of the Masonic ideal. Above all, you are to reverence yourself as a divine immortal soul, and respect others as such, since we all share the same divine nature, intelligence and ordeals. This requires boundless mutual assistance, compassion and, in a word, LOVE. Such is the True Word of the

THE JOURNEY OF THE ELU TO ENLIGHTENMENT

Master Mason, the True Royal Secret and the Holy Doctrine of True Masonic Brotherhood.

GLORIA DEI EST CELARE VERBUM. AMEN.

QUESTIONS TO CONTEMPLATE AS A MASTER OF THE ROYAL SECRET

1. What is a Soldier of Light? What does he seek?
2. What does a Soldier of Freedom fight? What freedoms is he fighting for?
3. To what is a Soldier of True Religion engaged? What principle of religion does he defend? Who are his enemies?
4. To what is a Soldier of the People pledged to protect people from? What is his main weapon?
5. What kinds of things does a Soldier of the Scottish Rite defend? Who or what does a Scottish Rite Mason do battle with?
6. What is the sacred reason a Scottish Rite Mason loves mankind?
7. What is the meaning of the "Words" in Masonry? The Lost Word, the True Word, the Sacred Word?
8. What is the Holy Doctrine?
9. What are some examples of each of the five equilibriums contained within the Holy Doctrine?
10. What is the Masonic Camp designed to do? How does it serve as a Memory Palace?
11. What is the Royal Secret?

XIII

WHITHER ARE WE TRAVELING?

"All good and evil lie in a man's will."

As a Master of the Royal Secret, you have made the most profound and meaningful journey of your life. You have encountered yourself, recognized your passions, limitations, and shortcomings for what they are. You have gained control over your passions, learned that your responsibility is literally to make a difference in the world, and that every act you do has repercussions far beyond yourself and your immediate surroundings. You have come to understand the glory of a great work. You have learned of the great enemies of human thought and liberty, and how easily they grow. Indeed, you have learned that you are as subject to temptations as any man alive. You have battled the ruffians within you. You have sharpened your skills, learned when to attack and when to defend.

You have been taught that the thoughts of great men outlive them, and that the Great Pathfinders—the sages, philosophers and thinkers of the past—stand ready to help and assist you at any time. You have seen truth as defined by many cultures and many systems of thought. You have realized your kinship with all those who, before you, have been the servants of Light. You have made a deep examination of yourself, and you have learned that a good Mason does the good thing which comes his way, and the love of duty commands his will to do it. He is true to his mind, his conscience, heart, soul, and will. You have learned that you have more goodness within you than the channels of your daily life will hold. And you have been counseled that the good man goes out to seek the good; he not only wills it, he has a longing to do good, to spread his truth, his justice, his generosity, his Masonry over all the world.

Thus, with the Light of Masonry now in your mind, body, and soul, what do you do with it? The big question before you as an Elu, is how do you turn what you have learned into action; into reality? How do you make the changes necessary for you to walk the walk as well as talk the talk?

It begins with will. Let us never forget the lesson of the 12°. Wisdom is not possible without the acquisition of knowledge. And knowledge requires a great will. Will is a motivating force. It is will alone which turns thought into action. In a real sense, we become what we desire the most, because we will what we desire to happen. The end we have in view is what we desire, and the faculty of desire constitutes our will to achieve it.

To give one example from my own experience, I mentioned in the preface of this work that my desire in life was to be a city manager. I knew when I was nine years old that I wanted to be a city manager. Being raised on a farm, our social conversations outside the home normally occurred when we visited the community that was closest to where we lived. This is where we went to church and enjoyed many of the festivals of our lives. And our little community had a great niche for putting on festivals. As a lad, it seemed to me at such events, that everything was arranged for everyone's enjoyment, and there was plenty for people of all ages to do. We would make a day of it; usually capped off by a baseball game, a rodeo, or some similar evening event. For the longest time, I couldn't figure out how all this happened. Then, when I was nine years old, it occurred to me that the city manager was the active force behind all this community good. I will never forget that I pointed my finger at him on that day and said; "I want to be like him because he makes a difference in everyone's life!" That was the motivating force which charted my drive to choose city management as a profession when I finished my education. And the path I took to achieve that end was *the will to achieve it.*

The distinction between thought and action sets the stage for the discovery of an influence which serves to connect them. Acting on a thing may follow the thinking of it, but not without the intervention of some desire or determination to translate those thoughts into deeds. One way your ability to reason becomes practical is when it is used to determine the choices that must be made to direct the action that you desire will result from it.

The same process is employed to convert what we have learned as Masons into action; that is, into living as Masons. It is having a great enough will, or the presence of mind, to actually become what we are capable of becoming; to live life as fully as we can, and in such a way that others will want to be like us. The best act of humanity that we can ever achieve is to live an exemplary life.

It is the choice we have because we have the free will to make the best of our life; that is, we possess the motivation to change our circumstances, to improve ourselves in Masonry; to be men of high character; to be virtuous men. So the path to distinguishing ourselves from the rest of the community is the journey that strong-willed men choose to take for themselves. It is our committed journey to enlightenment. And we do it because the obligations we have taken on the altars of Masonry, in the presence of God, is an eternal commitment we make to the Grand Architect to build a temple in His Holy name. We can never forget that most provocative passage in Paul's second letter to the church in Corinth (2 Corinthians 6:16) when he reminds them, we are "the Temple of the Living God!"

If you have the will, you have the ability to take the teachings of Masonry into your heart. A change of perspective is a change in heart. And you have been graced with a soul to inspire you to choose good over evil, love over hatred, happiness over despair, in whatever circumstance you encounter.

The degrees of Masonry have taught us that good and evil, light and darkness, knowledge and ignorance are always present in the human condition. These oppositions lie in the will of every man. But right thinking is the neutral sphere that brings will into the proper reckoning of these two great opposing forces. We have been taught to think about ourselves, about who we are, why we are here, and what we should be doing. We now know what is required of us to rediscover and affirm a higher self-esteem for ourselves.

And as we become more self-reliant on our abilities and judgments, then we have assurance of our own value, our own right to live the way we want to live. We need only to ask ourselves what we must do to generate good and healthy feelings about ourselves, and our relationships with others. What patterns of action must we adopt to be more responsible? More caring? Less judgmental? More loving? What is the desirable path to our own self-improvement and development? What practices need to be summoned that will assure us of a positive and healthy life?

We can choose who we will be, and what we will carry with us in our dealings with others. We can associate with people whom we most admire and want to emulate; people who can help us with our questions and challenges, and lead us to be better examples of integrity, love, and inspiration. The only thing that can truly be conceived in the world without qualifications is a Good Will. And a good will is not good because of what it performs or effects; it is simply good in itself.

My brethren, find and embrace the power of your will. Use it to become in word and deed a Master of the Royal Secret. And God's will, working within you, will lead you to a life of exemplary virtue. We have but one aim in view—to participate in the grand design of being happy, and communicating happiness.

References Cited

This book is not an academic treatise on the history of the Scottish Rite, or the origin of its Degrees, nor a treatise on the meaning of the many symbols, colors, numbers, words, regalia, and settings presented in the rituals and pageantry of the Rite.

It is an interpretative study of the overall themes, quests, meanings, and teachings given to those who are already Masters of the Royal Secret (32° Masons). It is also primarily written as a study guide for those who have received their Degrees in Orients (States, Territories) utilizing the adopted work of the Ancient and Accepted Scottish Rite of Freemasonry, Southern Jurisdiction, USA. The adopted ritual workings of the Rite in the Northern Masonic Jurisdiction, USA, Canada, Mexico, the British Isles, Europe, and in South America are not standardized; and, in some cases, are no longer connected to the French Rite from which they came. Thus, the degree titles, legends, and teachings represented in this book do not apply to every Scottish Rite Mason.

It was written to help bridge the gap between the more formal language, cultural understanding, and historical settings that existed during the period in which the degrees were originally penned (18th Century), and their practical application to contemporary life of men today. The philosophy, ethics, morals and civic lessons presented by the Rite are as important, significant, and relevant today as they were in the 1700's. There is no reason for there to be a disconnect between ancient teachings and contemporary life. Since this is primarily an interpretative work, the references used in this work are few, and are cited, as follows:

Chapter II

Lobinger, Charles Sumner, 33°, G∴C∴, The Ancient and Accepted Scottish Rite of Freemasonry, Standard Printing Co., Louisville, KY, 1932

Chapter III

Jacob, Margaret C., Living the Enlightenment: Freemasonry and Politics in Eighteenth Century Europe, Oxford University Press, New York, 1991

Cassirer, Earnest, The Philosophy of the Enlightenment, Princeton University Press, 1968

Angel Leonard, Enlightenment East & West, State University of New York Press, 1994

White, John, What Is Enlightenment. Exploring the Goal of the Spiritual Path, St. Martin's Press, New York, 1984

Chapter IV

Wolfe, Alan, Moral Freedom: The Search for Virtue in a World of Choice, W.W. Norton and Co., 2001

Comte-Sonville, Andre, A Small Treatise on the Great Virtues, Metropolitan Books, New York, 2001

Adler, Mortimer J., Great Ideas, A Treasury of Western Philosophy, MacMillan Publishing Co. New York, 1992

Davidson, Robert F., Philosophies Men Live By, Second Edition, Holt,Rinehart, and Winston, New York, 1974

Hayek, Friedrich A., The Constitution of Liberty, The University of Chicago Press, 1960

Chapter V

Mayor, Federico and Binde, Jerome, The World Ahead, Our Future in the Making, Zed Books, The University of Chicago Press, 2001

Jones, Peter, Essays on Toleration, ECPR Press, London, 2018

Chapter VIII

De Hoyos, Arturo, Scottish Rite Ritual Monitor and Guide, The Supreme Council, 33°, Southern Jurisdiction, Washington, DC, 2008

Naudon, Paul, Histoire, Rituels et Tuileur des Hauts Grades Maconniquies," Dervy Edition, 1993

Chapters IX – XIII

The Degrees of the Scottish Rite
4° - 32°

Pike, Albert: Morals & Dogma
    Liturgies of the Ancient and Accepted Scottish Rite
    The Magnum Opus or Great Work, 1857

Rituals of the Lodge of Perfection, Chapter of Rose Croix, Council of Kadosh, and Consistory, Volumes 1-IV

Tresner, Jim and Davis, Robert, The Stories, Lessons, and Applications of the Degrees of the Scottish Rite—a Syllabus for Scottish Rite Education, Guthrie College of the Consistory

Printed in France by Amazon
Brétigny-sur-Orge, FR